the HOLMES reader

The life, writings, speeches, constitutional decisions, etc., of the late Oliver Wendell Holmes, Associate Justice of the Supreme Court of the United States, as well as an evaluation of his work and achievements by eminent authorities.

Selected and Edited by
JULIUS J. MARKE
Law Librarian
New York University

OCEANA'S DOCKET BOOKS

New York City
Oceana Publications
1955

Library of Congress Card No. 55-5961

Printed in the U. S. A.

CONTENTS

CONTENTS—*continued*

PREFACE

It is the purpose of this collection to present the life and work of one of the greatest American jurists since Chief Justice John Marshall. Justice Holmes is particularly noted for his general work on the Anglo-American legal system published under the title *The Common Law* in 1881. This book is easily available in libraries and in bookstores by reason of the many reprints that have been published. The materials herein collected are not so easily available to the general public as they appeared in law reviews and books that on the whole are now out of print or difficult to obtain outside of law libraries.

The articles on Justice Holmes were written by contemporary legal scholars and philosophers who are considered today of leading importance. Through the "gathering of these little fragments of my fleece that I have left upon the hedges of life", as was so aptly stated by Justice Holmes himself, we can better understand the man and appreciate his philosophy of life and law. Justice Holmes looked upon his extra-judicial thoughts as "chance utterances of faith and doubt". As we read him today we can not help but recognize him as a "majestic intellect" still influential in our halls of learning and in the courts of our land.

The editor wishes to express his thanks and appreciation to the following authors, publishers and periodicals for granting permission to reprint material originally copyrighted by them:

The Honorable Felix Frankfurter, Associate Justice of The Supreme Court of The United States and The Harvard Law Review Association for "Mr. Justice Holmes and The Constitution" from *The Harvard Law Review,* December, 1929; The Honorable Charles E. Wyzanski, Jr., United States District Judge, District of Massachusetts and The Vanderbilt Law Review for "The Democracy of Justice Oliver Wendell Holmes" from *The Vanderbilt Law Review*, April, 1954; The American Bar Association Journal for "The Secret of Mr. Justice Holmes: An Analysis" by Harold R. McKinnon from *The American Bar Association Journal*, April, 1920; The Harvard Graduates' Magazine for "Oliver Wendell Holmes" by Arthur D. Hill from *The Harvard Graduates' Magazine*, March, 1931; Professor Mark de Wolfe Howe and The Harvard University Press for letters from *The Holmes-Pollock Letters*, 1874-1932, edited by Mark De Wolfe Howe, 1941; Little, Brown & Co. for the following speeches of Oliver Wendell Holmes: "The Law and the Court," "The Professor of the Law," "Learning and Science," Boston Bar Association Speech, Yale University Speech, "John Marshall" and "The Soldier's Faith" from *Speeches by Oliver Wendell Holmes*, 1913; The Harvard Law Review Association for "Mr. Justice Holmes" by Benjamin N. Cardozo from *Harvard Law Review*, March, 1931, "Mr. Justice Holmes" by Frederick Pollock from *Harvard Law Review*, March, 1931, "The Path of the Law" by Mr. Justice Holmes from *Harvard Law Review*, 1896, "The Theory of Legal Interpretation" by Mr. Justice Holmes from *Harvard Law Review*, 1899, "Natural Law" by Mr. Justice Holmes from *Harvard Law Review*, 1918, and "Law in Science and Science in Law" by Mr. Justice Holmes from *Harvard Law Review*, 1899; Northwestern University Law Review for "Ideals and Doubts" by Oliver Wendell Holmes from the *Illinois Law Review*, 1915.

JULIUS J. MARKE

PART I.

LIFE AND WORK OF MR. JUSTICE HOLMES

OLIVER WENDELL HOLMES,

JUSTICE OF THE SUPREME COURT OF THE UNITED STATES

By Arthur Dehon Hill

Reprinted from the Harvard Graduate Magazine, vol. 39, pp. 265-289, March, 1931.

This article was written one year before the retirement of Mr. Justice Holmes and four years before his death. Mr. Hill was a member of the Bar of Massachusetts and a professor of law at Harvard University, resigning in 1916. He died in 1947.

On March 8, 1931, Oliver Wendell Holmes, Justice of the Supreme Court of the United States, was ninety years old. . . . He was born at Boston on March 8, 1841, the son of Oliver Wendell Homes and his wife, Amelia Lee Jackson. Both his parents came of the old Puritan stock, and were members of the kind of families from which so largely have been drawn the clergy and teachers, the lawyers and doctors of New England, the type his father had christened "the Brahmin caste of New England." [1] He was brought up and educated in Boston and attended the school of Mr. Dixwell (whose daughter he afterwards married), went to Harvard College and graduated in the Class of 1861. The year of his graduation coincided with the outbreak of the Civil War, and, like a majority of his classmates, he at once enlisted in the Union Army. He served three years, 1861 to 1864, first as lieutenant and later as captain in the Twentieth Massachusetts Volunteers. His regiment formed part of the Army of the Potomac, and with it he took part in much fighting and was three times wounded. In his speech at the Fiftieth Anniversary of the Graduation of his class, he said:

> It has been my fortune to belong to two bodies that seemed to me somewhat alike—the 20th Massachusetts Regiment and the class of '61. The 20th never wrote about itself to the newspapers, but for its killed and wounded in battle it stood in the first half-dozen of all the regiments of the north. This little class never talked much about itself, but graduating just as the war of secession began, out of its eighty-one members it had fifty-one under arms, the largest proportion that any class sent to that war.[3]

A younger contemporary, Bishop Lawrence, has described how his service appeared to a boy in Boston:

> I watched his record, for we boys were alert to the heroes of those days and as he was brought back wounded again and again—at Ball's Bluff shot in the breast, at Antietam with a ball in the neck, at Fredericksburg wounded in the foot—he was seen on the streets in Boston, a handsome invalid, to the great delectation of the girls of the city. He was a romantic hero, built for it.[4]

Scattered in Justice Holmes's speeches and writings are vivid pictures of his war experiences:

> Most men who know battle know the cynic force with which the thoughts of common-sense will assail in times of stress, but they know that in their greatest moments faith has trampled those thoughts under foot.
>
> If you have been in line, suppose on Tremont Street Mall, ordered simply to wait and to do nothing, and have watched the enemy bring their guns to bear upon you down a gentle slope like that from Beacon Street, have seen the puff of the firing, have felt the burst of the spherical case shot as it came toward you, have heard and seen the shrieking fragments go tearing through your company, and have known that the next or the

> next shot carries your fate; if you have advanced in line and have seen ahead of you the spot which you must pass where the rifle bullets are striking; if you have ridden by night at a walk toward the blue line of fire at the dead angle of Spottsylvania, where for twenty-four hours the soldiers were fighting on the two sides of an earthwork, and in the morning the dead and dying lay piled in a row six deep, and as you rode have heard the bullets splashing in the mud and earth about you; if you have been on the picket line at night in a black and unknown wood, have heard the spat of the bullets upon the trees, and as you moved have felt your foot slip upon a dead man's body; if you have had a blind fierce gallop against the enemy, with your blood up and a pace that left no time for fear—if, in short, as some, I hope many, who hear me, have known, you have known the vicissitudes of terror and of triumph in war, you know that there is such a thing as the faith I spoke of.[5]

After the war he studied for two years at the Harvard Law School and received his degree in 1866. In 1867 he was admitted to the Bar and practised law in Boston, first as a student in the office of Robert M. Morse, and later with George Otis Shattuck and William A. Munroe, as a member of the firm of Shattuck, Holmes and Munroe. Between 1870 and 1882 he taught law at Harvard, first in the College as an instructor in constitutional law, and later in the Law School where he was successively a lecturer and professor. His appointment as professor came in 1882, and he resigned January 8, 1883, to become a member of the Massachusetts Bench. While at the Bar he edited the 12th Edition of Kent's Commentaries on *American Law,* was from 1870 to 1873 one of the editors of the *American Law Review,* in which he published a number of articles, and in the winter of 1880-81 delivered a course of lectures at the Lowell Institute, which he embodied in a book entitled ***The***

Common Law. This book attracted wide attention and at once put him in the first ranks of legal scholars. On December 5, 1882, at the age of forty-one, he was appointed as an Associate Justice of the Supreme Judicial Court of Massachusetts. He served until August 5, 1899, when he was promoted to Chief Justice, and he held this position until he became a member of the Supreme Court of the United States. On December 8, 1902, he was appointed to that Court by President Roosevelt, and is now its senior justice.[6]

Until his appointment to the Supreme Court made residence in Washington necessary, Justice Holmes had always lived in Massachusetts, and except for occasional brief visits to Europe had rarely left the Commonwealth. In winter he lived in Boston, in summer at Beverly Farms in Essex County on the North Shore. Even since he has moved to Washington he has returned to Beverly Farms each summer.

On June 17, 1872, he married Miss Fanny Dixwell of Cambridge. Her quick and vivid perception, her keen wit and vigorous judgment, and the originality and charm of her character cannot be forgotten by any one who knew her. It is impossible to think of Justice Holmes without thinking of her also. Her effect on his life and career can neither be omitted nor measured in any account of him. She died on April 30, 1929.

Justice Holmes's energies have been concentrated on his profession. Besides his edition of Kent and his book on the common law, his written work is contained in the volumes of reports issued since he has been on the Bench,[7] in a volume of *Collected Legal Papers* [8] and in a small volume of speeches [9] many, though not all, on subjects connected with the law. He has had few public activities outside the law, and this was so even before he went on the Bench. He has never taken any active part in politics. From 1876 to 1882 he was a member of the Board of Overseers of Harvard University. He has never associated himself with any of the public or semi-public institutions of which the Massachusetts General Hospital and the Boston

Athenaeum are the type, and whose affairs add to the work of so many Boston lawyers. Nor has he ever had any especial outside avocation.

All this does not mean that his life has been a narrow one. On the contrary, his interests have been many. Not only does he keep abreast of philosophic and economic thought, but he reads widely outside those special fields. No form of good book is wholly alien to him. He takes up and enjoys Thucydides, Horace Walpole, the work of Martin Dooley and *Gentlemen Prefer Blondes,* and finds something in each.

Nor are his tastes confined to books. Pictures, the theatre, and the simple natural things are all vivid to him. He values highly good talk and the free exchange of ideas and opinions. Not only has he been a social favorite in Washington, but he always has met each variety of man that life threw in his path with singular ease and understanding. He has had capacity for liking and appreciating widely varied types no matter how unlike his own. The men with whom he served in the war, the lawyers who were his fellows at the Bar or who appeared before him in Court, his fellow judges, the neighbors among whom he spent his summers in Essex County, all to him were subjects of vivid interest. He once said that so long as he could be wheeled in a chair to the street corner and talk with the passers-by he would be content to live.

Nor is he one of those—of whom Macaulay was the type—whose talk is a monologue. He is as eager to hear the ideas of others as he is to state his own. It is noteworthy how often in his writings he introduces something that has been said to him by some one else. His private speech is even better than his written work. No one can fully know his humor and deep human wisdom, his quick apprehension of new ideas, his brilliancy and his charm, who has not sat with him far into the night while the talk swept from the latest play or the latest decision to some new scientific or philosophic theory, some personal incident or some trait of character that had touched or amused him.

He has a great capacity for friendship and a generous appreciation of others. No one who has read it will forget the characterization in his speech at Keene on Memorial Day,[10] of the men with whom he served in the 20th Massachusetts, or his touching answers to the Resolutions of the Bar on the deaths of George Otis Shattuck,[11] of Justice William Allen,[12] and of Chief Justice Field.[13]

No man has ever had more friends and unlike most men the number of his friendships has increased with his years. It is told of a Harvard graduate of the last generation who received his degree at the age of seventeen, that his Commencement "part" began with the words, "I am past the age for forming friendships." Whenever that age should be fixed, Justice Holmes has not yet attained it. Each year his circle widens. With him difference of age is no barrier. When he was eighty-five, he impressed an acute observer as having "an intellectual youth that most men of forty cannot boast," and the same observer spoke of how he received the ideas of young men "with the courtesy, admiration, and speculative curiosity accorded to honored guests."[14] All this is just as true today. There is growing up around him an increasing circle of younger men who feel toward him an affection and respect impossible to be put into words. They think of him less as the great man that he is than as the friend he has proved himself to them—wise and kind in counsel and ready with sympathy and understanding. Each of them could say as he has said of his friendship, with his partner Shattuck: "My education would have been but a thin and poor thing had I missed the great experience."[15]

The bare facts of Justice Holmes's career would have sufficed to make him a national figure. Few men are successful both as scholars in the law and as active members of two courts. The mere length of his service, through its accumulation of experience and the authority such experience gives, has added to the value of his work. Its effect would be great even from its quantity alone. A judge who sits on an important state court for many years and follows that by long participation in decisions of the Supreme Court cannot fail to affect the development of the law. When, as in the case of Justice Holmes, there is added high intellectual ability, a rare bit of style, a character of unusual charm, and an integrity so obvious and complete as to be apparent to all the world, that effect could not be otherwise than great. Among American judges and lawyers he is today the foremost figure.

This is not the place to attempt to fix Justice Holmes's rank as a jurist. It is enough here to quote what a great scholar has said of his work:

> Mr. Justice Holmes was among the first in this country to work out a basis for the answering of new questions by discovery of starting points through historical investigation. Also, in his edition of Kent's Commentaries, he turned his back to the common law, where Kent had looked at our legal institutions in the light of Continental natural law and civilian universal conceptions. At the same time, in his lectures on the common law, he gave us models for analytical jurisprudence and was a pioneer for America in the method of reaching general results on the basis of a comparative analysis of the legal precepts of the time and place taken as they are. Here was one man's work in the science of law achieved before he went upon the bench. In his forty-eight years upon the bench, he has again done at least a man's full work as a judge. Yet he has not ceased to be a leader in juristic thought. As he had been among the first in the analytical and historical jurisprudence of the last generation, he has been easily first in the English-speaking world among those who have been bringing us to the sociological or social-scientific method of today. . . .
>
> His short, pointed opinions, going directly to the legal root of the matter, are exceptionally adapted to teaching and have been favorites with the

> teachers and the compilers of case books. Moreover, they have in them a scientific quality, an appreciation of what is significant for the future of the law, which will keep a place for them as long as American law is taught from reported judicial experience, and will be reflected in restatements and codifications and texts, if some day the bulk of our legal materials constrains us to put the law in that form.[16]

In his opinions there are many in which his learning has made plain that relation between old law and new which he first taught as a writer.[17] He says himself, "I have done my share of quotation from the Year Books," [18] and sometimes his opinions contain references to authorities from a past to which the Year Books seem modern.[19] But he recognizes the limited place of antiquarian learning in legal development. In a speech at the dedication of a new hall at Boston University he said:

> History must be a part of the study, because without it we cannot know the precise scope of rules which it is our business to know. It is a part of the rational study, because it is the first step toward an enlightened scepticism, that is, towards a deliberate reconsideration of the worth of those rules. When you get the dragon out of his cave on to the plain and in the daylight, you count his teeth and claws, and see just what is his strength. But to get him out is only the first step. The next is either to kill him, or to tame him and make him a useful animal. For the rational study of the law the black-letter man may be the man of the present, but the man of the future is the man of statistics and the master of economics. It is revolting to have no better reason for a rule of law than that so it was laid down in the time of Henry IV. It is still more revolting if the grounds upon which it was laid down have vanished long since, and the rule simply persists from blind imitation of the past.[20]

His style has added greatly to the effect of his opinions. Law books are generally difficult reading. The story of the English lawyer who told a youthful aspirant that he saw no reason why he should not be successful if he was able to eat sawdust without butter contains perhaps the best description of that mass of words in which the treasures of the common law lie buried. The work of even the ablest judges is seldom readable to any but an expert. It is, perhaps, unfair to instance giants of the past, like Holt and Mansfield in England, or Marshall and Story in this country. Taste in style changes. It is often hard for us to enjoy eighteenth century writing. But even modern legal opinions are difficult reading. If any one doubts this, let him attempt the last volume of the law reports of his own State. Judicial writings gain little from their form, whatever may be their merit in substance. The work of Justice Holmes is an exception. Law cannot be made as easy as a love story, or a detective novel, but to any one who is interested in the subject-matter his opinions are fascinating reading.

The old saying that the style is the man is peculiarly true of Justice Holmes. His style is not the product of a love of verbal expression; that delight in words for their own sake which often inspires literary work. It springs directly from the clarity of his thought and his attitude toward the Law. His greatest interests are ideas and action; that interplay of human forces, which with economic causes govern the lives of men and nations. To him an opinion is a statement of ideas as a basis for action, a means by which effect is given to the will of the State which finds expression in the judgment of its Court. His primary object is to make clear what lies behind his words; to leave no doubt just what it is that has been decided, and just what the State through its Court has ordered to be done. There is a sense of actuality. The reader never has the feeling that the Court has not allowed its mind to penetrate through the legal verbiage to the fact behind it. The decision is not an abstraction, but an act that vitally affects the lives of human beings.

There is a constant search for the origin of the rules under discussion; a constant refusal to be satisfied with anything less than a complete and candid statement of the question before the Court and the reasons for the conclusion reached. Take, as an example, his dissent in the wire-tapping cases:

> There is no body of precedents by which we are bound, and which confines us to logical deduction from established rules. Therefore we must consider the two objects of desire, both of which we cannot have, and make up our minds which to choose. It is desirable that criminals should be detected, and to that end that all available evidence should be used. It also is desirable that the Government should not itself foster and pay for other crimes, when they are the means by which the evidence is to be obtained.
>
> If it pays its officers for having got evidence by crime, I do not see why it may not as well pay them for getting it in the same way, and I can attach no importance to protestations of disapproval if it knowingly accepts and pays and announces that in future it will pay for the fruits. We have to choose, and for my part I think it a less evil that some criminals should escape than that the Government should play an ignoble part.[21]

It is not possible beyond a limited extent to estimate what a particular judge or lawyer has accomplished in any special branch of the law. Justice Holmes, himself, has well defined the place of the individual in legal work:

> The glory of lawyers, like that of men of science, is more corporate than individual. Our labor is an endless organic process. The organism whose being is recorded and protected by the law is the undying body of society. When I hear that one of the builders has ceased his toil, I do not

> ask what statue he has placed upon some conspicuous pedestal, but I think of the mighty whole, and say to myself, He has done his part to help the mysterious growth of the world along its inevitable lines towards its unknown end.[22]

Rarely, as in the case of Lord Mansfield's decisions as to Commercial Law, or in Marshall's moulding of American Constitutional doctrine, some peculiar circumstances enable us to identify what has been done by some one judge. Generally, however, the individual's work is merged in that of the court of which he is a member, and his personality shows only indirectly in the quality and reputation of the court, itself. The Court of Massachusetts has ranked high among the state tribunals. Toward the maintenance and strengthening of that standing, Justice Holmes contributed much, both by the high quality of his work and by the influence of his strong and vivid personality on the court. A leading Boston lawyer said of him, "Holmes is like rum to the other judges." No one could read the decisions while he was a member of the Massachusetts Court, and particularly those while he was Chief Justice, without feeling his influence, not only in the opinions written by him, but in the general tone of the court's work. The same thing is true of the Supreme Court since he became a member. It would be hard for any one to be associated with Justice Holmes and not to respond to his mind and character and be inspired to work of greater depth and vigor.

His opinions are individual to an unusual degree. As Dean Wigmore has said, he

> has framed for himself a system of legal ideas and general truths of life, and composed his opinions in harmony with the system already framed. His opinions present themselves as instances naturally serving to exhibit this general body of principles in application. The framework is his own, and not some orthodox commentator's.[23]

His opinions express his emotional as well as his intellectual character. His work has been an integral part of himself, not a task, from which he turned when accomplished to his individual life. He has had that passionate interest in law which a great painter feels for art, or a scientist for science. Early in his judicial career he said of the law:

> And what a profession it is! No doubt everything is interesting when it is understood and seen in its connection with the rest of things. Every calling is great when greatly pursued. But what other gives such scope to realize the spontaneous energy of one's soul? In what other does one plunge so deep in the stream of life—so share its passion, its battles, its despair, its triumphs, both as witness and actor? [24]

And again and again in later utterances he has sounded this note. When in the same speech he said, "If we are to speak of the law as our mistress, we who are here know that she is a mistress only to be wooed with sustained and lonely passion—only to be won by straining all the faculties by which man is likest to a god"—he not merely indulged in a kind of simile common to after-dinner speakers; he expressed his own deep feeling. He has given to the law that sort of devotion that the knight of legend gave to his lady; he has served it in the spirit that a devout priest gives to his religion, or a great statesman to the principles of his party. He has brought to it what he, himself, has called "the cold passion of the Puritan." [25] This devotion helps to give to Justice Holmes's opinions their vital quality. It also creates a peculiar unity between what he writes as a judge and the rest of his life. His service in the Army, his work as a law teacher and lawyer, his duties as a judge have each been done with the same enthusiasm and the same intensity of interest. His judicial opinions have the same qualities mental and spiritual as what he says in a speech or in private conversation. His beliefs and opinions have widened and strengthened with years and experience, but in essentials they have not changed.

Perhaps his most fundamental article of faith is that belief in liberty of thought and speech which was characteristic of Liberalism in the last century. Intellectually he is skeptical of dogmatic expression. In his view each belief and each opinion lies open to criticism and attack and is entitled to survive only if it can hold its own in the open combat of ideas. It is in such combat that he sees the hope of future progress. When he speaks of freedom his words have a touch of passion. In theory, indeed, he can recognize that the principle of free speech is itself debatable, but his life and writings show that he accepts it as a guide to conduct:

> Persecution for the expression of opinions seems to me perfectly logical. If you have no doubt of your premises or your power and want a certain result with all your heart you naturally express your wishes in law and sweep away all opposition. To allow opposition by speech seems to indicate that you think the speech impotent, as when a man says that he has squared the circle, or that you do not care whole-heartedly for the result, or that you doubt either your power or your premises. But when men have realized that time has upset many fighting faiths, they may come to believe even more than they believe the very foundations of their own conduct that the ultimate good desired is better reached by free trade in ideas—that the best test of truth is the power of the thought to get itself accepted in the competition of the market, and that truth is the only ground upon which their wishes safely can be carried out. That, at any rate, is the theory of our Constitution. It is an experiment, as all life is an experiment. Every year if not every day we have to wager our salvation upon some prophecy based upon imperfect knowledge. While that ex-

> periment is part of our system I think that we should be eternally vigilant against attempts to check the expression of opinions that we loathe and believe to be fraught with death, unless they so imminently threaten immediate interference with the lawful and pressing purposes of the law that an immediate check is required to save the country.[26]

The same Liberal faith is found where any question arises as to the right of an individual to freedom of thought or action:

> . . . if there is any principle of the Constitution that more imperatively calls for attachment than any other it is the principle of free thought—not free thought for those who agree with us but freedom for the thought that we hate. I think that we should adhere to that principle with regard to admission into, as well as to life within, this Country.[27]

Whenever he feels that no dominating authority restrains him, his impulse is to favor unrestricted thought and action.

In part, this deep-rooted belief in freedom is the result of the period in which he grew up and the community in which he passed the first part of his life. In the middle of the nineteenth century faith in the doctrines of the Benthamite Liberal School was at its height both in England and America. The principles of laissez-faire seemed permanently established, and the belief was generally held by intelligent people that it was unwise in other than exceptional instances to interfere with the operation of economic and social forces. In New England such belief was especially strong, both because the intellectual classes were greatly influenced by English opinion, and because it corresponded to the needs of the time. An exception, difficult in theory but easy in practice, was made in the matter of a protective tariff. Elsewhere until well after 1870 the only wish of the nineteenth century New Englander in economic matters was to be let alone. In intellectual affairs since the collapse in the late seventeenth century of the Puritan attempt to found a community of saints, free speech had been the rule and recognition of its advantage had grown steadily. Toleration was seldom gracious. Dissent from the prevalent opinion was allowed not so much because of any recognition of its possible value as because it had become recognized that suppression as a practical matter did not work. From time to time there were sporadic attempts to get rid by force of some unpopular manifestation of opinion like the Roman Catholic faith or the anti-slavery agitation. Such attempts, however, were remarkably ineffective and were rebuked by the most respected part of the community. Considering the violent passions roused by the controversies which existed, efforts at suppression of opinion were notably rare and feeble. It can fairly be said that the Massachusetts in which Justice Holmes grew up had accepted as fundamental dogmas that the individual should be let alone and that thought and talk and writing should be unrestrained by law. Even those guilty of occasional violations of faith had an uneasy sense of being wrong. Freedom was in the air.

Most men are influenced by the atmosphere about them. Particularly is this so in a nature as sensitve and quick as that of Justice Holmes to seize and assimilate ideas. Moreover, the prevailing tone of opinion was admirably adapted to his mind, at once daring in speculation, slow in reaching conclusions, and careful in taking action by reason of a deep distrust of human wisdom. His point of view is the philosophic embodiment of the conservative Liberalism of New England.

The intense patriotism of Justice Holmes is another notable trait. In scholarship and capacity for philosophic thought, in ability to meet and understand men and women of any nationality, he is a man of the world. In outlook and feeling he is intensely American and even New England. He has that double patriotism, possible only at its height in a country with a Federal Government. He has for Massachusetts and New England that sort of instinctive sentiment on which the ancient love of country was so largely based. In a speech at Ipswich made at the unveiling of tablets to the memory of certain Puritan worthies, he says:

> I love every brick and shingle of the old Massachusetts towns where once they worked and prayed, and I think it a noble and pious thing to do whatever we may by written word and moulded bronze and sculptured stone to keep our memories, our reverence and our love alive and to hand them on to new generations all too ready to forget.[28]

He has also in full measure that wider patriotism that Americans feel for the United States. They do not love it as they do their own States, as something they know and understand, that is a part of themselves. Rather they love it as an idea and almost a religion, a greater something that takes in not only their own State and region but many others, each different but all alike in finding their highest development through association. Justice Holmes feels the thrill that comes from the contemplation of the mighty structure of our Federal union. When the Massachusetss Court joined in a commemoration in honor of Marshall, Justice Holmes said the day stood:

> . . . to a patriot for the fact that time has been on Marshall's side, and that the theory for which Hamilton argued, and he decided, and Webster spoke, and Grant fought, and Lincoln died, is now our corner-stone. To the more abstract but farther-reaching contemplation of the lawyer, it stands for the rise of a new body of jurisprudence, by which guiding principles are raised above the reach of statute and State, and judges are entrusted with a solemn and hitherto unheard-of

> authority and duty. . . . It is all a symbol, if you like, but so is the flag. The flag is but a bit of bunting to one who insists on prose. Yet, thanks to Marshall and to the men of his generation—and for this above all we celebrate him and them—its red is our life-blood, its stars our world, its blue our heaven. It owns our land. At will it throws away our lives.[29]

He is able to fuse the two kinds of patriotism into the deep idea that underlies and unites them. In his speech at the 250th Anniversary of the First Church in Cambridge he said of the Puritans:

> These men and their fellows planted a congregational church, from which grew a democratic state. They planted something mightier even than institutions. Whether they knew it or not, they planted the democratic spirit in the heart of man. It is to them we owe the deepest cause we have to love our country—that instinct, that spark that makes the American unable to meet his fellow man otherwise than simply as a man, eye to eye, hand to hand, and foot to foot, wrestling naked on the sand. When the citizens of Cambridge forget that they too tread a sacred soil, that Massachusetts also has its traditions which grow more venerable and inspiring as they fade—when Harvard College is no longer dedicated to truth, and America to democratic freedom—then perhaps, but not till then, will the blood of the martyrs be swallowed in the sand, and the Puritan have lived in vain.[30]

Independence of mind and disinterestedness are inherent in one of Justice Holmes's origin. The tradition of the Puritan was one of free individual thought. His creed might be hard and narrow, but he was rarely sordid. At least he believed that he did his own thinking. The intellectual class in New England, the clergy, the teachers and the best of the professional men have never been wholly preoccupied with material ends. Certainly until recent times the standards of the Boston lawyers have not been commercial. A man's position at the Bar depended far more on his ability and character than on the amount he earned. The attitude toward money was well expressed in the current sayings that "A Boston Lawyer's estate consists of a share in the Athenaeum library and just enough money for an annuity for his widow" and that they "lived well, worked hard, and died poor." Justice Holmes counts the fact that to a lawyer money need never be the primary consideration as one of the advantages of his profession:

> I should say that one of the good things about the law is that it does not pursue money directly. When you sell goods the price which you get and your own interests are what you think about in the affair. When you try a case you think about the ways to win it and the interests of your client. In the long run this affects one's whole habit of mind, as any one will notice if he talks much with men.[31]

He has been consistently disinterested not only about money but about other things. He cares for place and promotion as affording opportunity through which honor may be won. Yet it may be doubted whether it ever entered his mind to trim his sails so as to help himself. He has been too engrossed in doing his work well for such considerations to intrude. His dissent in *Vegelahn* v. *Gunter*,[32] where he upheld the right of striking employees to picket their employer's premises provided no threats or violence were used, was written at a time when as Massachusett's opinion stood it seemed likely to end for him all prospect of judicial promotion. In the Northern Securities case[33] he decided against the view ardently held by the President who had just appointed him to the Court. No one reading these opinions could fail to feel that they were written by a man whose mind was wholly aloof from any consideration except that of reaching what seemed to him the correct result in the case before him.

Justice Holmes has reached his high place without any of those compromises either of conduct or mental integrity that often accompany success. It has come to him solely through such service as he described when he said at the Fiftieth Anniversary of his graduation:

> I learned in the regiment and in the class, the conclusion, at least, of what I think the best service that we can do for our country and for ourselves: To see so far as one may, and to feel, the great forces that are behind every detail . . . to hammer out as compact and solid a piece of work as one can, to try to make it first rate, and to leave it unadvertised.[34]

He is unusually exempt from those group loyalties, the product of business or political connections that so often unconsciously influence men's minds. At the Bar his practice was not of a kind to identify him with any particular economic interest. He has at no time shown any interest in party conflicts or the details of political life. His affiliation while in Massachusetts with the Republican Party was little more than the acquaintance of one naturally conservative in politics in the existing government. He was a Republican in Massachusetts, as he might have been a Democrat in Virginia. Nor has he ever had the sort of social relations that sometimes affect a judge's mind without his even realizing it. Intellectually hospitable to widely varied types of people, he has never been affiliated with any class or group so as to bias his judgment when its interests were concerned. He comes to each new case uninfluenced either by prejudice or passion. He fulfills to the full the noble aspiration of the Massachusetts Constitution that judges should be "as free, impartial and independent as the lot of humanity will admit."[35]

He approaches the cases that come before him with little regard to their apparent magnitude or the degree of public interest in their decision. As he has said of himself:

> My keenest interest is excited, not by what are called great questions and great cases, but by little decisions which the common run of selectors would pass by because they did not deal with the Constitution or a telephone company, yet which have in them the germ of some wider theory, and therefore of some profound interstitial change in the very tissue of the law.[36]

And in the Northern Securities case he emphasized the danger that such cases may make bad law:

> because of some accident of immediate overwhelming interest which appeals to the feelings and distorts the judgment.[37]

When such cases do come before him he deals with them as he does with his other work. One of his most conspicuous public services has been in constitutional cases.

In our American system the powers which the courts, and particularly the Supreme Court of the United States, are called upon to exercise require the utmost delicacy and judgment. The authority which interprets the law, whether written or spoken, to a large extent is in substance the lawmaker:

> Whoever hath an absolute authority to interpret any written or spoken laws, it is he who is truly the law-giver to all intents and purposes, and not the person who first wrote or spoke them.[38]

This is peculiarly true of Constitutions, which necessarily are couched in broad and general terms. Questions like what is included under words like "liberty" and "property," what is meant by phrases like "due process of law" and "equal protection of the laws," just how far the provision of the Constitution that gives Congress control over interstate and foreign commerce limits the rights of the States admit of wide differences of opinion. The answers given are likely to affect the interests and stir the feeling of the community. Moreover, the Court, while in form it is concerned merely with construction, in practice necessarily at times must seek to control the government of a State or the Federal Executive or Legislature. Such power inevitably involves danger both of excessive exercise by the Court and of unreasonable resentment in those who are restive under its control. That powers so great and unusual should have become so firmly established and so generally acquiesced in is due in large measure to the wise restraint with which they have been exercised. Marshall, himself, to whom more than any other one man our dictrine of constitutional law owes its origin, said in one of the later years of his life:

> No questions can be brought before a judicial tribunal of greater delicacy than those which involve the constitutionality of legislative acts. If they become indispensably necessary to the case, the court must meet and decide them; but if the case may be determined on other grounds, a just respect for the legislature requires that the obligation of its laws should not be unnecessarily and wantonly assailed.

and in 1831, at a speech in Philadelphia made in answer to a tribute from the Bar, he expressed the hope

> that if he might be permitted to claim for himself and his associates any part of the kind things they had said, it would be this, that they had "never sought to enlarge the judicial power beyond its proper bounds, nor feared to carry it to the fullest extent that duty required." [39]

It became the established rule that no statute should be held unconstitutional except when the case admitted of no other result.

During his entire judicial career, Justice Holmes has had this principle in mind. He has consistently refused to attempt unduly to narrow the Legislative power. Thus, in 1894, in answering a request of the Legislature as to whether under the Massachusetts Constitution an act could be passed granting to women the right to vote in town and city elections, which should take effect upon its acceptance by a majority of the voters, he said:

> I admit that the Constitution establishes a representative government, not a pure democracy. It establishes a General Court which is to be the lawmaking power. But the question is whether it puts a limit upon the power of that body to make laws. In my opinion the Legislature has the whole lawmaking power except so far as the words of the Constitution expressly or impliedly withhold it, and I think that in construing the Constitution we should remember that it is a frame of government for men of opposite opinions and for the future, and therefore not hastily import into it our own views, or unexpressed limitations derived merely from the practice of the past. I ask myself, as the only question, what words express or imply that a power to pass a law subject to rejection by the people is withheld? I find none which do so.[40]

During most of our history this principle has been adhered to, but there have been periods of social or political conflict when it has been forgotten. An instance of this occurred during the contest over slavery in the decision of the Supreme Court in the Dred Scot case.[41] It is recognized today that the Court was unwise and the case provoked such irritation as to cause criticism of the judges even by men as temperate and law-abiding as Lincoln himself. There has been another instance in our own time. In the reaction from the doctrine of laissez-faire that marked the end of the nineteenth century, there were enacted many statutes which interfered with freedom of contract, regulated business and imposed new and unheard-of restrictions on individual action. Such statutes were shocking to judges who had grown to maturity in an earlier school of opinion, and seemed to them assaults on rights the free exercise of which was essential to the public welfare. It was only natural that they should seek where possible to hold them inconsistent with constitutional provisions. What took place has been well stated by Justice Holmes:

> It is a misfortune if a judge reads his conscious or unconscious sympathy with one side or the other prematurely into the law, and forgets that what seem to him to be first principles are believed by half his fellow men to be wrong. I think that we have suffered from this misfortune, in State courts at least, and that this is another and very important truth to be extracted from the popular discontent. When twenty years ago a vague terror went over the earth and the word socialism began to be heard, I thought and still think that fear was translated into doctrines that had no proper place in the Constitution or the common law. Judges are apt to be naif, simple-minded men, and they need something of Mephistopheles. We, too, need education in the obvious—to learn to transcend our own convictions and to leave room for much that we hold dear to be done away with short of revolution by the orderly change of law.[42]

As a result of the attitude of the courts here described, there were a number of cases in which statutes were construed away or held unconstitutional. As Justice Holmes suggests in the quotation just given, the State courts were perhaps the ones to go farthest, but the Supreme Court of the United States was not exempt from the same tendency. It will be enough here to refer as instances to the Lochner case,[43] where a statute was held unconstitutional that limited employment in bakeries to ten hours a day, and *Adkins* v. *Children's Hospital*,[44] where a law enacting a minimum wage for women in the District of Columbia was set aside. It is not intended here to discuss the merits of such statutes or to criticize the court's decision in any individual case. The tendency of decisions like these is toward an extension of the powers of the court beyond anything which had gone before. They have created a widespread feeling that in social conflicts the courts are not impartial, that they try to perpetuate outworn economic theories and unduly to protect property and class interests. There has been criticism of the judges, much of it unjust and violent, and suggestions for limiting the power of the courts, many of them injudicious and none as yet in practicable form. The wise principle of restraint established by Marshall has been relaxed and a dangerous strain is put upon our institutions.

In the contest against the tendency involved in such decisions, Justice Holmes has been the leading figure. In opinion after opinion, sometimes carrying with him a majority of the Court, sometimes dissenting either alone or with one or more of his colleagues, he has upheld the right of the legislative branch of state or national government to give expression to the will of the majority unhampered by the doctrines of any special school of economic or social philosophy. As early as his dissenting opinion in the Lochner case, where the court divided five to four, he said:

> But a constitution is not intended to embody a particular economic theory, whether of paternalism and the organic relation of the citizen to the State or of *laissez-faire*. It is made for people of fundamentally differing views, and the accident of our finding certain opinions natural and familiar or novel and even shocking ought not to

> conclude our judgment upon the question whether statutes embodying them conflict with the Constitution of the United States.[45]

And earlier in the same decision: "The Fourteenth Amendment does not enact Mr. Herbert Spencer's Social Statics." To the principles he has here laid down he has steadily adhered.

The value of Justice Holmes's service does not lie in the fact that his view would permit the enactment of many statutes designed to remove social and economic ills. Whether such statutes in the long run do more good than harm is still an unsettled question and one upon which he does not enter since it lies outside his function. He speaks neither for the socialist's nor the individualist's theory of the State, but on behalf of the only safe and rational relation that under our system can be held by the judiciary toward the other branches of the government. The conservatism of his doctrine of constitutional law cannot be too strongly emphasized. It is a mere incident that under existing conditions the result should often coincide with the wish of those who hold socialistic views, just as it was a mere incident that Marshall's nationalistic doctrine enured to the immediate benefit of Jefferson whom he detested and the Democratic Party which he despised. What is essential in the position of both Holmes and Marshall is their method of approach, which has an importance that far transcends the political or social doctrines that for the time being command a popular majority. Expressed in more philosophic form and with a greater sense of historical perspective than was possible in earlier days, Justice Holmes's opinions represent a return to the wise and temperate spirit that governed our judiciary during the early years of our national life.

It is right and proper that in the reading room of the Harvard Law School the portrait of Holmes should face in equal honor the portrait of Marshall. Unlike in many things, differing in viewpoint, in temperament, in background and intellectual outlook, the two men are alike in wise statesmanship, in sagacious moderation, and in that noble humility of view that keeps men from pressing to extremes even the convictions which they hold most dear. Justice Holmes has expressed truly what this portrait and its position represent when, in a letter acknowledging notice of what was to be done, he said:

> I feel deeply the great honor that you do me. To have the picture placed where I understand it is to be, in your magnificent hall—worthy of the noble corps of professors and instructors who teach there—seems to mark the culmination of my life and leaves me ready to say "Now lettest thou thy servant depart in peace." [46]

A belief in socialism would be against all Justice Holmes's traditions and beliefs. As Mr. Wigmore has well said in his article already quoted, one of the most recurrent principles in Justice Holmes's philosophy is that "life, as a fact, is a stern, endless struggle of interests, and government can merely mitigate and regulate its conditions." [47] In his speech at the dinner of the Harvard Law School Association in 1913, he expounded his belief in individualism and said:

> . . . that the great body of property is socially administered now, and that the function of private ownership is to divine in advance the equilibrium of social desires—which socialism equally would have to divine, but which, under the illusion of self-seeking, is more poignantly and shrewdly foreseen.[48]

His views are again stated in a more recent utterance where he makes plain his fundamental distrust of socialistic legislation, though he recognizes the idealism that underlies it.

> But I hold to a few articles of a creed that I do not expect to see popular in my day. I believe that

> the wholesale social regeneration which so many now seem to expect, if it can be helped by conscious, coordinated human effort, cannot be affected appreciably by tinkering with the institution of property, but only by taking in hand life and trying to build a race. That would be my starting point for an ideal for the law. The notion that with socialized property we should have women free and a piano for everybody seems to me an empty humbug.[49]

And ends in words of generous moderation:

> It is fashionable nowadays to emphasize the criterion of social welfare as against the individualistic eighteenth century bills of rights. I may venture to refer to a book of mine published thirty-four years ago to show that it is no novelty. The trouble with some of those who hold to that modest platitude is that they are apt to take the general premise as a sufficient justification for specific measures. One may accept the premise in good faith and yet disbelieve all the popular conceptions of socialism, or even doubt whether there is a panacea in giving women votes. Personally I like to know what the bill is going to be before I order a luxury. But it is a pleasure to see more faith and enthusiasm in the young men; and I thought that one of them made a good answer to some of my skeptical talk when he said, "You would base legislation upon regrets rather than upon hopes."[50]

When he upholds the power of the Legislature, it is not because he believes in the wisdom of what it has done, but because he is unable to find any constitutional prohibition against it, and because, this being so, the only criterion of its validity is whether, considering the end in view, the statute passes the point of reason and assumes the character of a merely arbitrary fiat. As he said in *Bartels* v. *Iowa*:

> I think I appreciate the objection to the law but it appears to me to present a question upon which men reasonably might differ and therefore I am unable to say that the Constitution of the United States prevents the experiment being tried.[51]

Wherever he feels free to do so, the whole tendency of his mind is against legal restrictions and in favor of freedom for individuals, even to the extent of allowing freedom of combination. Indeed, his reluctance to interfere with Legislative action is to a large degree based on his distrust of limitations imposed upon liberty by human wisdom. Legislation in his view may be wrong, and is very likely to be wrong, but so, for that matter, may be the court, and it is better that the dominant majority in the State should be able within the widest limits possible to express its will by legislation. This, he feels, is true of the national government, and truer yet of the States.

In one of his wisest opinions he has deprecated the use of the Federal Constitution beyond the absolute compulsion of its words

> to prevent the making of social experiments that an important part of the community desires, in the insulated chambers afforded by the several States, even though the experiments may seem futile or even noxious to me and to those whose judgment I most respect.[52]

Over and above what Justice Holmes has done for his country in war and in the law, he has served it well in being among those who have stood for the romantic ideal in a time largely given over to material success. Not insensible to worldly rewards, he has always placed above them honor and those vivid sensations that to the romantic make life worth living:

> . . . who of us could endure a world, although cut up into five-acre lots and having no man upon it who was not well fed and well housed,

> without the divine folly of honor, without the senseless passion for knowledge out-reaching the flaming bounds of the possible, without ideals the essence of which is that they never can be achieved? [53]

And in all the noise and turmoil, he hears the note of the ideal:

> When one listens from above to the roar of a great city, there comes to one's ears—almost indistinguishable, but there—the sound of church bells, chiming the hours, or offering a pause in the rush, a moment for withdrawal and prayer. Commerce has outsoared the steeples that once looked down upon the marts, but still their note makes music of the din. For those of us who are not churchmen the symbol still lives. Life is a roar of bargain and battle, but in the very heart of it there rises a mystic spiritual tone that gives meaning to the whole. It transmutes the dull details into romance. It reminds us that our only but wholly adequate significance is as parts of the unimaginable whole. It suggests that even while we think that we are egotists we are living to ends outside ourselves.[54]

Nowhere does the romantic unity of his life and thought better appear than in his attitude toward War. He realizes fully its tedium and brutality.

"War, when you are at it, is horrible and dull," [55] he has said, and in Memorial Day reunions he remembers vividly its intense discomforts:

> On this day we still meet our companions in the freezing winter bivouacs and in those dreadful summer marches where every faculty of the soul seemed to depart one after another, leaving only a dumb animal power to set the teeth and to persist—a blind belief that somewhere and at last there was rest and water.[56]

Yet the dominant impressions made on him were not of War's hideous and wasteful brutality and suffering, but of its spiritual values. In the sentences that immediately follow that in which he calls War horrible, tedious and dull, he says:

> It is only when time has passed that you see that its message was divine. I hope it may be long before we are called again to sit at that master's feet. But some teacher of the kind we all need. In this snug, over-safe corner of the world we need it, that we may realize that our comfortable routine is no eternal necessity of things, but merely a little space of calm in the midst of the tempestuous untamed streaming of the world, and in order that we may be ready for danger.[67]

Years before he showed what to him had been War's deepest meaning:

> To fight out a war, you must believe something and want something with all your might. So must you do to carry anything else to an end worth reaching. More than that, you must be willing to commit yourself to a course, perhaps a long and hard one, without being able to foresee exactly where you will come out. All that is required of you is that you should go some-whither as hard as ever you can. The rest belongs to fate. One may fall—at the beginning of the charge or at the top of the earthworks; but in no other way can he reach the rewards of victory.[58]

War remains to him primarily a great experience, the most intense expression of life's activities, and it is characteristic that the speech in which he has set forth most fully his own beliefs should be entitled "The Soldier's Faith." It was natural, too, that at a dinner given in his honor by the members of the Middlesex Bar, when he was appointed to the Supreme Court of the United States, that he should have ended his speech with the words:

> As I have said, I have felt very sad at the thought of all that I leave, and sad with the wonder whether the work of twenty years on which I have spent the passion of my heart will be adjudged to have been nobly done. I have felt sad, too, with a different sadness in thinking of the future. It is an adventure into the unknown. No man can go far who never sets down his foot until he knows that the sidewalk is under it.
>
> But, gentlemen, it is a great adventure, and that thought brings with it a mighty joy. To have the chance to do one's share in shaping the laws of the whole country, spreads over me the hush that one used to feel when one was awaiting the beginning of a battle. . . .
>
> We will not falter. We will not fail. We will reach the earth works if we live, and if we fail we will leave our spirit in those who follow, and they will not turn back. All is ready. Bugler, blow the charge.[59]

He has done his work on the Supreme Court in the same spirit of devotion, with the same singleness of purpose that as a young man he fought his battle in the Army of the Potomac.

Perhaps it is his romantic spirit as much as any other one thing which has made Justice Holmes the great influence he has been on the younger men who have followed him. It has been the fashion in our time to express the world in prosaic words. Understatement, and not overstatement, is the order of the day. Our youth avoid romantic extravagances and romantic terms, but though the form changes the spirit beneath it does not. Men, and especially young men, will always be attracted by the man whose zest for life is full and complete, and who confronts every activity from a battle to a lawsuit with a sort of rapturous delight in each new experience. There will always be many like those to whom Justice Holmes spoke in 1886, when, in a lecture on the profession of the law delivered to Harvard undergraduates, he said:

And now, perhaps, I ought to have done. But I know that some spirit of fire will feel that his main question has not been answered. He will ask: What is all this to my soul? You do not bid me sell my birthright for a mess of pottage; what have you said to show that I can reach my own spiritual possibilities through such a door as this? How can the laborious study of a dry and technical system, the greedy watch for clients and practice of shop-keepers' arts, the mannerless conflicts over often sordid interests, make out a life? Gentlemen, I admit at once that these questions are not futile, that they may prove unanswerable, that they have often seemed to me unanswerable. And yet I believe there is an answer. They are the same questions that meet you in any form of practical life. If a man has the soul of Sancho Panza, the world to him will be Sancho Panza's world, but if he has the soul of an idealist, he will make—I do not say find—his world ideal. Of course, the law is not the place for the artist or the poet. The law is the calling of thinkers. But to those who believe with me that not the least godlike of man's activities is the large survey of causes, that to know is not less than to feel, I say—and I say no longer with any doubt—that a man may live greatly in the law as well as elsewhere; that there as well as elsewhere his thought may find its unity in an infinite perspective; that there as well as elsewhere he may wreak himself upon life, may drink the bitter cup of heroism, may wear his heart out after the unattainable.[60]

[EDITOR'S NOTE: Justice Holmes began to feel the effects of his great age when he was 91. One day he found it necessary to be assisted to his seat on the Bench. On that very afternoon he told his attendant at the Supreme Court, "I won't be in tomorrow" and on January 12, 1931 he submitted his resignation to President Hoover. "The time has come and I bow to the inevitable," he wrote in his own characteristic handwriting. President Hoover replied, "I know of no American retiring from public service with such a sense of affection and devotion of the whole people." Chief Justice Hughes voiced the true sentiment of the Supreme Court Justices, when he wrote to Justice Holmes on this occasion. "Your profound learning and philosophic outlook have found expression in opinions which have become classics, enriching the literature of the law as well as its substance. . . . While we are losing the privilege of daily companionship, the most precious memories of your unfailing kindness and generous nature abide with us and these memories will ever be one of the choicest traditions of the Court." Justice Holmes was touched. He replied, "For such little time as may be left to me I shall treasure it as adding gold to the sunset."

He spent his last remaining years, still mentally alert, gentle, studious, finding comfort in his friendships. The end came on March 6, 1935.

His death stirred the country. Eulogies, articles, letters on his life and work appeared everywhere. Mr. Justice Brandeis, his friend and closest colleague epitomized this tremendous surge of feeling: "And so the great man is gone."

He was buried on his 94th birthday, March 8, 1935, with full military honors in the Arlington National Cemetery alongside his wife and the Civil War veterans of the Army of the Potomac.

His last will and testament reflected his way of life. He left $283,500 to relatives, friends and servants and institutions, and the residue of the estate of $553,752 to the United States of America without restriction.

President Roosevelt in a message to Congress on April 25, 1935 commented that Holmes was "one who in war and peace devoted his life to the service of his country. Clearly he thereby sought by his gift to the nation with a generous emphasis, to mark the full measure of his faith in those principles of freedom which the country was founded to preserve." President Roosevelt continued that he hoped that the Congress would "translate this gift into a form that may serve as a permanent impulse for the maintenance of the deepest tradition that Mr. Justice Holmes embodied." President Roosevelt interpreted that tradition as "a faith in the creative possibilities of the law. For him law was an instrument of just relations between man and man. With an insight into its history that no American scholar has surpassed, with a capacity to mold ancient principles or present needs, unique in range and remarkable in prophetic power, with a grasp of its significance as the basis upon which the purposes of men are shaped, Mr. Justice Holmes sought to make the jurisprudence of the United States fulfill the great ends our nation was established to accomplish."

NOTES

OLIVER WENDELL HOLMES by Arthur Dehon Hill.

[1] "Harvard College in the War" (1884). *Speeches,* 13, 14.
[2] *Elsie Venner* (1886), 17. (31st Edition.)
[3] Speech at Fiftieth Anniversary of the Class of '61 (1911). *Speeches,* 95, 96.
[4] Speech of Bishop Lawrence at Presentation of Portrait of Mr. Justice Holmes, March 20, 1930. 32 *Harvard Alumni Bulletin,* 741, 747.
[5] "The Soldier's Faith" (1895). *Speeches,* 56, 59, 60. [Reprinted on pp. 148-156, *Infra.*]
[6] Among the services of George Frisbie Hoar and Henry Cabot Lodge to the Commonwealth and the United States should be reckoned the fact that as Senators from Massachusetts they cooperated in this nomination. See *Selections from the Correspondence of Theodore Roosevelt and Henry Cabot Lodge* (1925), 517, 525.
[7] *Massachusetts Reports, volumes* 134-182. *United States Reports, volumes* 187-282.
[8] *Collected Legal Papers by Oliver Wendell Holmes.* New York, Harcourt, Brace and Howe, 1920.
[9] *Speeches by Oliver Wendell Holmes.* Boston, Little, Brown & Co., 1918.
[10] *Speeches,* 1, 5, *et seq.*
[11] "George Otis Shattuck" (1897). *Speeches,* 70.
[12] William Allen" (1891). *Speeches,* 52.
[13] "Walbridge Abner Field" (1899). *Speeches,* 75.
[14] Elizabeth Shepley Sergeant, in *Fire under the Andes,* "Oliver Wendell Holmes" (1927), 307, 319.
[15] George Otis Shattuck" (1897). *Speeches,* 70.
[16] Speech of Dean Pound at Presentation of Portrait of Mr. Justice Holmes, March 20, 1930, 32 *Harvard Alumni Bulletin,* 741, 745, 746. See also Dean Wigmore, "Justice Holmes and the Law of Torts" (1916), 29 *Harvard Law Review,* 601.
[17] See for instance *Commonwealth* v. *Rubin,* 165 Mass. 453, and for an illustration of a case where his learning has been used by a court of which he was not then a member see the following: "As matter of history a man was once responsible for all harm done by animals or things which belonged to him regardless of his negligence. Mr. Justice Holmes sketches the development of this doctrine from Exodus xxi, 28, to comparatively recent years in *The Common Law,* pages 7 to 35." (Rugg, C. J. in *Nash* v. *Lang,* S. J. C. Mass., Sept. 16, 1929; A. S. 1841-1845.)
[18] "Learning and Science" (1895). *Speeches,* 67, 68. [Reprinted on pp. 106-107, *Infra.*]
[19] See as an illustration, *Grant Timber etc. Co.* v. *Gray* (1915), 236 U. S. 133, 134.
[20] "The Path of the Law" (1897), *Collected Legal Papers,* 167, 186, 187. [Reprinted on pp. 59-85, *Infra.*]

[21] *Olmstead, et al.* v. *United States* (1928), 277 U. S. 438, 470.

[22] "Daniel S. Richardson" (1890). *Speeches*, 46, 47, 48.

[23] "Justice Holmes and the Law of Torts" (1916), 29 *Harvard Law Review*, 601.

[24] "The Law," Speech at Suffolk Bar Association Dinner (1885). *Speeches*, 16, 17. [Reprinted on pp. 91-93, *Infra.*]

[25] "The Puritan," Speech at 250th Anniversary of the First Church in Cambridge (1886). *Speeches*, 19, 21.

[26] *Abrams* v. *United States* (1919), 250 U. S. 616, 630.

[27] *United States* v. *Schwimmer* (1929), 279 U. S. 644, 654, 655.

[28] Ipswich (1902). *Speeches*, 92.

[29] "John Marshall" (1901). *Speeches*, 87, 90, 91. [Reprinted on pp. 114-117, *Infra.*]

[30] *Speeches*, 19, 20.

[31] "The Bar as a Profession." Article in *Youth's Companion* (1896), reprinted in *Collected Legal Papers*, 153.

[32] *Vegelahn* v. *Gunter* (1896), 167 Mass. 92, 104.

[33] *Northern Securities Co.* v. *United States* (1903), 193 U. S. 400.

[34] The Class of '61 (1911). *Speeches*, 95, 96.

[35] *Constitution of Massachusetts. Declaration of Rights*, Article XXIX.

[36] "John Marshall" (1901). *Speeches*, 87, 90. [Reprinted on pp. 114-117, *Infra.*]

[37] *Northern Securities Co.* v. *United States* (1903), 193 U. S. 197, 400.

[38] Quotation from sermon by Bishop Hoadley in Gray, *Nature and Sources of the Law* (2d ed., 1921), 102, 125, 172.

[39] *John Marshall, by James B. Thayer* (1901), 105, 106.

[40] Opinions of the Justices (1894), 160 Mass. 586, 594.

[41] *Dred Scott* v. *Sandford* (1856), 19 Howard, 393.

[42] "Law and the Court," speech at dinner of the Harvard Law School Association of New York (1913). *Speeches*, 98, 101, 102. [Reprinted on pp. 94-98, *Infra.*]

[43] *Lochner* v. *New York* (1905), 198 U. S. 45.

[44] *Adkins* v. *Children's Hospital* (1923), 261 U. S. 525.

[45] *Lochner* v. *New York*, 198 U. S. 45, 75.

[46] Letter to Professor Joseph H. Beale (1930), 32 *Harvard Alumni Bulletin*, 748.

[47] Justice Holmes and the Law of Torts (1916), 29 *Harvard Law Review*, 601, 603.

[48] "Law and the Court" (1913). *Speeches*, 98, 100. [Reprinted on pp. 94-98, *Infra.*]

Justice Holmes's doctrine in constitutional cases will be found more fully stated in an article by Professor Frankfurter, published in the *Harvard Law Review* for April, 1916 (29 *Harvard Law Review*, 683), reprinted as No. 4 Dunster House Papers, Dunster House Bookshop, Cambridge, Massachusetts. In an appendix to that article is given a digest of the Justice's opinions in such cases. For the benefit of readers who are not lawyers or conversant with legal matters, it should be stated that some of the views held by Justice Holmes, as well as some of those put forward by Professor Frankfurter, or stated in this article, might not be universally accepted by the legal profession. As all lawyers know, there are substantial differences of opinion on what is the true doctrine of constitutional law. *Editor's Note*—The article by Prof. Frankfurter referred to above was revised and published in 41 Harvard Law Review 121-173, December 1929. It is reprinted on pp. 173-230, *Infra*, without the appendix.

49 "Ideals and Doubts," 10 *Ill. Law Review* (1915). Reprinted in *Collected Legal Papers*, 303, 306, 307. [Reprinted on pp. 102-105, *Infra*.]

50 *Ibid.*

51 *Bartels* v. *Iowa* (1923), 262 U. S. 404, 412.

52 *Truax* v. *Corrigan* (1921), 257 U. S. 312, 344.

53 "The Soldier's Faith" (1895). *Speeches*, 56, 59. [Reprinted on pp. 148-156, *Infra*.]

54 The Class of '61. *Speeches*, 95, 97.

55 "The Soldier's Faith" (1895). *Speeches*, 56, 62. [Reprinted on pp. 148-156, *Infra*.]

56 Address, Memorial Day (1886). *Speeches*, 1, 10.

57 "The Soldier's Faith" (1895). *Speeches*, 56, 62. [Reprinted on pp. 148-156, *Infra*.]

58 Speech on Memorial Day, Keene, N. H. (1884). *Speeches*, 1, 3.

59 Report of speech in *Boston Advertiser* of December 4, 1902.

60 "The Profession of the Law" (1886). *Speeches*, 22, 23. [Reprinted on pp. 99-101, *Infra*.]

MR. JUSTICE HOLMES

By Benjamin N. Cardozo

Reprinted from the *Harvard Law Review*, volume 44, pp. 682-692, March 1931.

This article was written in celebration of the ninetieth birthday of Mr. Justice Holmes. Benjamin Cardozo was a judge of the Court of Appeals of New York at the time he wrote this article. He was appointed Associate Justice of the U. S. Supreme Court on February 15, 1932, by President Hoover. He died July 9, 1938. Mr. Justice Cardozo has been acknowledged as one of the great legal minds of the 20th century. He is noted also as the author of the Jurisdiction of the New York Court of Appeals, 1909; The Nature of the Judicial Process, 1921; The Growth of the Law, 1924; The Paradoxes of Legal Science, 1928; Law and Literature and Other Essays, 1931, and many important law review articles.

How can I praise thee, and not overpraise,
And yet not mar the grace by stint thereof?
EURIPIDES, IPHIGENIA AT AULIS,
translated by Arthur S. Way.

To the lips of eager youth comes at times the halting doubt whether law in its study and its profession can fill the need for what is highest in the yearnings of the human spirit. Thus challenged, I do not argue. I point the challenger to Holmes. In those hours of discouragement to which not even experience is a stranger, I feel at moments the same doubt, paralyzing effort with its whispers of futility. The district is shamed and silenced by the vision of a great example.

Historian he is and scholar, a master of the learning of the law and of its traditional technique. High praise this would be for many. One almost feels the need of an apology in saying it of him, in saying it of one who is famed for so much else. There are things one takes for granted in those who stand upon the heights. The learning proper to his calling is visible at every turn, in his slightest work as in his greatest, yet a learning that knows its place, a learning subdued and harnessed to the service of philosophy. He may be groping for things vanished. He gives us glimpses of the things eternal. There are rifts in the common air that reveal an aether more luminous in the unmeasured depths beyond. Little side-remarks and comments, falling from his lips incidentally and casually, thrown off by the way in the discussion of a larger theme, have in them stuff sufficient for a treatise or a library. Who else has been able to pack a whole philosophy of legal method into a fragment of a paragraph, as in those reverberating sentences on the opening page of his lectures on *The Common Law*, written in comparative youth a half century ago? One can not renounce the joy of quoting them, familiar though they are. "The life of the law has not been logic: it has been experience. The felt necessities of the time, the prevalent moral and political theories, intuitions of public policy, avowed or unconscious, even the prejudices which judges share with their fellow-men, have had a good deal more to do than the syllogism in determining the rules by which men should be governed. The law embodies the story of a nation's development through many centuries, and it cannot be dealt with as if it contained only the axioms and corollaries of a book of mathematics." The student of juristic method, bewildered in a maze of precedents, feels the thrill of a new apocalypse in the flash of this revealing insight. Here is the text to be unfolded. All that is to come will be development and commentary.

Flashes there are like this in his earlier manner as in his latest, yet the flashes grow more frequent, the thunder peals more resonant, with the movement of the years. At the outset he was more preoccupied with learning as a present end. One sees the marks of the preoccupation in the lectures on *The Common Law*; one sees it in other essays, the studies of early English equity, and of the law of executors and agents, and in many of the opinions written while he was still a judge in Massachusetts. This does not mean, indeed, that in seeking the present end he was forgetful, even at the beginning, of the relation of that end to others more nearly ultimate in value. History for him at all times has been something more than archaeology. He has relished the study of the past for its own interest and savor, but even more for its capacity to give coherence and significance to the study of the present. He has gone down into the depths, but he has remembered that the depths are the foundations of the heights. Yet withal, a change of emphasis has declared itself with the passing of the years. As time goes on, he is less content than of old with adherence to a method whereby research into the recesses of the past holds the centre of the stage in the unfolding through the ages of the endless drama of the law. Perhaps this is merely because he has explored the depths already and wrung from their recesses whatever secrets they can tell. One seems to read in him at all events the tokens of a growing sympathy with the present and the future when their voices are heard decrying all this deference for things departed, are heard pleading with some petulance their own capacity and privilege to hold the centre of the stage themselves. "It is revolting," he responds, "to have no better reason for a rule of law than that so it was laid down in the time of Henry IV. It is still more revolting if the grounds upon which it was laid down have vanished long since, and the rule simply persists from blind imitation of the past. For the rational study of the law the black-letter man may be the man of the present, but the man of the future is the man of statistics and the master of economics."[1] This is 1897, eleven years before the coming of *Muller v. Oregon.*[2] In processing the new ardor, he can still be loyal to the old love. "I have done some black-letter reading of my own," he tells us in one of his addresses, though I quote him from uncertain and perhaps imperfect recollection. One detects a lingering note of tenderness, a note halfway between pride and elegiac reminiscence.

As historian and mere technician his place would be secure in any survey of the legal scene. But he has come in these later years to fill another place also, and that still more august. He is today for all students of the law and for all students of human society the philosopher and the seer, the greatest of our age in the domain of jurisprudence, and one of the greatest of the ages. So deeply infused is his philosophy into the texture of his creative work that to separate it from its setting, to make explicit what is implicit everywhere, is not an easy task, not easy because the light seems to lose a little of its mellow radiance when extracted and diverted into a concentrated ray. What is law? What is its origin? What are its capacities and its limits? What its ends and aims, the purpose of its being? In this complex modern world of ours, questions such as these are at the root of many a legal problem which to the thought of a simpler age could have been solved by a mere comparison of precedents without summoning divine philosophy. Our philosopher has known better. Zones, of course, there are where precedents are so controlling that choice is predetermined. These are the trodden highways, builded by the centuries, builded as long ago at times as the roads of ancient Rome. But highways are not everywhere. Once turn into the fields and you will hardly stir a step in the solution of a novel problem, in particular a problem in the domain of public law, without finding yourself face to face with queries that are ultimate.

Is a legal concept a finality, or only a pragmatic tool? Shall we think of liberty as a constant, or, better, as a variable that may shift from age to age? Is its content given us by deduction from unalterable premises, or by a toilsome process of induction from circumstances of time and place? Shall we say that restraints and experiments will be permitted if all that is affected is the liberty to act, when experiment or restraint will be forbidden if the result is an encroachment upon liberty of thought or speech? In the development of a system of case-law is logic one organon among many, or an umpire that displaces rivals? Are the origins of a precept subordinate to its ends, or are ends to be sacrificed if to adhere to them is to be unfaithful to beginnings?

I do not dare to say how Holmes would make answer to these queries or others like to them in spirit. All that I can say with certitude is that such queries are slumbering within many a common lawsuit, which can be lifted from meanness up to dignity if the great judge is by to see what is within. I may think that I am able, however dumbly or intuitively, to divine the tenor of his answers, but safer it will be by the touchstones of a few examples to let him answer for himself. The examples that I choose are part of the common coinage of juristic thought, a little worn, some of them, in passing constantly from hand to hand, but recognized as legal tender wherever truth is sovereign.

"The Fourteenth Amendment does not enact Mr. Herbert Spencer's Social Statics." [3] "While the courts must exercise a judgment of their own, it by no means is true that every law is void which may seem to the judges who pass upon it, excessive, unsuited to its ostensible end, or based upon conceptions of morality with which they disagree. Considerable latitude must be allowed for difference of view as well as for possible peculiar conditions which this court can know but imperfectly, if at all. Otherwise a constitution, instead of embodying only relatively fundamental rules of right, as generally understood by all English-speaking communities, would become the partisan of a particular set of ethical or economical opinions, which by no means are held *semper ubique et ab omnibus*." [4] "When men have realized that time has upset many fighting faiths, they may come to believe even more than they believe the very foundations of their own conduct that the ultimate good desired is better reached by free trade in ideas—that the best test of truth is the power of the thought to get itself accepted in the competition of the market, and that truth is the only ground upon which their wishes safely can be carried out. That at any rate is the theory of our Constitution. It is an experiment, as all life is an experiment." [5] "When a legal distinction is determined, as no one doubts that it may be, between night and day, childhood and maturity, or any other extremes, a point has to be fixed or a line has to be drawn, or gradually picked out by successive decisions, to mark where the change takes place. Looked at by itself without regard to the necessity behind it the line or point seems arbitrary. It might as well or nearly as well be a little more to one or the other. But when it is seen that a line or point there must be, and that there is no mathematical or logical way of fixing it precisely, the decision of the legislature must be accepted unless we can say that it is very wide of any reasonable mark." [6] "In the organic relations of modern society it may sometimes be hard to draw the line that is supposed to limit the authority of the legislature to exercise or delegate the power of eminent domain. But to gather the streams from waste and to draw from them energy, labor without brains, and so to save mankind from toil that it can be spared, is to supply what, next to intellect, is the very foundation of all our achievements and all our welfare. If that purpose be not public we should be at a loss to say what is." [7]

There is a famous passage in the essay on the Study of Poetry where Matthew Arnold tells us how to separate the gold from the alloy in the coinage of the poets by the test of a few lines which we are to carry in our thoughts. The lines that I have quoted from a few opinions among many may do the like for those who would know the philosophic mind in law. How he views as from a peak the horizon of the lives of men, the whole scene of their activities with all its regions ands its divisions, whether of nature or of art! There is the keenness of perception that marks the little barriers between one region and another, but along with this there is the humor, the charity, the sense of historic values, that recalls with plangent iteration how many another barrier, as lofty and intimidating, has been leveled to the dust. "I have labored carefully," says Spinoza in that famous statement of his outlook upon life which time and repetition are without capacity to mar, "I have labored carefully not to mock, lament and execrate the actions of men; I have labored to understand them." An echo of that cadence is sounding in our day and land.

Men speak of him as a great Liberal, a lover of Freedom and its apostle. All this in truth he is, yet in his devotion to Freedom he has not been willing to make himself the slave of a mere slogan. No one has labored more incessantly to demonstrate the truth that rights are absolute, though they are ever struggling and tending to declare themselves as such. "There is nothing that I more deprecate than the use of the Fourteenth Amendment beyond the absolute compulsion of its words to prevent the making of social experiments that an important part of the community desires, in the insulated chambers afforded by the several States, even though the experiment may seem futile or even noxious to me and to those whose judgment I most respect." [8] He has known how to distinguish between one freedom and another. He has vividly perceived what was pointed out by de Tocqueville a century ago that one kind of liberty may cancel and destroy another, and that stronger even than the love of liberty is the passion for something different, different in name and yet at its core the same, the passion for equality. Restrictions, vexations if viewed alone, may be seen to be necessary in the long run "to establish the equality of position." [9] in which true liberty begins. Many an appeal to freedom is the masquerade of privilege or inequality seeking to intrench itself behind the catchword of a principle. There must be give and take at many points, allowance must be made for the play of the machine, or in the clash of jarring rivalries the pretending absolutes will destroy themselves and ordered freedom too. Only in one field is compromise to be excluded, or kept within the narrowest limits. There shall be no compromise of the freedom to think one's thoughts and speak them, except at those extreme borders where thought merges into action. There is to be no compromise here, for thought freely communicated, if I may borrow my own words, is the indispensable condition of intelligent experimentation, the one test of its validity. There is no freedom without choice, and there is no choice without knowledge—or none that is not illusory. Here are goods to be conserved, however great the seeming sacrifice. We may not squander the thought that will be the inheritance of the ages.

No one has been able to combat more effectively than he the repression of a formula, the tyranny of tags and tickets. Is it a question of the competence of a legislature to respond by novel legislation to the call of an emergent need? Fettered by the word, we are too often satisfied to say that competence exists if it can be brought within a cliché, "the police power" of the state; and at home in the protective phrase, we settle back at peace. Is it a question of the quality of the need, the pressure of the emergency, that will bring the power into play? We say the need must have relation to an activity "affected with a public interest"; and again at home in the protective phrase, we are happy in the thought that while we keep within that shelter there can come no damage to the state. The familiar form beguiles into an assurance of security. Danger as well as deception may indeed be lurking ill concealed, danger as well as deception in a false appearance of exactitude. The threat is too remote to jolt us out of the deeply-cloven ruts. In the end we may find we have been sinking a little deeper than we willed. For a cliché is not a barrier to power intent upon its aims, though sluggishness of thought may lead us for a season to act as if it were. A label is not a dyke or dam that will repel the onset of the flood—the rush of an emergent need—though it may breed a sense of safety till the flood has swept beyond. All this the great master has been quick to see.[10] He has seen it when, paternally indulgent, he has been willing for the hour to let the cramping phrases pass, to let them pass with a word of warning that the need may yet arrive to throw them over or expand them, to pull out of the rut at whatever cost of pain and effort. The repetition of a catchword can hold analysis in fetters for fifty years and more.[11]

There are other marks of greatness that even the briefest survey will be reluctant to ignore. In our homage to the philosopher we must pause to pay homage to the literary craftsman. "I am studying law," writes the youthful James Russell Lowell in a letter to a comrade, "and shall probably become Chief Justice of the United States." Unfortunately for the law, and perhaps also for the Chief Justiceship, he was enticed into the paths of literature, though every now and then one will find in his essays the phrases and allusions that bespeak the training of the lawyer. The professions look with jealous eyes upon genius and scholarship kidnapped and converted. "I wish," says Leslie Stephen, "that Disraeli could have stuck to his novels instead of rising to be Prime Minister of England." One does not need, when one thinks of Holmes, to lament the decline or the rise—according to one's point of view—of a great writer into a jurist. One does not need to lament, for here is one who has known how to combine the two callings, and to combine them to the glory of each. Law in his hands has been philosophy, but it has been literature too. If any one has ever been sceptical of the transfiguring power of style, let him look to these opinions. They will put scepticism to flight. How compact they are, a sentence where most of us would use a paragraph, a paragraph for a page. What a tang in their pointed phrases; what serenity in their placid depths; what a glow and a gleam when they become radiant with heat. One almost writhes in despair at the futility, too painfully apparent, of imitation or approach. These qualities of style are visible, of course, when he has spoken in great causes. What interests me as much is to find them as clearly visible in causes less pretentious, causes that to an art less consistent or fastidious might have seemed trivial and humble. He has known that greatness in such matters can be independent of the stakes. "Great cases," he tells us, "are called great, not by reason of their real importance in shaping the law of the future, but because of some accident of immediate overwhelming interest which appeals to the feelings and distorts the judgment."[12] Many a time, in turning the pages of an opinion devoted to a humdrum theme, some problem perhaps of contract or of negligence, I have come across a winged sentence that seemed with its wings to chase obscurity away. Curious, I have gone back to the beginning, to find the name of Holmes.

There is a fine conscience in such matters, a conscience that is scornful, even in trifles, of work lower than one's best. Not even the draftsman of an ordinary lease. we are reminded by Sir Frederick Pollock, can produce really good work "unless he has a share of artistic feeling in the eminent sense, and takes a certain artistic pride in the quality of his workmanship, apart from the reward he will get for it." More recently Dr. Whitehead has been preaching the same lesson. "Style," he says, "is the ultimate morality of mind." "The administrator with a sense of style hates waste; the engineer with a sense of style economizes his material; the artisan with a sense of style prefers good work"; to which we may add that the judge with a sense of style will balk at inaccurate and slipshod thought. Style is thus a form of honor and courage, just as, Santayana tells us, is the pursuit of truth always. One can not read these opinions without seeing honor and courage written down on every page.

The calendar tells us he is old, as longevity is reckoned by the generations that wither like the grass. So, I suppose, he is, for the volume following this preface has been planned to be a tribute of devotion at the end of ninety years. One speaks a commonplace, however, when one says that his spirit is still young. Perhaps we may find in his own words the key to the mystery, or at least the keynote of his thought. "One of my favorite paradoxes," he writes in a letter to a friend, "is that everything is dead in twenty-five (or fifty) years. The author no longer says to you what he meant to say. If he is original, his new truths have been developed and become familiar in improved form—his errors exploded. If he is not a philosopher but an artist, the emotional emphasis has changed." There is little danger that a mind impressed so deeply with a sense of the transient and ephemeral in the achievement of the human spirit will lose the spring of its fine coils with the rust of the corroding years.

Reading these pages over, I am haunted by the fear that I may have given an impression of aloofness, of a being less or more than human. Those of us who know him can bear devoted witness that the impression, if given, would be woefully at odds with truth. A majestic intellect is there, as any one would know after the privilege of the barest glimpse. Wit there is, too, and eager interest, and nimbleness of thought and fancy. But there are many things besides. Serenity is there, and gentleness, and most of all benignancy—the benignancy of a soul that has fashioned its own scale of values, and in those deeply graven markings has found the quietude of peace. Not even benignancy, however, sums up the tale of the impression. A pervasive sense one has of something not to be defined, a quality which, for lack of a better term, one may speak of as simplicity. I do not mean that he is without the pride of mind inseparable from gifts so rare. No one favored so superbly by the gods and the muses could be lacking altogether in a sense of his own powers. The knowledge has not saved him from something like a shy distrust, a questioning and a doubting, as if he felt the need to reassure himself that in looking into his own soul he was viewing something more than the gleam of a mirage. Sceptic of many things, of many boasted certainties, he is sceptic even of himself.

Among my hoarded treasures is a letter from his hand. He has given me his consent to quote from it. "I always have thought," he writes, "that not place or power or popularity makes the success that one desires, but the trembling hope that one has come near to an ideal. The only ground that warrants a man for thinking that he is not living the fool's paradise if he ventures such a hope is the voice of a few masters. . . . I feel it so much that I don't want to talk about it." This from the great overlord of the law and its philosophy.

One does not know where to match the thought in its perfection and engaging modesty unless in the "trembling hope" of another worshipper of truth and beauty. The wistful words of Keats re-echo through the spaces of a century. "I think I shall be among the English poets after my death."

There was no "fool's paradise" for Keats, nor will there be for Holmes.

NOTES

MR. JUSTICE HOLMES by Benjamin N. Cardozo

* This essay [is] the introduction to a volume entitled MR. JUSTICE HOLMES (Coward-McCann, Inc.).

1 *The Path of the Law,* COLLECTED LEGAL PAPERS (1920) 167, 186, 187. [Reprinted on pp. 59-85, *Infra.*]

2 208 U. S. 412 (1908).

3 Lochner v. New York, 198 U. S. 45, 75 (1905).

4 Otis v. Parker, 187 U. S. 606, 608-09 (1903).

5 Abrams v. United States, 250 U. S. 616, 630 (1919).

6 Louisville Gas Co. v. Coleman, 277 U. S. 32, 41 (1927).

7 Mount Vernon Co. v. Alabama Power Co., 240 U. S. 30, 32 (1916).

8 Truax v. Corrigan, 257 U. S. 312, 344 (1921).

9 Coppage v. Kansas, 236 U. S. 1, 27 (1915).

10 See, *e. g.,* Frost v. California, 271 U. S. 583, 600 (1926); Tyson & Bro. v. Banton, 273 U. S. 418, 445 (1927); Liggett Co. v. Baldridge, 278 U. S. 105, 114 (1928); *cf. Law in Science and Science in Law,* COLLECTED LEGAL PAPERS 210, 230. [Reprinted on pp. 124-147, *Infra.*]

11 *Law in Science and Science in Law,* COLLECTED LEGAL PAPERS 210, 230. [Reprinted on pp. 124-147, *Infra.*]

12 Northern Securities Co. v. United States, 193 U. S. 197, 400 (1904).

MR. JUSTICE HOLMES

By Sir Frederick Pollock

Reprinted from *Harvard Law Review,* volume 44, pp. 693-696, March, 1931.

This article was written in celebration of the 90th birthday of Mr. Justice Holmes. Sir Frederick Pollock was born in 1845 and was almost a life-long friend of Mr. Justice Holmes. He corresponded with Justice Holmes continually from 1874, to the day of his death. See *Holmes-Pollock Letters,* edited by Mark de Wolfe Howe, 1941, 2v. At the time he wrote this article he was a judge of the Admiralty Court of Cinque Ports, and a noted author of English law and history. He edited the *Law Quarterly Review,* a leading English legal periodical, from 1885 to 1919, and was editor of the *Law Reports* from 1895 to 1935. During his long life he wrote Principles of Contract, 1876; Digest of the Law of Partnership, 1877; the Law of Torts, 1887; Possession in the Common Law (with Sir R. S. Wright), 1888; History of English Law (with F. W. Maitland), 1895; 2nd ed. 1898; Selden's Table Talk, 1927; Spinoza, His Life and Philosophy, 1880 and 1912. His books were quite popular and ran into many editions. He died in 1937.

I FIND myself in some difficulty in complying with your request to say something on this occasion. To frame a considered estimate of my friend Mr. Justice Holmes' work and its value would not be possible for me—nor, I think, for any man—within the time allowed. You know, of course, that I do not pretend to be impartial. On the whole I will take refuge in falling back upon the past.

It may be of some little interest to my learned friends in New England if not in any wider circle to recall the memory of what I said about Holmes on *The Common Law* when it was new, in an article in the old *Saturday Review,* necessarily unsigned according to the custom of most journals at that time. It was a time, let me remind your younger readers—A.D. 1881 to wit—when English-speaking law schools were in their infancy and serious law reviews, in English at any rate, not yet born, when current text-books were with few exceptions merely empirical, and most practicing lawyers believed that law could be learnt only by rule of thumb (as some still do) and that professed teachers of law were no better than impostors (as indeed some were not). Here follow some of the words I wrote then.

"Mr. O. W. Holmes's simple and general title covers something quite different from the string of maxims and rules, supported by more or less relevant examples and more or less plausible reasons, which we have to be content with in most legal expositions. He gives us a searching historical and analytical criticism of several of the leading notions of English law; not an antiquarian discussion first and a theoretical discussion afterwards, but a continuous study in the joint light of policy and history. He shows us how dimly felt grounds of expediency, struggling with traditional rules of which the real grounds were mostly forgotten, have issued in the establishment of principles which are now capable of being expressed in a rational form for the most part, though many minute irregularities in their application, and now and then downright anomalies, preserve the memory of conflict and compromise."—My young friends who were born in the twentieth century, does this now read to you like common learning? If it does, you have Mr. Justice Holmes to thank for it more than any other man.

I went on to mention the chapters on the grounds of liability in general (Lectures II, III, IV) as being to my mind the best part of the book, and summarized their doctrines. "Blameworthiness [in criminal law] is the ultimate ground of liability, but the actual measure of liability is not what is blameworthy in the particular individual, but what would, in his circumstances, be blameworthy in a man of ordinary knowledge and capacities [*et inde vide plura postea per* Holmes, J., in *Commonwealth v. Pierce,* 138 Mass. 165, 180 (1884)]. An external standard of conduct is established, to which the subject is bound to come up at his peril. Whether it has been conformed to in a particular case is a question in general independent of the person's actual state of mind. . . . If he had a chance sufficient for a reasonable man he is liable, notwithstanding that his individual ability or perceptions were not up to the average. . . . Mr. Holmes goes on to show that the same principle of the external standard holds in the theory of civil wrongs, and particularly in that much confused subject [as it was fifty years ago] the law of negligence. What the law means by negligence, he strongly points out, is not as assumed by some modern teachers [and still maintained by a few], a state of the party's mind. This is more clearly seen by taking it as what it really is, a negative term. Negligence is the want of diligence. But diligence is not something in the party's mind; it is a matter of external conduct, the actual exercise of a certain measure of intelligence and caution."

Finally I wrote: "Altogether, Mr. Holmes's book will be a most valuable—we should almost say an indispensable—companion to the scientific student of legal history." The prophecy has been fulfilled, and I suppose the event appears to our younger brethren as quite in the natural or even necessary course of things. In fact it did not come about immediately. A certain library committee, presumably composed of learned persons, actually refused to buy *The Common Law.* There is no reason to name it. So I take a certain satisfaction at this day in having prophesied not only aright but speedily and confidently.

Mr. Justice Holmes did not invent the external standard of prudence or discover the Reasonable Man. They may be traced through our medieval sages and the canonists to the classical Roman lawyers, back to the Greek philosophers, especially the Stoics, and ultimately to Aristotle; and the doctrine was enounced in a practical form by English judges of the nineteenth century, to whom due honour is rendered in *The Common Law*. But Holmes was the first to perceive the far-reaching importance of the doctrine and to set it forth in an orderly and convincing exposition. The like observation might be made on several other matters discussed in *The Common Law*.

Concerning Mr. Justice Holmes' judicial opinions Professor Frankfurter lately said, consciously or unconsciously using a classical figure of Eastern poetry: "To consider Mr. Justice Holmes' opinions is to string pearls." But so large a number of those opinions deal with questions peculiar to American constitutional law that an English workman is hardly competent to handle them. Also much has already been written, and very well written, about them. I will, therefore, within my proper limits, only give thanks for two pretty recent contributions to sound learning in questions of pure common law. *United Zinc & Chemical Co. v. Britt,* 258 U. S. 268 (1922), gave a timely check to the persistent attempts made through a long course of years to deny, in effect, that a child below the age of discretion can in any circumstances be a trespasser. Our House of Lords has taken the same line in *Robert Addie & Sons (Collieries) v. Dumbrech,* [1929] A. C. 358. And in *Baltimore & Ohio R. R. v. Goodman,* 275 U. S. 66 (1927), the Court, *per* Holmes, J., tend to remind every man who drives or walks over a grade crossing that he must stop for the train, not the train stop for him, and he must use reasonable caution accordingly. Why this decision surprised any one I can not understand.

Some people seem to think that Mr. Justice Holmes is always dissenting. Does he really dissent much oftener than his learned brethren, or is the impression due to the weight rather than the number of the dissents? I read in an able tract I have already cited that nearly one fifth of Mr. Justice Miller's opinions were dissenting ones. Being acquainted with only a fraction of Mr. Justice Holmes' opinions I can not guess what the result of similar computation would be. As to those I do know I have found that, whether they speak with the voice of the Court or only with his own, I almost always agree with them. But, as I said at the outset, I am not impartial.

PART II.

SPEECHES AND WRITINGS OF MR. JUSTICE HOLMES

THE PATH OF THE LAW

An address delivered by Mr. Justice Holmes at the dedication of the new hall of the Boston University School of Law, on January 8, 1897. At the time he was a justice of the Supreme Judicial Court of Massachusetts.

Reprinted from Harvard Law Review, volume 10, pp. 457-478 (1896).

WHEN we study law we are not studying a mystery but a well known profession. We are studying what we shall want in order to appear before judges, or to advise people in such a way as to keep them out of court. The reason why it is a profession, why people will pay lawyers to argue for them or to advise them, is that in societies like ours the command of the public force is intrusted to the judges in certain cases, and the whole power of the state will be put forth, if necessary, to carry out their judgments and decrees. People want to know under what circumstances and how far they will run the risk of coming against what is so much stronger than themselves, and hence it becomes a business to find out when this danger is to be feared. The object of our study, then, is prediction, the prediction of the incidence of the public force through the instrumentality of the courts.

The means of the study are a body of reports, of treatises, and of statutes, in this country and in England, extending back for six hundred years, and now increasing annually by hundreds. In these sibylline leaves are gathered the scattered prophecies of the past upon the cases in which the axe will fall. These are what properly have been called the oracles of the law. For the most important and pretty nearly the whole meaning of every new effort of legal thought is to make these prophecies more precise, and to generalize them into a thoroughly connected system. The process is one, from a lawyer's statement of a case, eliminating as it does all the dramatic elements with which his client's story has clothed it, and retaining only the facts of legal import, up to the final analyses and abstract universals of theoretic jurisprudence. The reason why a lawyer does not mention that his client wore a white hat when he made a contract, while Mrs. Quickly would be sure to dwell upon it along with the parcel gilt goblet and the sea-coal fire, is that he foresees that the public force will act in the same way whatever his client had upon his head. It is to make the prophesies easier to be remembered and to be understood that the teachings of the decisions of the past are put into general propositions and gathered into text-books, or that statutes are passed in a general form. The primary rights and duties with which jurisprudence busies itself again are nothing but prophecies. One of the many evil effects of the confusion between legal and moral ideas, about which I shall have something to say in a moment, is that theory is apt to get the cart before the horse, and to consider the right or the duty as something existing apart from and independent of the consequences of its breach, to which certain sanctions are added afterward. But, as I shall try to show, a legal duty so called is nothing but a prediction that if a man does or omits certain things he will be made to suffer in this or that way by judgment of the court;—and so of a legal right.

The number of our predictions when generalized and reduced to a system is not unmanageably large. They present themselves as a finite body of dogma which may be mastered within a reasonable time. It is a great mistake to be frightened by the ever increasing number of reports. The reports of a given jurisdiction in the course of a generation take up pretty much the whole body of the law, and restate it from the present point of view. We could reconstruct the corpus from them if all that went before were burned. The use of the earlier reports is mainly historical, a use about which I shall have something to say before I have finished.

I wish, if I can, to lay down some first principles for the study of this body of dogma or systematized prediction which we call the law, for men who want to use it as the instrument of their business to enable them to prophesy in their turn, and, as bearing upon the study, I wish to point out an ideal which as yet our law has not attained.

The first thing for a business-like understanding of the matter is to understand its limits, and therefore I think it desirable at once to point out and dispel a confusion between morality and law, which sometimes rises to the height of conscious theory, and more often and indeed constantly is making trouble in detail without reaching the point of consciousness. You can see very plainly that a bad man has as much reason as a good one for wishing to avoid an encounter with the public force, and therefore you can see the practical importance of the distinction between morality and law. A man who cares nothing for an ethical rule which is believed and practised by his neighbors is likely nevertheless to care a good deal to avoid being made to pay money, and will want to keep out of jail if he can.

I take it for granted that no hearer of mine will misrepresent what I have to say as the language of cynicism. The law is the witness and external deposit of our moral life. Its history is the history of the moral development of the race. The practice of it, in spite of popular jests, tends to make good citizens and good men. When I emphasize the difference between law and morals I do so with reference to a single end, that of learning and understanding the law. For that purpose you must definitely master its specific marks, and it is for that that I ask you for the moment to imagine yourselves indifferent to other and greater things.

I do not say that there is not a wider point of view from which the distinction between law and morals becomes of secondary or no importance, as all mathematical distinctions vanish in presence of the infinite. But I do say that that distinction is of the first importance for the object which we are here to consider, a right study and mastery of the law as a business with well understood limits, a body of dogma enclosed within definite lines. I have just shown the practical reason for saying so. If you want to know the law and nothing else, you must look at it as a bad man, who cares only for the material consequences which such knowledge enables him to predict, not as a good one, who finds his reasons for conduct, whether inside the law or outside of it, in the vaguer sanctions of conscience. The theoretical importance of the distinction is no less, if you would reason on your subject aright. The law is full of phraseology drawn from morals, and by the mere force of language continually invites us to pass from one domain to the other without perceiving it, as we are sure to do unless we have the boundary constantly before our minds. The law talks about rights, and duties, and malice, and intent, and negligence, and so forth, and nothing is easier, or, I may say, more common in legal reasoning, than to take these words in their moral sense, at some stage of the argument, and so to drop into fallacy. For instance, when we speak of the rights of man in a moral sense, we mean to mark the limits of interference with individual freedom which we think are prescribed by conscience, or by our ideal, however reached. Yet it is certain that many laws have been enforced in the past, and it is likely that some are enforced now, which are condemned by the most enlightened opinion of the time, or which at all events pass the limit of interference as many consciences would draw it. Manifestly, therefore, nothing but confusion of thought can result from assuming that the rights of man in a moral sense are equally rights in the sense of the Constitution and the law. No doubt simple and extreme cases can be put of imaginable laws which the statute-making power would not dare to enact, even in the absence of written constitutional prohibitions, because the community would rise in rebellion and fight; and this gives some plausibility to the proposition that the law, if not a part of morality, is limited by it. But this limit of power is not coextensive with any system of morals. For the most part it falls far within the lines of any such system, and in some cases may extend beyond them, for reasons drawn from the habits of a particular people at a particular time. I once heard the late Professor Agassiz say that a German population would rise if you added two cents to the price of a glass of beer. A statute in such a case would be empty words, not because it was wrong, but because it could not be enforced. No one will deny that wrong statutes can be and are enforced, and we should not all agree as to which were the wrong ones.

The confusion with which I am dealing besets confessedly legal conceptions. Take the fundamental question, What constitutes the law? You will find some text writers telling you that it is something different from what is decided by the courts of Massachusetts or England, that it is a system of reason, that it is a deduction from principles of ethics or admitted axioms or what not, which may or may not coincide with the decisions. But if we take the view of our friend the bad man we shall find that he does not care two straws for the axioms or deductions, but that he does want to know what the Massachusetts or English courts are likely to do in fact. I am much of this kind. The prophecies of what the courts will do in fact, and nothing more pretensions, are what I mean by the law.

Take again a notion which as popularly understood is the widest conception which the law contains;—the notion of legal duty, to which already I have referred. We fill the word with all the content which we draw from morals. But what does it mean to a bad man? Mainly, and in the first place, a prophecy that if he does certain things he will be subjected to disagreeable consequences by way of imprisonment or compulsory payment of money. But from his point of view, what is the difference between being fined and being taxed a certain sum for doing a certain thing? That his point of view is the test of legal principles is shown by the many discussions which have arisen in the courts on the very question whether a given statutory liability is a penalty or a tax. On the answer to this question depends the decision whether conduct is legally wrong or right, and also whether a man is under compulsion or free. Leaving the criminal law on one side, what is the difference between the liability under the mill acts or statutes authorizing a taking by eminent domain and the liability for what we call a wrongful conversion of property where restoration is out of the question? In both cases the party taking another man's property has to pay its fair value as assessed by a jury, and no more. What significance is there in calling one taking right and another wrong from the point of view of the law? It does not matter, so far as the given consequence, the compulsory payment, is concerned, whether the act to which it is attached is described in terms of praise or in terms of blame, or whether the law purports to prohibit it or to allow it. If it matters at all, still speaking from the bad man's point of view, it must be because in one case and not in the other some further disadvantages, or at least some further consequences, are attached to the act by the law. The only other disadvantages thus attached to it which I ever have been able to think of are to be found in two somewhat insignificant legal doctrines, both of which might be abolished without much disturbance. One is, that a contract to do a prohibited act is unlawful, and the other, that, if one of two or more joint wrongdoers has to pay all the damages, he cannot recover contribution from his fellows. And that I believe is all. You see how the vague circumference of the notion of duty shrinks and at the same time grows more precise when we wash it with cynical acid and expel everything except the object of our study, the operations of the law.

Nowhere is the confusion between legal and moral ideas more manifest than in the law of contract. Among other things, here again the so-called primary rights and duties are invested with a mystic significance beyond what can be assigned and explained. The duty to keep a contract at common law means a prediction that you must pay damages if you do not keep it,—and nothing else. If you commit a tort, you are liable to pay a compensatory sum. If you commit a contract, you are liable to pay a compensatory sum unless the promised event comes to pass, and that is all the difference. But such a mode of looking at the matter stinks in the nostrils of those who think it advantageous to get as much ethics into the law as they can. It was good enough for Lord Coke, however, and here, as in many other cases, I am content to abide with him. In Bromage *v.* Genning,[1] a prohibition was sought in the King's Bench against a suit in the marches of Wales for the specific performance of a covenant to grant a lease, and Coke said that it would subvert the intention of the covenantor, since he intends it to be at his election either to lose the damages or to make the lease. Sergeant Harris for the plaintiff confessed that he moved the matter against his conscience, and a prohibition was granted. This goes further than we should go now, but it shows what I venture to say has been the common law point of view from the beginning, although Mr. Harriman, in his very able little book upon Contracts has been misled, as I humbly think, to a different conclusion.

I have spoken only of the common law, because there are some cases in which a logical justification can be found for speaking of civil liabilities as imposing duties in an intelligible sense. These are the relatively few in which equity will grant an injunction, and will enforce it by putting the defendant in prison or otherwise punishing him unless he complies with the order of the court. But I hardly think it advisable to shape general theory from the exception, and I think it would be better to cease troubling ourselves about primary rights and sanctions altogether, than to describe our prophecies concerning the liabilities commonly imposed by the law in those inappropriate terms.

I mentioned, as other examples of the use by the law of words drawn from morals, malice, intent, and negligence. It is enough to take malice as it is used in the law of civil liability for wrongs,—what we lawyers call the law of torts,—to show you that it means something different in law from what it means in morals, and also to show how the difference has been obscured by giving to principles which have little or nothing to do with each other the same name. Three hundred years ago a parson preached a sermon and told a story out of Fox's Book of Martyrs of a man who had assisted at the torture of one of the saints, and afterward died, suffering compensatory inward torment. It happened that Fox was wrong. The man was alive and chanced to hear the sermons, and thereupon he sued the parson. Chief Justice Wray instructed the jury that the defendant was not liable, because the story was told innocently, without malice. He took malice in the moral sense, as importing a malevolent motive. But nowadays no one doubts that a man may be liable without any malevolent motive at all, for false statements manifestly calculated to inflict temporal damage. In stating the case in pleading, we still should call the defendant's conduct malicious; must, in my opinion at least, the word means nothing about motives, or even about the defendant's attitude toward the future, but only signifies that the tendency of his conduct under the known circumstances was very plainly to cause the plaintiff temporal harm.[2]

In the law of contract the use of moral phraseology has led to equal confusion, as I have shown in part already, but only in part. Morals deal with the actual internal state of the individual's mind, what he actually intends. From the time of the Romans down to now, this mode of dealing has affected the language of the law as to contract, and the language used has reacted upon the thought. We talk about a contract as a meeting of the minds of the parties, and thence it is inferred in various cases that there is no contract because their minds have not met; that is, because they have intended different things or because one party has not known of the assent of the other. Yet nothing is more certain than that parties may be bound by a contract to things which neither of them intended, and when one does not know of the other's assent. Suppose a contract is executed in due form and in writing to deliver a lecture, mentioning no time. One of the parties thinks that the promise will be construed to them at once, within a week. The other thinks that it means when he is ready. The court says that it means within a reasonable time. The parties are bound by the contract as it is interpreted by the court, yet neither of them meant what the court declares that they have said. In my opinion no one will understand the true theory of contract or be able even to discuss some fundamental questions intelligently until he has understood that all contracts are formal, that the making of a contract depends not on the agreement of two minds in one intention, but on the agreement of two sets of external signs,—not on the parties' having *meant* the same thing but on their having *said* the same thing. Furthermore, as the signs may be addressed to one sense or another,—to sight or to hearing—on the nature of the sign will depend the moment when the contract is made. If the sign is tangible, for instance, a letter, the contract is made when the letter of acceptance is delivered. If it is necessary that the minds of the parties meet, there will be no contract until the acceptance can be read,—none, for example, if the acceptance be snatched from the hand of the offerer by a third person.

This is not the time to work out a theory in detail, or to answer many obvious doubts and questions which are suggested by these general views. I know of none which are not easy to answer, but what I am trying to do now is only by a series of hints to throw some light on the narrow path of legal doctrine, and upon two pitfalls which, as it seems to me, lie perilously near to it. Of the first of these I have said enough. I hope that my illustrations have shown the danger, both to speculation and to practice, of confounding morality with law, and the trap which legal language lays for us on that side of our way. For my own part, I often doubt whether it would not be a gain if every word of moral significance could be banished from the law altogether, and other words adopted which should convey legal ideas uncolored by anything outside the law. We should lose the fossil records of a good deal of history and the majesty got from ethical associations, but by ridding ourselves of an unnecessary confusion we should gain very much in the clearness of our thought.

So much for the limits of the law. The next thing which I wish to consider is what are the forces which determine its content and its growth. You may assume, with Hobbes and Bentham and Austin, that all law emanates from the sovereign, even when the first human beings to enunciate it are the judges, or you may think that law is the voice of the Zeitgeist, or what you like. It is all one to my present purpose. Even if every decision required the sanction of an emperor with despotic power and a whimsical turn of mind, we should be interested none the less, still with a view to prediction, in discovering some order, some rational explanation, and some principle of growth for the rules which he laid down. In every system there are such explanations and principles to be found. It is with regard to them that a second fallacy comes in, which I think it important to expose.

The fallacy to which I refer is the notion that the only force at work in the development of the law is logic. In the broadest sense, indeed, that notion would be true. The postulate on which we think about the universe is that there is a fixed quantitative relation between every phenomenon and its antecedents and consequents. If there is such a thing as a phenomenon without these fixed quantitative relations, it is a miracle. It is outside the law of cause and effect, and as such transcends our power of thought, or at least is something to or from which we cannot reason. The condition of our thinking about the universe is that it is capable of being thought about rationally, or, in other words, that every part of it is effect and cause in the same sense in which those parts are with which we are most familiar. So in the broadest sense it is true that the law is a logical development, like everything else. The danger of which I speak is not the admission that the principles governing other phenomena also govern the law, but the notion that a given system, ours, for instance, can be worked out like mathematics from some general axioms of conduct. This is the natural error of the schools, but it is not confined to them. I once heard a very eminent judge say that he never let a decision go until he was absolutely sure that it was right. So judicial dissent often is blamed, as if it meant simply that one side or the other were not doing their sums right, and, if they would take more trouble, agreement inevitably would come.

This mode of thinking is entirely natural. The training of lawyers is a training in logic. The processes of analogy, discrimination, and deduction are those in which they are most at home. The language of judicial decision is mainly the language of logic. And the logical method and form flatter that longing for certainty and for repose which is in every human mind. But certainty generally is illusion, and repose is not the destiny of man. Behind the logical form lies a judgment as to the relative worth and importance of competing legislative grounds, often an inarticulate and unconscious judgment, it is true, and yet the very root and nerve of the whole proceeding. You can give any conclusion a logical form. You always can imply a condition in a contract. But why do you imply? It is because of some belief as to the practice of the community or of a class, or because of some opinion as to policy, or, in short, because of some attitude of yours upon a matter not capable of founding exact logical conclusions. Such matters really are battle grounds where the means do not exist for determinations that shall be good for all time, and where the decision can do no more than embody the preference of a given body in a given time and place. We do not realize how large a part of our law is open to reconsideration upon a slight change in the habit of the public mind. No concrete proposition is self-evident, no matter how ready we may be to accept it, not even Mr. Herbert Spencer's. Every man has a right to do what he wills, provided he interferes not with a like right on the part of his neighbors.

Why is a false and injurious statement privileged, if it is made honestly in giving information about a servant? It is because it has been thought more important that information should be given freely, than that a man should be protected from what under other crcumstances would be an actionable wrong. Why is a man at liberty to set up a business which he knows will ruin his neighbor? It is because the public good is supposed to be best subserved by free competition. Obviously such judgments of relative importance may vary in different times and places. Why does a judge instruct a jury that an employer is not liable to an employee for an injury received in the course of his employment unless he is negligent, and why do the jury generally find for the plaintiff if the case is allowed to go to them? It is because the traditional policy of our law is to confine liability to cases where a prudent man might have foreseen the injury, or at least the danger, while the inclination of a very large part of the community is to make certain classes of persons insure the safety of those with whom they deal. Since the last words were written, I have seen the requirement of such insurance put forth as part of the programme of one of the best known labor organizations. There is a concealed, half conscious battle on the question of legislative policy, and if any one thinks that it can be settled deductively, or once for all, I only can say that I think he is theoretically wrong, and that I am certain that his conclusion will not be accepted in practice *semper ubique et ab omnibus.*

Indeed, I think that even now our theory upon this matter is open to reconsideration, although I am not prepared to say how I should decide if a reconsideration were proposed. Our law of torts comes from the old days of isolated, ungeneralized wrongs, assaults, slanders, and the like, where the damages might be taken to lie where they fell by legal judgment. But the torts with which our courts are kept busy today are mainly the incidents of certain well known businesses. They are injuries to person or property by railroads, factories, and the like. The liability for them is estimated, and sooner or later goes into the price paid by the public. The public really pays the damages, and the question of liability, if pressed far enough, is really the question how far it is desirable that the public should insure the safety of those whose work it uses. It might be said that in such cases the chance of a jury finding for the defendant is merely a chance, once in a while rather arbitrarily interrupting the regular course of recovery, most likely in the case of an unusually conspicuous plaintiff, and therefore better done away with. On the other hand, the economic value even of a life to the community can be estimated, and no recovery, it may be said, ought to go beyond that amount. It is conceivable that some day in certain cases we may find ourselves imitating, on a higher plane, the tariff for life and limb which we see in the Leges Barbarorum.

I think that the judges themselves have failed adequately to recognize their duty of weighing considerations of social advantage. The duty is inevitable, and the result of the often proclaimed judicial aversion to deal with such considerations is simply to leave the very ground and foundation of judgments inarticulate, and often unconscious, as I have said. When socialism first began to be talked about, the comfortable classes of the community were a good deal frightened. I suspect that this fear has influenced judicial action both here and in England, yet it is certain that it is not a conscious factor in the decisions to which I refer. I think that something similar has led people who no longer hope to control the legislatures to look to the courts as expounders of the Constitutions, and that in some courts now principles have been discovered outside the bodies of those instruments, which may be generalized into acceptance of the economic doctrines which prevailed about fifty years ago, and a wholesale prohibition of what a tribunal of lawyers does not think about right. I cannot but believe that if the training of lawyers led them habitually to consider more definitely and explicitly the social advantage on which the rule they lay down must be justified, they sometimes would hesitate where now they are confident, and see that really they were taking sides upon debatable and often burning questions.

So much for the fallacy of logical form. Now let us consider the present condition of the law as a subject for study, and the ideal toward which it tends. We still are far from the point of view which I desire to see reached. No one has reached it or can reach it as yet. We are only at the beginning of a philosophical reaction, and of a reconsideration of the worth of doctrines which for the most part still are taken for granted without any deliberate, conscious, and systematic questioning of their grounds. The development of our law has gone on for nearly a thousand years, like the development of a plant, each generation taking the inevitable next step, mind, like matter, simply obeying a law of spontaneous growth. It is perfectly natural and right that it should have been so. Imitation is a necessity of human nature, as has been illustrated by a remarkable French writer, M. Tarde, in an admirable book, "Les Lois de l'Imitation." Most of the things we do, we do for no better reason than that our fathers have done them or that our neighbors do them, and the same is true of a larger part than we suspect of what we think. The reason is a good one, because our short life gives us no time for a better, but it is not the best. It does not follow, because we all are compelled to take on faith at second hand most of the rules on which we base our action and our thought, that each of us may not try to set some corner of his world in the order of reason, or that all of us collectively should not aspire to carry reason as far as it will go throughout the whole domain. In regard to the law, it is true, no doubt, that an evolutionist will hesitate to affirm universal validity for his social ideals, or for the principles which he thinks should be embodied in legislation. He is content if he can prove them best for here and now. He may be ready to admit that he knows nothing about an absolute best in the cosmos, and even that he knows next to nothing about a permanent best for men. Still it is true that a body of law is more rational and more civilized when every rule it contains is referred articulately and definitely to an end which it subserves, and when the grounds for desiring that end are stated or are ready to be stated in words.

At present, in very many cities, if we want to know why a rule of law has taken its particular shape, and more or less if we want to know why it exists at all, we go to tradition. We follow it into the Year Books, and perhaps beyond them to the customs of the Salian Franks, and somewhere in the past, in the German forests, in the needs of Norman kings, in the assumptions of a dominant class, in the absence of generalized ideas, we find out the practical motive for what now best is justified by the mere fact of its acceptance and that men are accustomed to it. The rational study of law is still to a large extent the study of history. History must be a part of the study, because without it we cannot know the precise scope of rules which it is our business to know. It is a part of the rational study, because it is the first step toward a deliberate reconsideration of the worth of those rules. When you get the dragon out of his cave on to the plain and in the daylight, you can count his teeth and claws, and see just what is his strength. But to get him out is only the first step. The next is either to kill him, or to tame him and make him a useful animal. For the rational study of the law the black-letter man may be the man of the present, but the man of the future is the man of statistics and the master of economics. It is revolting to have no better reason for a rule of law than that so it was laid down in the time of Henry IV. It is still more revolting if the grounds upon which it was laid down have vanished long since, and the rule simply persists from blind imitation of the past. I am thinking of the technical rule as to trespass *ab initio,* as it is called, which I attempted to explain in a recent Massachusetts case.[3]

Let me take an illustration, which can be stated in a few words, to show how the social end which is aimed at by a rule of law is obscured and only partially attained in consequence of the fact that the rule owes its form to a gradual historical development, instead of being reshaped as a whole, with conscious articulate reference to the end in view. We think it desirable to prevent one man's property being misappropriated by another, and so we make larceny a crime. The evil is the same whether the misappropriation is made by a man into whose hands the owner has put the property, or by one who wrongfully takes it away. But primitive law in its weakness did not get much beyond an effort to prevent violence, and very naturally made a wrongful taking, a trespass, part of its definition of the crime. In modern times the judges enlarged the definition a little by holding that, if the wrong-doer gets possession by a trick or device, the crime is committed. This really was giving up the requirement of a trespass, and it would have been more logical, as well as truer to the present object of the law, to abandon the requirement altogether. That, however, would have seemed too bold, and was left to statute. Statutes were passed making embezzlement a crime. But the force of tradition caused the crime of embezzlement to be regarded as so far distinct from larceny that to this day, in some jurisdictions at least, a slip corner is kept open for thieves to contend, if indicted for larceny, that they should have been indicted for embezzlement, and if indicted for embezzlement, that they should have been indicted for larceny, and to escape on that ground.

Far more fundamental questions still await a better answer than that we do as our fathers have done. What have we better than a blind guess to show that the criminal law in its present form does more good than harm? I do not stop to refer to the effect which it has had in degrading prisoners and in plunging them further into crime, or to the question whether fine and imprisonment do not fall more heavily on a criminal's wife and children than on himself. I have in mind more far-reaching questions. Does punishment deter? Do we deal with criminals on proper principles? A modern school of Continental criminalists plumes itself on the formula, first suggested, it is said, by Gall, that we must consider the criminal rather than the crime. The formula does not carry us very far, but the inquiries which have been started look toward an answer of my questions based on science for the first time. If the typical criminal is a degenerate, bound to swindle or to murder by as deep seated an organic necessity as that which makes the rattlesnake bite, it is idle to talk of deterring him by the classical method of imprisonment. He must be got rid of; he cannot be improved, or frightened out of his structural reaction. If, on the other hand, crime, like normal human conduct, is mainly a matter of imitation, punishment fairly may be expected to help to keep it out of fashion. The study of criminals has been thought by some well known men of science to sustain the former hypothesis. The statistics of the relative increase of crime in crowded places like large cities, where example has the greatest chance to work, and in less populated parts, where the contagion spreads more slowly, have been used with great force in favor of the latter view. But there is weighty authority for the belief that, however this may be, "not the nature of the crime, but the dangerousness of the criminal, constitutes the only reasonable legal criterion to guide the inevitable social reaction against the criminal." [4]

The impediments to rational generalization, which I illustrated from the law of mercy, are shown in the other branches of the law, as well as in that of crime. Take the law of tort or civil liability for damages apart from contract and the like. Is there any general theory of such liability, or are the cases in which it exists simply to be enumerated, and to be explained each on its special ground, as is easy to believe from the fact that the right of action for certain well known classes of wrongs like trespass or slander has its special history for each class? I think that there is a general theory to be discovered, although resting in tendency rather than established and accepted. I think that the law regards the infliction of temporal damage by a responsible person as actionable, if under the circumstances known to him the danger of his act is manifest according to common experience, or according to his own experience if it is more than common, except in cases where upon special grounds of policy the law refuses to protect the plaintiff or grants a privilege to the defendant.[5] I think that commonly malice, intent, and negligence mean only that the danger was manifest to a greater or less degree, under the circumstances known to the actor, although in some cases of privilege malice may mean an actual malevolent motive, and such a motive may take away a permission knowingly to inflict harm, which otherwise would be granted on this or that ground of dominant public good. But when I stated my view to a very eminent English judge the other day, he said: "You are discussing what the law ought to be; as the law is, you must show a right. A man is not liable for negligence unless he is subject to a duty." If our difference was more than a difference in words, or with regard to the proportion between the exceptions and the rule, then, in his opinion, liability for an act cannot be referred to the manifest tendency of the act to cause temporal damage in general as a sufficient explanation, but must be referred to the special nature of the damage, or must be derived from some special circumstances outside of the tendency of the act, for which no generalized explanation exists. I think that such a view is wrong, but it is familiar, and I dare say generally is accepted in England.

Everywhere the basis of principle is tradition, to such an extent that we even are in danger of making the role of history more important than it is. The other day Professor Ames wrote a learned article to show, among other things, that the common law did not recognize the defense of fraud in actions upon specialties, and the moral might seem to be that the personal character of that defence is due to its equitable origin. But if, as I have said, all contracts are formal, the difference is not merely historical, but theoretic, between defects of form which prevent a contract from being made, and mistaken motives which manifestly could not be considered in any system that we should call rational except against one who was privy to those motives. It is not confined to specialties, but is of universal application. I ought to add that I do not suppose that Mr. Ames would disagree with what I suggest.

However, if we consider the law of contract, we find it full of history. The distinctions between debt, covenant, and assumpsit are merely historical. The classification of certain obligations to pay money, imposed by the law irrespective of any bargain as quasi contracts, is merely historical. The doctrine of consideration is merely historical. The effect given to a seal is to be explained by history alone.—Consideration is a mere form. Is it a useful form? If so, why should it not be required in all contracts? A seal is a mere form, and is vanishing in the scroll and in enactments that a consideration must be given, seal or no seal.—Why should any merely historical distinction be allowed to affect the rights and obligations of business men?

Since I wrote this discourse I have come on a very

good example of the way in which tradition not only overrides rational policy, but overrides it after first having been misunderstood and having been given a new and broader scope than it had when it had a meaning. It is the settled law of England that a material alteration of a written contract by a party avoids it as against him. The doctrine is contrary to the general tendency of the law. We do not tell a jury that if a man ever has lied in one particular he is to be presumed to lie in all. Even if a man has tried to defraud, it seems no sufficient reason for preventing him from proving the truth. Objections of like nature in general go to the weight, not to the admissibility, of evidence. Moreover, this rule is irrespective of fraud, and is not confined to evidence. It is not merely that you cannot use the writing, but that the contract is at an end. What does this mean? The existence of a written contract depends on the fact that the offerer and offeree have interchanged their written expressions, not on the continued existence of those expressions. But in the case of a bond the primitive notion was different. The contract was inseparable from the parchment. If a stranger destroyed it, or tore off the seal, or altered it, the obligee could not recover, however free from fault, because the defendant's contract, that is, the actual tangible bond which he had sealed, could not be produced in the form in which it bound him. About a hundred years ago Lord Kenyon undertook to use his reason on this tradition, as he sometimes did to the detriment of the law, and, not understanding it, said he could see no reason why what was true of a bond should not be true of other contracts. His decision happened to be right, as it concerned a promissory note, where again the common law regarded the contract as inseparable from the paper on which it was written, but the reasoning was general, and soon was extended to other written contracts, and various absurd and unreal grounds of policy were invented to account for the enlarged rule.

I trust that no one will understand me to be speaking with disrespect of the law, because I criticise it so freely. I venerate the law, and especially our system of law, as one of the vastest products of the human mind. No one knows better than I do the countless number of great intellects that have spent themselves in making some addition or improvement, the greatest of which is trifling when compared with the mighty whole. It has the final title to respect that it exists, that it is not a Hegelian dream, but a part of the lives of men. But one may criticise even what one reveres. Law is the business to which my life is devoted, and I should show less than devotion if I did not do what in me lies to improve it, and, when I perceive what seems to me the ideal of its future, if I hesitated to point it out and to press toward it with all my heart.

Perhaps I have said enough to show the part which the study of history necessarily plays in the intelligent study of the law as it is today. In the teaching of this school and at Cambridge it is in no danger of being undervalued. Mr. Bigelow here and Mr. Ames and Mr. Thayer there have made important contributions which will not be forgotten, and in England the recent history of early English law by Sir Frederick Pollock and Mr. Maitland has lent the subject an almost deceptive charm. We must beware of the pitfall of antiquarianism, and must remember that for our purposes our only interest in the past is for the light it throws upon the present. I look forward to a time when the part played by history in the explanation of dogma shall be very small, and instead of ingenious research we shall spend our energy on a study of the ends sought to be attained and the reasons for desiring them. As a step toward that ideal it seems to me that every lawyer ought to seek an understanding of economics. The present divorce between the schools of political economy and law seems to me an evidence of how much progress in philosophical study still remains to be made. In the present state of political economy, indeed, we come again upon history on a larger scale, but there we are called on to consider and weigh the ends of legislation, the means of attaining them, and the cost. We learn that for everything we have to give up something else, and we are taught to set the advantage we gain against the other advantage we lose, and to know what we are doing when we elect.

There is another study which sometimes is undervalued by the practical minded, for which I wish to say a good word, although I think a good deal of pretty poor stuff goes under that name. I mean the study of what is called jurisprudence. Jurisprudence, as I look at it, is simply law in its most generalized part. Every effort to reduce a case to a rule is an effort of jurisprudence, although the name as used in English is confined to the broadest rules and most fundamental conceptions. One mark of a great lawyer is that he sees the application of the broadest rules. There is a story of a Vermont justice of the peace before whom a suit was brought by one farmer against another for breaking a churn. The justice took time to consider, and then said that he had looked through the statutes and could find nothing about churns, and gave judgment for the defendant. The same state of mind is shown in all our common digests and textbooks. Applications of rudimentary rules of contract or tort are tucked away under the head of Railroads or Telegraphs or go to swell treatises on historical subdivisions, such as Shipping or Equity, or are gathered under an arbitrary title which is thought likely to appeal to the practical mind, such as Mercantile Law. If a man goes into law it pays to be a master of it, and to be a master of it means to look straight through all the dramatic incidents and to discern the true basis of prophecy. Therefore, it is well to have an accurate notion of what you mean by law, by a right, by a duty, by malice, intent, and negligence, by ownership, by possession, and so forth. I have in my mind cases in which the highest courts seem to me to have floundered because they had no clear ideas on some of these themes. I have illustrated their importance already. If a further illustration is wished, it may be found by reading the Appendix to Sir James Stephen's Criminal Law on the subject of possession, and then turning to Pollock and Wright's enlightened book. Sir James Stephen is not the only writer whose attempts to analyze legal ideas have been confused by striving for a useless quintessence of all systems, instead of an accurate anatomy of one. The trouble with Austin was that he did not know enough English law. But still it is a practical advantage to master Austin, and his predecessors, Hobbes and Bentham, and his worthy successors, Holland and Pollock. Sir Frederick Pollock's recent little book is touched with the felicity which marks all his works, and is wholly free from the perverting influence of Roman models.

The advice of the elders to young men is very apt to be as unreal as a list of the hundred best books. At least in my day I had my share of such counsels, and high among the unrealities I place the recommendation to study the Roman law. I assume that such advice means more than collecting a few Latin maxims with which to ornament the discourse,—the purpose for which Lord Coke recommanded Bracton. If that is all that is wanted, the title "De Regulis Juris Antiqui" can be read in an hour. I assume that, if it is well to study the Roman law, it is well to study it as a working system. That means mastering a set of technicalities more difficult and less understood than our own, and studying another course of history by which even more than our own the Roman law must be explained. If any one doubts me, let him read Keller's "Der Romische Civil Process und die Actionen," a treatise on the praetor's edict, Muirhead's most interesting "Historical Introduction to the Private Law of Rome," and, to give him the best chance possible, Sohm's admirable Institutes. No. The way to gain a liberal view of your subject is not to read something else, but to get to the bottom of the subject itself. The means of doing that are, in the first place, to follow the existing body of dogma into its highest generalizations by the help of jurisprudence; next, to discover from history how it has come to be what it is; and, finally, so far as you can, to consider the ends which the several rules seek to accomplish, the reasons why those ends are desired, what is given up to gain them, and whether they are worth the price.

We have too little theory in the law rather than too much, especially on this final branch of study. When I was speaking of history, I mentioned larceny as an example to show how the law suffered from not having embodied in a clear form a rule which will accomplish its manifest purpose. In that case the trouble was due to the survival of forms coming from a time when a more limited purpose was entertained. Let me now give an example to show the practical importance, for the decision of actual cases, of understanding the reasons of the law, by taking an example from rules which, so far as I know, never have been explained or theorized about in any adequate way. I refer to statutes of limitation and the law of prescription. The end of such rules is obvious, but what is the justification for depriving a man of his rights, a pure evil as far as it goes, in consequence of the lapse of time? Sometimes the loss of evidence is referred to, but that is a secondary matter. Sometimes the desirability of peace, but why is peace more desirable after twenty years than before? It is increasingly likely to come without the aid of legislation. Sometimes it is said that, if a man neglects to enforce his rights, he cannot complain if, after a while, the law follows his example. Now if this is all that can be said about it, you probably will decide a case I am going to put, for the plaintiff; if you take the view which I shall suggest, you possibly will decide it for the defendant. A man is sued for trespass upon land, and justifies under a right of way. He proves that he has used the way openly and adversely for twenty years, but it turns out that the plaintiff had granted a license to a person whom he reasonably supposed to be the defendant's agent, although not so in fact, and therefore had assumed that the use of the way was permissive, in which case no right would be gained. Has the defendant gained a right or not? If his gaining it stands on the fault and neglect of the landowner in the ordinary sense, as seems commonly to be supposed, there has been no such neglect, and the right of way has not been acquired. But if I were the defendant's counsel, I should suggest that the foundation of the acquisition of rights by lapse of time is to be looked for in the position of the person who gains them, not in that of the loser. Sir Henry Maine has made it fashionable to connect the archaic notion of property with prescription. But the connection is further back than the first recorded history. It is in the nature of man's mind. A thing which you have enjoyed and used as your own for a long time, whether property or an opinion, takes root in your being and cannot be torn away without your resenting the act and trying to defend yourself, however you came by it. The law can ask no better justification than the deepest instincts of man. It is only by way of reply to the suggestion that you are disappointing the former owner, that you refer to his neglect having allowed the gradual dissociation between himself and what he claims, and the gradual association of it with another. If he knows that another is doing acts which on their face show that he is on the way toward establishing such an association, I should argue that in justice to that other he was bound at his peril to find out whether the other was acting under his permission, to see that he was warned, and, if necessary, stopped.

I have been speaking about the study of the law, and I have said next to nothing of what commonly is talked about in that connection,—text-books and the case system, and all the machinery with which a student comes most immediately in contact. Nor shall I say anything about them. Theory is my subject, not practical details. The modes of teaching have been improved since my time, no doubt, but ability and industry will master the raw material with any mode. Theory is the most important part of the dogma of the law, as the architect is the most important man who takes part in the building of a house. The most important improvements of the last twenty-five years are improvements in theory. It is not to be feared as unpractical, for, to the competent, it simply means going to the bottom of the subject. For the incompetent, it sometimes is true, as has been said, that an interest in general ideas means an absence of particular knowledge. I remember in army days reading of a youth who, being examined for the lowest grade and being asked a question about squadron drill, answered that he never had considered the evolutions of less than ten thousand men. But the weak and foolish must be left to their folly. The danger is that the able and practical minded should look with indifference or distrust upon ideas the connection of which with their business is remote. I heard a story, the other day, of a man who had a valet to whom he paid high wages, subject to deduction for faults. One of his deductions was, "For lack of imagination, five dollars." The lack is not confined to valets. The object of ambition, power, generally presents itself nowadays in the form of money alone. Money is the most immediate form, and is a proper object of desire. "The fortune," said Rachel, "is the measure of the intelligence." That is a good text to waken people out of a fool's paradise. But, as Hegel says,[6] "It is in the end not the appetite, but the opinion, which has to be satisfied." To an imagination of any scope the most far-reaching form of power is not money, it is the command of ideas. If you want great examples read Mr. Leslie Stephen's "History of English Thought in the Eighteenth Century," and see how a hundred years after his death the abstract speculations of Descartes had become a practical force controlling the conduct of men. Read the works of the great German jurists, and see how much more the world is governed to-day by Kant than by Bonaparte. We cannot all be Descartes or Kant, but we all want happiness. And happiness, I am sure from having known many successful men, cannot be won simply by being counsel for great corporations and having an income of fifty thousand dollars. An intellect great enough to win the prize needs other food beside success. The remoter and more general aspects of the law are those which give it universal interest. It is through them that you not only become a great master in your calling, but connect your subject with the universe and catch an echo of the infinite, a glimpse of its unfathomable process, a hint of the universal law.

NOTES

THE PATH OF THE LAW

1 1 Roll. Rep. 368.

2 See Hanson v. Globe Newspaper Co., 159 Mass. 293, 302.

3 Commonwealth v. Rubin, 165 Mass. 453.

4 Havelock Ellis, "The Criminal," 41 citing Garofalo. See also Ferri, "Sociologie Criminelle," *passim.* Compare Tarde, "La Philosophie Pénale."

5 An example of the law's refusing to protect the plaintiff is when he is interrupted by a stranger in the use of a valuable way, which he has travelled adversely for a week less than the period of prescription. A week later he will have gained a right, but now he is only a trespasser. Examples of privilege I have given already. One of the best is competition in business.

6 Phil. des Rechts, § 190.

THE THEORY OF LEGAL INTERPRETATION

Reprinted from *Harvard Law Review*, volume 12, pp. 417-420, 1899.

THE paper upon the Principles of Legal Interpretation by Mr. F. Vaughan Hawkins, reprinted in Professor Thayer's recently published and excellent Preliminary Treatise on Evidence, induces me to suggest what seems to me to be the theory of our rules of interpretation,—a theory which I think supports Lord Wensleydale and the others whom Mr. Hawkins quotes and disapproves, if I correctly understand their meaning and his.

It is true that in theory any document purporting to be serious and to have some legal effect has one meaning and no other, because the known object is to achieve some definite result. It is not true that in practice (and I know no reason why theory should disagree with the facts) a given word or even a given collocation of words has one meaning and no other. A word generally has several meanings, even in the dictionary. You have to consider the sentence in which it stands to decide which of those meanings it bears in the particular case, and very likely will see that it there has a shade of significance more refined than any given in the word-book. But in this first step, at least, you are not troubling yourself about the idiosyncracies of the writer, you are considering simply the general usages of speech. So when you let whatever galvanic current may come from the rest of the instrument run through the particular sentence, you still are doing the same thing.

How is it when you admit evidence of circumstances and read the document in the light of them?

Is this trying to discover the particular intent of the individual, to get into his mind and to bend what he said to what he wanted? No one would contend that such a process should be carried very far, but, as it seems to me, we do not take a step in that direction. It is not a question of tact in drawing a line. We are after a different thing. What happens is this. Even the whole document is found to have a certain play in the joints when its words are translated into things by parol evidence, as they have to be. It does not disclose one meaning conclusively according to the laws of language. Thereupon we ask, not what this man meant, but what those words would mean in the mouth of a normal speaker of English, using them in the circumstances in which they were used, and it is to the end of answering this last question that we let in evidence as to what the circumstances were. But the normal speaker of English is merely a special variety, a literary form, so to speak, of our old friend the prudent man. He is external to the particular writer, and a reference to him as the criterion is simply another instance of the externality of the law.

But then it is said, and this is thought to be the crux, In the case of a gift of Blackacre to John Smith, when the donor owned two Blackacres and the directory reveals two John Smiths, you may give direct evidence of the donor's intention, and it is only an anomaly that you cannot give the same evidence in every case. I think, on the contrary, that the exceptional rule is a proof of the instinctive insight of the judges who established it. I refer again to the theory of our language. By the theory of our language, while other words may mean different things, a proper name means one person or thing and no other. If language perfectly performed its function, as Bentham wanted to make it, it would point out the person or thing named in every case. But under our random system it sometimes happens that your name is *idem sonans* with mine, and it may be the same even in spelling. But it never means you or me indifferently. In theory of speech your name means you and my name means me, and the two names are different.

They are different words. *Licet idem sit nomen, tamen diversum est propter diversitatem personae.*[1] In such a case we let in evidence of intention not to help out what theory recognizes as an uncertainty of speech, and to read what the writer meant into what he has tried but failed to say, but, recognizing that he has spoken with theoretic certainly, we inquire what he meant in order to find out what he has said. It is on this ground that there is no contract when the proper name used by one party means one ship, and that used by the other means another.[2] The mere difference of intent as such is immaterial. In the use of common names and words a plea of different meaning from that adopted by the court would be bad, but here the parties have said different things and never have expressed a contract. If the donor, instead of saying "Blackacre," had said "my gold watch" and had owned more than one, inasmuch as the words, though singular, purport to describe any such watch belonging to the speaker, I suppose that no evidence of intention would be admitted. But I dare say that evidence of circumstances sufficient to show that the normal speaker of English would have meant a particular watch if the same words would be let in.

I have stated what I suppose to be our general theory of construction. It remains to say a few words to justify it. Of course, the purpose of written instruments is to express some intention or state of mind of those who write them, and it is desirable to make that purpose effectual, so far as may be, if instruments are to be used. The question is how far the law ought to go in aid of the writers. In the case of contracts, to begin with them, it is obvious that they express the wishes not of one person but of two, and those two adversaries. If it turns out that one meant one thing and the other another, speaking generally, the only choice possible for the legislator is either to hold both parties to the judge's interpretation of the words in the sense which I have explained, or to allow the contract to be avoided because there has been no meeting of minds. The latter course not only would greatly enhance the difficulty of enforcing contracts against losing parties, but would run against a plain principle of justice. For each party to a contract has notice that the other will understand his words according to the usage of the normal speaker of English under the circumstances, and therefore cannot complain if his words are taken in that sense.[3]

Different rules conceivably might be laid down for the construction of different kinds of writing. In the case of a statute, to turn from contracts to the opposite extreme, it would be possible to say that as we are dealing with the commands of the sovereign the only thing to do is to find out what the sovereign wants. If supreme power resided in the person of a despot who would cut off your hand or your head if you went wrong, probably one would take every available means to find out what was wanted. Yet in fact we do not deal differently with a statute from our way of dealing with a contract. We do not inquire what the legislature meant; we ask only what the statute means. In this country, at least, for constitutional reasons, if for no other, if the same legislature that passed it should declare at a later date a statute to have a meaning which in the opinion of the court the words did not bear, I suppose that the declaratory act would have no effect upon intervening transactions unless in a place and case where retrospective legislation was allowed. As retrospective legislation it would not work by way of construction except in form.

So in the case of a will. It is true that the testator is a despot, within limits, over his property, but he is required by statute to express his commands in writing, and that means that his words must be sufficient for the purpose when taken in the sense in which they would be used by the normal speaker of English under his circumstances.

I may add that I think we should carry the external principle of construction even further than I have indicated. I do not suppose that you could prove, for purposes of construction as distinguished from avoidance, an oral declaration or even an agreement that words in a dispositive instrument making sense as they stand should have a different meaning from the common one; for instance, that the parties to a contract orally agreed that when they wrote five hundred feet it should mean one hundred inches, or that Bunker Hill Monument should signify Old South Church.[4] On the other hand, when you have the security of a local or class custom or habit of speech, it may be presumed that the writer conforms to the usage of his place or class when that is what a normal person in his situation would do. But these cases are remote from the point of theory upon which I started to speak.

It may be, after all, that the matter is one in which the important thing, the law, is settled, and different people will account for it by such theory as pleases them best, as in the ancient controversy whether the finder of a thing which had been thrown away by the owner got a title in privity by gift, or a new title by abandonment. That he got a title no one denied. But although practical men generally prefer to leave their major premises inarticulate, yet even for practical purposes theory generally turns out the most important thing in the end. I am far from saying that it might not make a difference in the old question to which I have referred.

NOTES

THE THEORY OF LEGAL INTERPRETATION

1 Bract. 190 *a*.

2 Raffles v. Wichelhaus, 2 H. & C. 906. See Mead v. Phenix Insurance Co., 158 Mass. 124; Hanson v. Globe Newspaper Co., 159 Mass. 293, 305.

3 In Nash v. Minnesota Title Insurance & Trust Co., 163 Mass. 574, I thought that this principle should be carried further than the majority of the court were willing to go.

4 Goode v. Riley, 153 Mass. 585, 586.

THE LAW

Address delivered to the Suffolk Bar Association Dinner, February 5, 1885. Reprinted from Speeches by Oliver Wendell Holmes, Boston, Little Brown & Co., 1913. pp. 16-18.

MR. CHAIRMAN AND GENTLEMEN OF THE BAR:—

The Court and the Bar are too old acquaintances to speak much to each other of themselves, or of their mutual relations. I hope I may say we are too old friends to need to do it. If you did not believe it already, it would be useless for me to affirm that, in the judges' half of our common work, the will at least is not wanting to do every duty of their noble office; that every interest, every faculty, every energy, almost every waking hour, is filled with their work; that they give their lives to it, more than which they cannot do. But if not of the Bench, shall I speak of the Bar? Shall I ask what a court would be, unaided? The law is made by the Bar, even more than by the Bench; yet do I need to speak of the learning and varied gifts that have given the bar of this State a reputation throughout the whole domain of the common law? I think I need not, nor of its high and scrupulous honor. The world has its fling at lawyers sometimes, but its very denial is an admission. It feels, what I believe to be the truth, that of all secular professions this has the highest standards.

And what a profession it is! No doubt everything is interesting when it is understood and seen in its connection with the rest of things. Every calling is great when greatly pursued. But what other gives such scope to realize the spontaneous energy of one's soul? In what other does one plunge so deep in the stream of life,—so share its passions, its battles, its despair, its triumphs, both of witness and actor?

But that is not all. What a subject is this in which we are united,—this abstraction called the the Law, wherein, as in a magic mirror, we see reflected, not only our own lives, but the lives of all men that have been! When I think on this majestic theme, my eyes dazzle. If we are to speak of the law as our mistress, we who are here know that she is a mistress only to be wooed with sustained and lonely passion,—only to be won by straining all the faculties by which man is likest to a god. Those who, having begun the pursuit, turn away uncharmed, do so either because they have not been vouchsafed the sight of her divine figure, or because they have not the heart for so great a struggle. To the lover of the law, how small a thing seem the novelist's tales of the loves and fates of Daphnis and Chloe! How pale a phantom even the Circe of poetry, transforming mankind with intoxicating dreams of fiery ether, and the foam of summer sea, and glowing greensward, and the white arms of women! For him no less a history will suffice than that of the moral life of his race. For him every text that he deciphers, every doubt that he resolves, adds a new feature to the unfolding panorama of man's destiny upon this earth. Nor will his task be done until, by the farthest stretch of human imagination, he has seen as with his eyes the birth and growth of society, and by the farthest stretch of reason he has understood the philosophy of its being. When I think thus of the law, I see a princess mightier than she who once wrought at Bayeux, eternally weaving into her web dim figures of the ever-lengthening past, —figures too dim to be noticed by the idle, too symbolic to be interpreted except by her pupils, but to the discerning eye disclosing every painful step and every world-shaking contest by which mankind has worked and fought its way from savage isolation to organic social life.

But we who are here know the Law even better in another aspect. We see her daily, not as anthropologists, not as students and philosophers, but as actors in a drama of which she is the providence and overruling power. When I think of the Law as we know her in the courthouse and the market, she seems to me a woman sitting by the wayside, beneath whose overshadowing hood very man shall see the countenance of his deserts or needs. The timid and overborne gain heart from her protecting smile. Fair combatants, manfully standing to their rights, see her keeping the lists with the stern and discriminating eye of even justice. The wretch who has defied her most sacred commands, and has thought to creep through ways where she was not, finds that his path ends with her, and beholds beneath her hood the inexorable face of death.

Gentlemen, I shall say no more. This is not the moment for disquisitions. But when for the first time I was called to speak on such an occasion as this, the only thought that could come into my mind, the only feeling that could fill my heart, the only words that could spring to my lips, were a hymn to her in whose name we are met here to-night,—to our mistress, the Law.

LAW AND THE COURT

Speech at a dinner of The Harvard Law School Association of New York on February 15, 1913.

Reprinted from Speeches by Oliver Wendell Holmes, Boston, Little, Brown & Co., 1913. pp. 98-103.

Mr. Chairman and Gentlemen:

Vanity is the most philosophical of those feelings that we are taught to despise. For vanity recognizes that if a man is in a minority of one we lock him up, and therefore longs for an assurance from others that one's work has not been in vain. If a man's ambition is the thirst for a power that comes not from office but from within, he never can be sure that any happiness is not a fool's paradise—he never can be sure that he sits on that other bench reserved for the masters of those who know. Then, too, at least until one draws near to seventy, one is less likely to hear the trumpets than the rolling fire of the front. I have passed that age, but I still am on the firing line and it is only in rare moments like this that there comes a pause and for half an hour one feels a trembling hope. They are the rewards of a lifetime's work.

But let me turn to more palpable realities—to that other visible Court to which for ten new accomplished years it has been my opportunity to belong. We are very quiet there, but it is the quiet of a storm centre, as we all know. Science has taught the world scepticism and has made it legitimate to put everything to the test of proof. Many beautiful and noble reverences are impaired, but in these days no one can complain if any institution, system, or belief is called on to justify its continuance in life. Of course we are not excepted and have not escaped. Doubts are expressed that go to our very being. Not only are we told that when Marshall pronounced an Act of Congress unconstitutional he usurped a power that the Constitution did not give, but we are told that we are the representatives of a class—a tool of the money power. I get letters, not always anonymous, intimating that we are corrupt. Well, gentlemen, I admit that it makes my heart ache. It is very painful, when one spends all the energies of one's soul in trying to do good work, with no thought but that of solving a problem according to the rules by which one is bound, to know that many see sinister motives and would be glad of evidence that one was consciously bad. But we must take such things philosophically and try to see what we can learn from hatred and distrust and whether behind them there may not be some germ of inarticulate truth.

The attacks upon the Court are merely an expression of the unrest that seems to wonder vaguely whether law and order pay. When the ignorant are taught to doubt they do not know what they safely may believe. And it seems to me that at this time we need education in the obvious more than investigation of the obscure. I do not see so much immediate use in committees on the high cost of living and inquiries how far it is due to the increased production of gold, how far to the narrowing of cattle ranges and the growth of population, how far to the bugaboo, as I do in bringing home to people a few social and economic truths. Most men think dramatically, not quantitively, a fact that the rich would be wise to remember more than they do. We are apt to contrast the palace with the hovel, the dinner at Sherry's with the working man's pail, and never ask how much or realize how little is withdrawn to make the prizes of success (subordinate prizes—since the only prize much cared for by the powerful is power. The prize of the general is not a bigger tent, but command). We are apt to think of ownership as a terminus, not as a gateway, and not to realize that except the tax levied for personal consumption large ownership means investment, and investment means the direction of labor towards the production of the greatest returns—returns that so far as they are great show by that very fact that they are consumed by the many, not alone by the few. If I may ride a hobby for an instant, I should say we need to think things instead of words—to drop ownership, money, etc., and to think of the stream of products of wheat and cloth and railway travel. When we do it is obvious that the many consume them; that they now as truly have substantially all there is, as if the title were in the United States, that the great body of property is socially administered now, and that the function of private ownership is to divine in advance the equilibrium of social desires—which socialism equally would have to divine, but which, under the illusion of self-seeking, is more poignantly and shrewdly foreseen.

I should like to see it brought home to the public that the question of fair prices is due to the fact that none of us can have as much as we want of all the things we want; that as less will be produced than the public wants, the question is how much of each product it will have and how much go without; that thus the final competition is between the objects of desire, and therefore between the producers of those objects; that when we oppose labor and capital, labor means the group that is selling its product and capital all the other groups that are buying it. The hated capitalist is simply the mediator, the product, the adjuster according to his divination of the future desire. If you could get that believed, the body of the people would have no doubt as to the worth of law.

That is my outside thought on the present discontents. As to the truth embodied in them, in part it cannot be helped. It cannot be helped, it is as it should be, that the law is behind the times. I told a labor leader once that what they asked was favor, and if a decision was against them they called it wicked. The same might be said of their opponents. It means that the law is growing. As law embodies beliefs that have triumphed in the battle of ideas and then have translated themselves into action, while there still is doubt, while opposite convictions still keep a battle front against each other, the time for law has not come; the notion destined to prevail is not yet entitled to the field. It is a misfortune if a judge reads his conscious or unconscious sympathy with one side or the other prematurely into the law, and forgets that what seem to him to be first principles are believed by half his fellow men to be wrong. I think that we have suffered from this misfortune, in State courts at least, and that this is another and very important truth to be extracted from the popular discontent. When twenty years ago a vague terror went over the earth and the word socialism began to be heard, I thought and still think that fear was translated into doctrines that had no proper place in the Constitution or the common law. Judges are apt to be naif, simple-minded men, and they need something of Mephistopheles. We too need education in the obvious—to learn to transcend our own convictions and to leave room for much that we hold dear to be done away with short of revolution by the orderly change of law.

I have no belief in panaceas and almost none in sudden ruin. I believe with Montesquieu that if the chance of a battle—I may add, the passage of a law—has ruined a state, there was a general cause at work that made the state ready to perish by a single battle or law. Hence I am not much interested one way or the other in the nostrums now so strenuously urged. I do not think the United States would come to an end if we lost our power to declare an Act of Congress void. I do think the Union would be imperiled if we could not make that declaration as to the laws of the several States. For one in my place sees how often a local policy prevails with those who are not trained to national views and how often action is taken that embodies what the Commerce Clause was meant to end. But I am not aware that there is any serious desire to limit the Court's power in this regard. For most of the things that properly can be called evils in the present state of the law I think the main remedy, as for the evils of public opinion, is for us to grow more civilized.

If I am right it will be a slow business for our people to reach rational views, assuming that we are allowed to work peaceably to that end. But as I grow older I grow calm. If I feel what are perhaps an old man's apprehensions, that competition from new races will cut deeper than working men's disputes and will test whether we can hang together and can fight; if I fear that we are running through the world's resources at a pace that we cannot keep; I do not lose my hopes. I do not pin my dreams for the future to my country or even to my race. I think it probable that civilization somehow will last as long as I care to look ahead—perhaps with smaller numbers, but perhaps also bred to greatness and splendor by science. I think it not improbable that man, like the grub that prepares a chamber for the winged thing it never has seen but is to be—that man may have cosmic destinies that he does not understand. And so beyond the vision of battling races and an impoverished earth I catch a dreaming glimpse of peace.

The other day my dream was pictured to my mind. It was evening. I was walking homeward on Pennsylvania Avenue near the Treasury, and as I looked beyond Sherman's Statue to the west the sky was aflame with scarlet and crimson from the setting sun. But, like the note of downfall in Wagner's opera, below the sky line there came from little globes the pallid discord of the electric lights. And I thought to myself the Gotterdammerung will end, and from those globes clustered like evil eggs will come the new masters of the sky. It is like the time in which we live. But then I remembered the faith that I partly have expressed, faith in a universe not measured by our fears, a universe that has thought and more than thought inside of it, and as I gazed, after the sunset and above the electric lights there shone the stars.

THE PROFESSION OF THE LAW

Conclusion of a lecture delivered to undergraduates of Harvard University on February 17, 1886.

Reprinted from Speeches by Oliver Wendell Holmes, Boston, Little, Brown & Co., 1913. pp. 22-25.

AND now, perhaps, I ought to have done. But I know that some spirit of fire will feel that his main question has not been answered. He will ask, What is all this to my soul? You do not bid me sell my birthright for a mess of pottage; what have you said to show that I can reach my own spiritual possibilities through such a door as this? How can the laborious study of a dry and technical system, the greedy watch for clients and practice of shopkeepers' arts, the mannerless conflicts over often sordid interests, make out a life? Gentlemen, I admit at once that these questions are not futile, that they may prove unanswerable, that they have often seemed to me unanswerable. And yet I believe there is an answer. They are the same questions that meet you in any form of practical life. If a man has the soul of Sancho Panza, the world to him will be Sancho Panza's world; but if he has the soul of an idealist, he will make—I do not say find—his world ideal. Of course, the law is not the place for the artist or the poet. The law is the calling of thinkers. But to those who believe with me that not the least godlike of man's activities is the large survey of causes, that to know is not less than to feel, I say—and I say no longer with any doubt—that a man may live greatly in the law as well as elsewhere; that there as well as elsewhere his thought may find its unity in an infinite perspective; that there as well as elsewhere he may wreak himself upon life, may drink the bitter cup of heroism, may wear his heart out after the unattainable. All that life offers any man from which to start his thinking or his striving is a fact. And if this universe is one universe, if it is so far thinkable that you can pass in reason from one part of it to another, it does not matter very much what that fact is. For every fact leads to every other by the path of the air. Only men do not yet see how, always. And your business as thinkers is to make plainer the way from some thing to the whole of things; to show the rational connection between your fact and the frame of the universe. If your subject is law, the roads are plain to anthropology, the science of man, to political economy, the theory of legislation, ethics, and thus by several paths to your final view of life. It would be equally true of any subject. The only difference is in the ease of seeing the way. To be master of any branch of knowledge, you must master those which lie next to it; and thus to know anything you must know all.

Perhaps I speak too much the language of intellectual ambition. I cannot but think that the scope for intellectual, as for physical adventure, is narrowing. I look for a future in which the ideal will be content and dignified acceptance of life, rather than aspiration and the passion for achievement. I see already that surveys and railroads have set limits to our intellectual wildernesses,—that the lion and the bison are disappearing from them, as from Africa and the no longer boundless West. But that undelightful day which I anticipate has not yet come. The human race has not changed, I imagine, so much between my generation and yours but that you still have the barbaric thirst for conquest, and there is still something left to conquer. There are fields still open for occupation in the law, and there are roads from them that will lead you where you will.

But do not think I am pointing you to flowery paths and beds of roses,—to a place where brilliant results attend your work, which shall be at once easy and new. No result is easy which is worth having. Your education begins when what is called your education is over,—when you no longer are stringing together

the pregnant thoughts, the "jewels five words long," which great men have given their lives to cut from the raw material for results which you do not see, cannot predict, and which may be long in coming,—when you take the fact which life offers you for your appointed task. No man has earned the right to intellectual ambition until he has learned to lay his course by a star which he has never seen,—to dig by the divining rod for springs which he may never reach. In saying this, I point to that which will make your study heroic. For I say to you in all sadness of conviction, that to think great thoughts you must be heroes as well as idealists. Only when you have worked alone,—when you have felt around you a black gulf of solitude more isolating than that which surrounds the dying man, and in hope and in despair have trusted to your own unshaken will,—then only will you have achieved. Thus only can you gain the secret isolated joy of the thinker, who knows that, a hundred years after he is dead and forgotten, men who never heard of him will be moving to the measure of his thoughts,—the subtile rapture of a postponed power, which the world knows not because it has no external trappings, but which to his prophetic vision is more real than that which commands an army. And if this joy should not be yours, still it is only thus that you can know that you have done what it lay in you to do,—can say that you have lived, and be ready for the end.

IDEALS AND DOUBTS

Reprinted from the Illinois Law Review [now Northwestern University Law Review], volume 10, May, 1915, pp. 1-4.

For the last thirty years we have been preoccupied with the embryology of legal ideas; and explanations, which, when I was in college meant a reference to final causes, later came to mean tracing origin and growth. But fashion is as potent in the intellectual world as elsewhere, and there are signs of an inevitable reaction. The reaction, if there is one, seems to me an advance, for it is toward the ultimate question of worth. That is the text of an excellent article, "History versus Value," by Morris R. Cohen in the Journal of Philosophy, Psychology and Scientific Methods, and, although perhaps rather in the form of conservation than of advance, of Del Vecchio's "Formal Bases at Law" in the Modern Legal Philosophical Series. To show that it has my sympathy I may refer to the Law Quarterly Review.[1] But perhaps it will not be out of place to express the caution with which I am compelled to approach any general recension from which the young hope so much.

The first inquiry is for the criterion. If I may do Del Vecchio the wrong of summing up in a sentence or two what from a hasty reading I gather to be his mode of reaching one, it is that of a Neo-Kantian idealist. Experience takes place and is organized as consciousness, by its machinery and according to its laws, such as the category of cause and effect. Therefore, consciousness constructs the universe and as the fundamental fact is entitled to fundamental reverence. From this it is easy to proceed to the Kantian injunction to regard every human being as an end in himself and not as a means.

I confess that I rebel at once. If we want conscripts, we march them up to the front with bayonets in their rear to die for a cause in which perhaps they do not believe. The enemy we treat not even as a means but as an obstacle to be abolished, if so it may be. I feel no pangs of conscience over either step, and naturally am slow to accept a theory that seems to be contradicted by practices that I approve. In fact, it seems to me that the idealists give away their case when they write books. For it shows that they have done the great act of faith and decided that they are not God. If the world were my dream, I should be God in the only universe I know. But although I cannot prove that I am awake, I believe that my neighbors exist in the same sense that I do, and if I admit that, it is easy to admit also that I am in the universe, not it in me.

When I say that a thing is true, I mean that I cannot help believing it. I am stating an experience as to which there is no choice. But as there are many things that I cannot help doing that the universe can, I do not venture to assume that my inabilities in the way of thought are inabilities of the universe. I therefore define the truth as the system of my limitations, and leave absolute truth for those who are better equipped. With absolute truth I leave absolute ideals of conduct equally on one side.

But although one believes in what commonly, with some equivocation, is called necessity; that phenomena always are found to stand in quantitatively fixed relations to earlier phenomena; it does not follow that without such absolute ideals we have nothing to do but to sit still and let time run over us. As I wrote many years ago, the mode in which the inevitable comes to pass is through effort. Consciously or unconsciously we all strive to make the kind of a world that we like. And although with Spinoza we may regard criticism of the past as futile, there is every reason for doing all that we can to make a future such as we desire.

There is every reason also for trying to make our

desires intelligent. The trouble is that our ideals for the most part are inarticulate, and that even if we have made them definite we have very little experimental knowledge of the way to bring them about. The social reformers of today seem to me so far to forget that we no more can get something for nothing by legislation than we can by mechanics as to be satisfied if the bill to be paid for their improvements is not presented in a lump sum. Interstitial detriments that may far outweigh the benefit promised are not bothered about. Probably I am too skeptical as to our ability to do more than shift disagreeable burdens from the shoulders of the stronger to those of the weaker. But I hold to a few articles of a creed that I do not expect to see popular in my day. I believe that the wholesale social regeneration which so many now seem to expect, if it can be helped by conscious, co-ordinated human effort, cannot be affected appreciably by tinkering with the institution of property, but only by taking in hand life and trying to build a race. That would be my starting point for an ideal for the law. The notion that with socialized property we should have women free and a piano for everybody seems to me an empty humbub.

To get a little nearer to the practical, our current ethics and our current satisfaction with conventional legal rules, it seems to me, can be purged to a certain extent without reference to what our final ideal may be. To rest upon a formula is a slumber that, prolonged, means death. Our system of morality is a body of imperfect social generalizations expressed in terms of emotion. To get at its truth, it is useful to omit the emotion and ask ourselves what those generalizations are and how far they are confirmed by fact accurately ascertained. So in regard to the formulas of the law, I have found it very instructive to consider what may be the postulates implied. They are generically two: that such and such a condition or result is desirable and that such and such means are appropriate to bring it about. In all debatable matters there are conflicting desires to be accomplished by inconsistent means, and the further question arises, which is entitled to prevail in the specific case? Upon such issues logic does not carry us far, and the practical solution sometimes may assume a somewhat cynical shape. But I have found it a help to clear thinking to try to get behind my conventional assumptions as a judge whose first business is to see that the game is played according to the rules whether I like them or not. To have doubted one's own first principles is the mark of a civilized man. To know what you want and why you think that such a measure will help it is the first but by no means the last step towards intelligent legal reform. The other and more difficult one is to realize what you must give up to get it, and to consider whether you are ready to pay the price.

It is fashionable nowadays to emphasize the criterion of social welfare as against the individualistic eighteenth century bills of rights. I may venture to refer to a book of mine published thirty-four years ago to show that it is no novelty.[2] The trouble with some of those who hold to that modest platitude is that they are apt to take the general premise as a sufficient justification for specific measures. One may accept the premise in good faith and yet disbelieve all the popular conceptions of socialism, or even doubt whether there is a panacea in giving women votes. Personally I like to know what the bill is going to be before I order a luxury. But it is a pleasure to see more faith and enthusiasm in the young men; and I thought that one of them made a good answer to some of my skeptical talk when he said, "You would base legislation upon regrets rather than upon hopes."

NOTES

IDEALS AND DOUBTS

[1] 25 Law Quarterly Review, 412, 414, Oct., 1909.
[2] The Common Law, pp. 43, 44, 48.

LEARNING AND SCIENCE

Speech at a dinner of the Harvard Law School Association in honor of Professor C. C. Langdell, June 25, 1895.
Reprinted from Speeches by Oliver Wendell Holmes, Boston, Little, Brown & Co., 1913, pp. 67-69.

MR. PRESIDENT AND GENTLEMEN OF THE ASSOCIATION:

As most of those here have graduated from the Law School within the last twenty-five years, I know that I am in the presence of very learned men. For my own part, lately my thoughts have been turned to

> "old, unhappy, far-off things,
> And battles long ago;"

and when once the ghosts of the dead fifers of thirty years since begin to play in my head, the laws are silent. And yet as I look around me, I think to myself, like Correggio, "I too am or at least have been, a pedagogue." And as such I will venture a reflection.

Learning, my learned brethren, is a very good thing. I should be the last to undervalue it, having done my share of quotation from the Year Books. But it is liable to lead us astray. The law, so far as it depends on learning, is indeed, as it has been called, the government of the living by the dead. To a very considerable extent no doubt it is inevitable that the living should be so governed. The past gives us our vocabulary and fixes the limits of our imagination; we cannot get away from it. There is, too, a peculiar logical pleasure in making manifest the continuity between what we are doing and what has been done before. But the present has a right to govern itself so far as it can; and it ought always to be remembered that historic continuity with the past is not a duty, it is only a necessity.

I hope that the time is coming when this thought will bear fruit. An ideal system of law should draw its postulates and its legislative justification from science. As it is now, we rely upon tradition, or vague sentiment, or the fact that we never thought of any other way of doing things, as our only warrant for rules which we enforce with as much confidence as if they embodied revealed wisdom. Who here can give reasons of any different kind for believing that half the criminal law does not do more harm than good? Our forms of contract, instead of being made once for all, like a yacht, on lines of least resistance, are accidental relics of early notions, concerning which the learned dispute. How much has reason had to do in deciding how far, if at all, it is expedient for the State to meddle with the domestic relations? And so I might go on through the whole law.

The Italians have begun to work upon the notion that the foundations of the law ought to be scientific, and, if our civilization does not collapse, I feel pretty sure that the regiment or division that follows us will carry that flag. Our own word seems the last always; yet the change of emphasis from an argument in Plowden to one in the time of Lord Ellenborough, or even from that to one in our own day, is as marked as the difference between Cowley's poetry and Shelley's. Other changes as great will happen. And so the eternal procession moves on, we in the front for the moment; and, stretching away against the unattainable sky, the black spearheads of the army that has been passing in unbroken line already for near a thousand years.

SPEECH AT A DINNER GIVEN TO CHIEF JUSTICE HOLMES

Dinner given by The Bar Association of Boston on March 7, 1900.

Reprinted from Speeches by Oliver Wendell Holmes, Boston, Little, Brown & Co., 1913. pp. 82-86.

GENTLEMEN OF THE SUFFOLK BAR:—

THE kindness of this reception almost unmans me, and it shakes me the more when taken with a kind of seriousness which the moment has for me. As with a drowning man, the past is telescoped into a minute, and the stages are all here at once in my mind. The day before yesterday I was at the law school, fresh from the army, arguing cases in a little club with Goulding and Beaman and Peter Olney, and laying the dust of pleading by certain sprinklings which Huntington Jackson, another ex-soldier and I managed to contrive together. A little later in the day, in Bob Morse's office, I saw a real writ, acquired a practical conviction of the difference between assumpsit and trover, and marvelled open-mouthed at the swift certainty with which a master of his business turned it off.

Yesterday I was at the law school again, in the chair instead of on the benches, when my dear partner, Shattuck, came out and told me that in one hour the Governor would submit my name to the council for a judgeship, if notified of my assent. It was a stroke of lightning which changed the whole course of my life.

And the day before yesterday, gentlemen, was thirty-five years, and yesterday was more than eighteen years, ago. I have gone on feeling young, but I have noticed that I met fewer of the old to whom to show my deference, and recently I was startled by being told that ours is an old bench. Well, I accept the fact, although I find it hard to realize, and I ask myself, what is there to show for this half lifetime that has passed? I look into my book in which I keep a docket of the decisions of the full court which fall to me to write, and find about a thousand cases. A thousand cases, many of them upon trifling or transitory matters, to represent nearly half a lifetime! A thousand cases, when one would have liked to study to the bottom and to say his say on every question which the law ever has presented, and then to go on and invent new problems which should be the test of doctrine, and then to generalize it all and write it in continuous, logical, philosophical exposition, setting forth the whole corpus with its roots in history and its justifications of expedience real or supposed!

Alas, gentlemen, that is life. I often imagine Shakespeare or Napoleon summing himself up and thinking: "Yes, I have written five thousand lines of solid gold and a good deal of padding—I, who would have covered the milky way with words which outshone the stars!" "Yes, I beat the Austrians in Italy and elsewhere: I made a few brilliant campaigns, and I ended in middle life in a *cul-de-sac*—I, who had dreamed of a world monarchy and Asiatic power." We cannot live our dreams. We are lucky enough if we can give a sample of our best, and if in our hearts we can feel that it has been nobly done.

Some changes come about in the process, changes not necessarily so much in the nature as in the emphasis of our interest. I do not mean in our wish to make a living and to succeed—of course, we all want those things—but I mean in our ulterior intellectual or spiritual interest, in the ideal part, without which we are but snails or tigers.

One begins with a search for a general point of view. After a time he finds one, and then for a while he is absorbed in testing it, in trying to satisfy himsef whether it is true. But after many experiments or investigations all have come out one way, and his theory is confirmed and settled in his mind, he knows in advance that the next case will be but another verification, and the stimulus of anxious curiosity is gone. He realizes that his branch of knowledge only presents more illustrations of the universal principle; he sees it all as another case of the same old ennui, or the same sublime mystery,—for it does not matter what epithets you apply to the whole of things, they are merely judgments of yourself. At this stage the pleasure is no less, perhaps, but it is the pure pleasure of doing the work, irrespective of further aims, and when you reach that stage you reach, as it seems to me, the triune formula of the joy, the duty, and the end of life.

It was of this that Malebranche was thinking when he said that, if God held in one hand truth, and in the other the pursuit of truth, he would say: "Lord, the truth is for thee alone; give me the pursuit." The joy of life is to put out one's power in some natural and useful or harmless way. There is no other. And the real misery is not to do this. The hell of the old world's literature is to be taxed beyond one's powers. This country has expressed in story—I suppose because it has experienced it in life—a deeper abyss of intellectual asphyxia or vital ennui, when powers conscious of themselves are denied their chance.

The rule of joy and the law of duty seem to me all one. I confess that altruistic and cynically selfish talk seem to me about equally unreal. With all humility, I think "Whatsoever thy hand findeth to do, do it with thy might," infinitely more important than the vain attempt to love one's neighbor as one's self. If you want to hit a bird on the wing, you must have all your will in a focus, you must not be thinking about yourself, and, equally, you must not be thinking about your neighbor; you must be living in your eye on that bird. Every achievement is a bird on the wing.

The joy, the duty, and, I venture to add, the end of life. I speak only of this world, of course, and of the teachings of this world. I do not seek to trench upon the province of spiritual guides. But from the point of view of the world the end of life is life. Life is action, the use of one's powers. As to use them to their height is our joy and duty, so it is the one end that justifies itself. Until lately the best thing that I was able to think of in favor of civilization, apart from blind acceptance of the order of the universe, was that it made possible the artist, the poet, the philosopher, and the man of science. But I think that is not the greatest thing. Now I believe that the greatest thing is a matter that comes directly home to us all. When it is said that we are too much occupied with the means of living to live, I answer that the chief worth of civilization is just that it makes the means of living more complex; that it calls for great and combined intellectual efforts, instead of simple, uncoördinated ones, in order that the crowd may be fed and clothed and housed and moved from place to place. Because more complex and intense intellectual efforts mean a fuller and richer life. They mean more life. Life is an end in itself, and the only question as to whether it is worth living is whether you have enough of it.

I will add but a word. We all are very near despair. The sheathing that floats us over its waves is compounded of hope, faith in the unexplainable worth and sure issue of effort, and the deep, subconscious content which comes from the exercise of our powers. In the words of a touching negro song,—

> Sometimes I's up, sometimes I's down,
> Sometimes I's almost to the groun';

but these thoughts have carried me, as I hope they will carry the young men who hear me, through long years of doubt, self-distrust, and solitude. They do now, for, although it might seem that the day of trial was over, in fact it is renewed each day. The kindness which you have shown me makes me bold in happy moments to believe that the long and passionate struggle has not been quite in vain.

SPEECH ON RECEIVING THE DEGREE OF DOCTOR OF LAWS

Yale University Commencement, June 30, 1886.
Reprinted from Speeches by Oliver Wendell Holmes, Boston, Little, Brown & Co., 1913. pp. 26-27.

Mr. President and Gentlemen:—
I know of no mark of honor which this country has to offer that I should value so highly as this which you have conferred upon me. I accept it proudly as an accolade, like the little blow upon the shoulder from the sword of a master of war which in ancient days adjudged that a soldier had won his spurs and pledged his life to decline no combat in the future.

The power of honor to bind men's lives is not less now than it was in the Middle Ages. Now as then it is the breath of our nostrils; it is that for which we live, for which, if need be, we are willing to die. It is that which makes the man whose gift is the power to gain riches sacrifice health and even life to the pursuit. It is that which makes the scholar feel that he cannot afford to be rich.

One would sometimes think, from the speech of young men, that things had changed recently, and that indifference was now the virtue to be cultivated. I never heard any one profess indifference to a boat race. Why should you row a boat race? Why endure long months of pain in preparation for a fierce half-hour that will leave you all but dead? Does any one ask the question? Is there any one who would not go through all it costs, and more, for the moment when anguish breaks into triumph,—or even for the glory of having nobly lost? Is life less than a boat race? If a man will give all the blood in his body to win the one, will he not spend all the might of his soul to prevail in the other?

I know, Mr. President, that there is a motive above even honor which may govern men's lives. I know that there are some rare spirits who find the inspiration of every moment, the aim of every act, in holiness. I am enough of a Puritan, I think, to conceive the exalted joy of those who look upon themselves only as instruments in the hands of a higher power to work out its designs. But I think that most men do and must reach the same result under the illusion of self-seeking. If the love of honor is a form of that illusion, it is no ignoble one. If it does not lift a man on wings to the sky, at least it carries him above the earth and teaches him those high and secret pathways across the branches of the forest the travellers on which are only less than winged.

Not the least service of this great University and its sister from which I come is, that by their separate teaching and by their mutual rivalry they have fostered that lofty feeling among their graduates. You have done all that a university can do to fan the spark in me. I will try to maintain the honor you have bestowed.

SPEECH ON JOHN MARSHALL

In answer to a motion that the court adjourn, on February 4, 1901, the One Hundredth Anniversary of the day on which Marshall took his seat as Chief Justice.

Reprinted from Speeches by Oliver Wendell Holmes, Boston, Little, Brown & Co., 1913. pp. 87-91.

AS WE walk down Court Street in the midst of a jostling crowd, intent like us upon to-day and its affairs, our eyes are like to fall upon the small, dark building that stands at the head of State Street, and, like an ominous reef, divides the stream of business in its course to the gray cliffs that tower beyond. And, whoever we may be, we may chance to pause and forget our hurry for a moment, as we remember that the first waves that foretold the coming storm of the Revolution broke around that reef. But, if we are lawyers, our memories and our reverence grow more profound. In the old State House, we remember, James Otis argued the case of the writs of assistance, and in that argument laid one of the foundations for American constitutional law. Just as that little building is not diminished, but rather is enhanced and glorified, by the vast structures which somehow it turns into a background, so the beginnings of our national life, whether in battle or in law, lose none of their greatness by contrast with all the mighty things of later date, beside which, by every law of number and measure, they ought to seem so small. To us who took part in the Civil War, the greatest battle of the Revolution seems little more than a reconnaissance in force, and Lexington and Concord were mere skirmishes that would not find mention in the newspapers. Yet veterans who have known battle on a modern scale, are not less aware of the spiritual significance of those little fights, I venture to say, than the enlightened children of commerce who tell us that soon war is to be no more.

If I were to think of John Marshall simply by number and measure in the abstract, I might hesitate in my superlatives, just as I should hesitate over the battle of the Brandywine if I thought of it apart from its place in the line of historic cause. But such thinking is empty in the same proportion that it is abstract. It is most idle to take a man apart from the circumstances which, in fact, were his. To be sure, it is easier in fancy to separate a person from his riches than from his character. But it is just as futile. Remove a square inch of mucous membrane, and the tenor will sing no more. Remove a little cube from the brain, and the orator will be speechless; or another, and the brave, generous and profound spirit becomes a timid and querulous trifler. A great man represents a great ganglion in the nerves of society, or, to vary the figure, a strategic point in the campaign of history, and part of his greatness consists in his being *there.* I no more can separate John Marshall from the fortunate circumstance that the appointment of Chief Justice fell to John Adams, instead of to Jefferson a month later, and so gave it to a Federalist and loose constructionist to start the working of the Constitution, than I can separate the black line through which he sent his electric fire at Fort Wagner from Colonel Shaw. When we celebrate Marshall we celebrate at the same time and indivisibly the inevitable fact that the oneness of the nation and the supremacy of the national Constitution were declared to govern the dealings of man with man by the judgments and decrees of the most august of courts.

I do not mean, of course, that personal estimates are useless or teach us nothing. No doubt to-day there will be heard from able and competent persons such estimates of Marshall. But I will not trench upon their field of work. It would be out of place when I am called on only to express the answer to a motion addressed to the court and when many of those who are here are to listen this afternoon to the accomplished teacher who has had every occasion to make a personal study of the judge, and again this evening to a gentleman who shares by birth the traditions of the man. My own impressions are only those that I have gathered in the common course of legal education and practice. In them I am conscious, perhaps, of some little revolt from our purely local or national estimates, and of a wish to see things and people judged by more cosmopolitan standards. A man is bound to be parochial in his practice—to give his life, and if necessary his death, for the place where he has his roots. But his thinking should be cosmopolitan and detached. He should be able to criticise what he reveres and loves.

The Federalist, when I read it many years ago, seemed to me a truly original and wonderful production for the time. I do not trust even that judgment unrevised when I remember that the Federalist and its authors struck a distinguished English friend of mine as finite; and I should feel a greater doubt whether, after Hamilton and the Constitution itself, Marshall's work proved more than a strong intellect, a good style, personal ascendancy in his court, courage, justice and the convictions of his party. My keenest interest is excited, not by what are called great questions and great cases, but by little decisions which the common run of selectors would pass by because they did not deal with the Constitution or a telephone company, yet which have in them the germ of some wider theory, and therefore of some profound interstitial change in the very tissue of the law. The men whom I should be tempted to commemorate would be the originators of transforming thought. They often are half obscure, because what the world pays for is judgment, not the original mind.

But what I have said does not mean that I shall join in this celebration or in granting the motion before the court in any half-hearted way. Not only do I recur to what I said in the beginning, and remembering that you cannot separate a man from his place, remember also that there fell to Marshall perhaps the greatest place that ever was filled by a judge; but when I consider his might, his justice, and his wisdom, I do fully believe that if American law were to be represented by a single figure, sceptic and worshipper alike would agree without dispute that the figure could be one alone, and that one John Marshall.

A few words more and I have done. We live by symbols, and what shall be symbolized by any image of the sight depends upon the mind of him who sees it. The setting aside of this day in honor of a great judge may stand to a Virginian for the glory of his glorious State; to a patriot for the fact that time has been on Marshall's side, and that the theory for which Hamilton argued, and he decided, and Webster spoke, and Grant fought, and Lincoln died, is now our corner-stone. To the more abstract but farther-reaching contemplation of the lawyer, it stands for the rise of a new body of jurisprudence, by which guiding principles are raised above the reach of statute and State, and judges are entrusted with a solemn and hitherto unheard-of authority and duty. To one who lives in what may seem to him a solitude of thought, this day—as it marks the triumph of a man whom some Presidents of his time bade carry out his judgments as he could—this day marks the fact that all thought is social, is on its way to action; that, to borrow the expression of a French writer, every idea tends to become first a catechism and then a code; and that according to its worth his unhelped meditation may one day mount a throne, and without armies, or even with them, may shoot across the world the electric despotism of an unresisted power. It is all a symbol, if you like, but so is the flag. The flag is but a bit of bunting to one who insists on prose. Yet, thanks to Marshall and to the men of his generation—and for this above all we celebrate him and them—its red is our life-blood, its stars our world, its blue our heaven. It owns our land. At will it throws away our lives.

The motion of the bar is granted, and the court will now adjourn.

NATURAL LAW [1]

Reprinted from Harvard Law Review, volume 32, pp. 40-44, November, 1918.

IT IS not enough for the knight of romance that you agree that his lady is a very nice girl—if you do not admit that she is the best that God ever made or will make, you must fight. There is in all men a demand for the superlative, so much so that the poor devil who has no other way of reaching it attains it by getting drunk. It seems to me that this demand is at the bottom of the philosopher's effort to prove that truth is absolute and of the jurist's search for criteria of universal validity which he collects under the head of natural law.

I used to say, when I was young, that truth was the majority vote of that nation that could lick all others. Certainly we may expect that the received opinion about the present war will depend a good deal upon which side wins, (I hope with all my soul it will be mine), and I think that the statement was correct in so far as it implied that our test of truth is a reference to either a present or an imagined future majority in favor of our view. If, as I have suggested elsewhere, the truth may be defined as the system of my (intellectual) limitations, what gives it objectivity is the fact that I find my fellow man to a greater or less extent (never wholly) subject to the same *Can't Helps.* If I think that I am sitting at a table I find that the other persons present agree with me; so if I say that the sum of the angles of a triangle is equal to two right angles. If I am in a minority of one they send for a doctor or lock me up; and I am so far able to transcend the to me convincing testimony of my senses or my reason as to recognize that if I am alone probably something is wrong with my works.

Certitude is not the test of certainty. We have been cock-sure of many things that were not so. If I may quote myself again, property, friendship, and truth have a common root in time. One can not be wrenched from the rocky crevices into which one has grown for many years without feeling that one is attacked in one's life. What we most love and revere generally is determined by early associations. I love granite rocks and barberry bushes, no doubt because with them were my earliest joys that reach back through the past eternity of my life. But while one's experience thus makes certain preferences dogmatic for oneself, recognition of how they came to be so leaves one able to see that others, poor souls, may be equally dogmatic about something else. And this again means scepticism. Not that one's belief or love does not remain. Not that we would not fight and die for it if important—we all, whether we know it or not, are fighting to make the kind of a world that we should like—but that we have learned to recognize that others will fight and die to make a different world, with equal sincerity or belief. Deep-seated preferences can not be argued about—you can not argue a man into liking a glass of beer—and therefore, when differences are sufficiently far reaching, we try to kill the other man rather than let him have his way. But that is perfectly consistent with admitting that, so far as appears, his grounds are just as good as ours.

The jurists who believe in natural law seem to me to be in that naive state of mind that accepts what has been familiar and accepted by all men everywhere. No doubt it is true that, so far as we can see ahead, some arrangements and the rudiments of familiar institutions seem to be necessary elements in any society that may spring from our own and that would seem to us to be civilized—some form of permanent association between the sexes—some residue of property individually owned—some mode of binding oneself to specified future conduct—to the bottom of all, some protection for the person. But without speculating whether a group is imaginable in which all but the last of these might disappear and the last be subject to qualifications that most of us would abhor, the question remains as to the *Ought* of natural law.

It is true that beliefs and wishes have a transcendental basis in the sense that their foundation is arbitrary. You can not help entertaining and feeling them, and there is an end of it. As an arbitrary fact people wish to live, and we say with various degrees of certainty that they can do so only on certain conditions. To do it they must eat and drink. That necessity is absolute. It is a necessity of less degree but practically general that they should live in society. If they live in society, so far as we can see, there are further conditions. Reason working on experience does tell us, no doubt, that if our wish to live continues, we can do it only on those terms. But that seems to me the whole of the matter. I see no *a priori* duty to live with others and in that way, but simply a statement of what I must do if I wish to remain alive. If I do live with others they tell me that I must do and abstain from doing various things or they will put the screws on to me. I believe that they will, and being of the same mind as to their conduct I not only accept the rules but come in time to accept them with sympathy and emotional affirmation and begin to talk about duties and rights. But for legal purposes a right is only the hypostasis of a prophecy—the imagination of a substance supporting the fact that the public force will be brought to bear upon those who do things said to contravene it—just as we talk of the force of gravitation accounting for the conduct of bodies in space. One phrase adds no more than the other to what we know without it. No doubt behind these legal rights is the fighting will of the subject to maintain them, and the spread of his emotions to the general rules by which they are maintained; but that does not seem to me the same thing as the supposed *a priori* discernment of a duty or the assertion of a preexisting right. A dog will fight for his bone.

The most fundamental of the supposed preexisting rights—the right to life— is sacrificed without a scruple not only in war, but whenever the interest of society, that is, of the predominant power in the community, is thought to demand it. Whether that interest is the interest of mankind in the long run no one can tell, and as, in any event, to those who do not think with Kant and Hegel it is only an interest, the sanctity disappears. I remember a very tender-hearted judge being of opinion that closing a hatch to stop a fire and the destruction of a cargo was justified even if it was known that doing so would stifle a man below. It is idle to illustrate further, because to those who agree with me I am uttering commonplaces and to those who disagree I am ignoring the necessary foundations of thought. The *a priori* men generally call the dissentients superficial. But I do agree with them in believing that one's attitude on these matters is closely connected with one's general attitude toward the universe. Proximately, as has been suggested, it is determined largely by early associations and temperament, coupled with the desire to have an absolute guide. Men to a great extent believe what they want to—although I see in that no basis for a philosophy that tells us what we should want to want.

Now when we come to our attitude toward the universe I do not see any rational ground for demanding the superlative—for being dissatisfied unless we are assured that our truth is cosmic truth, if there is such a thing—that the ultimates of a little creature on this little earth are the last word of the unimaginable whole. If a man sees no reason for believing that significance, consciousness and ideals are more than marks of the finite, that does not justify what has been familiar in French sceptics; getting upon a pedestal and professing to look with haughty scorn upon a world in ruins. The real conclusion is that the part can not swallow the whole—that our categories are not, or may not be, adequate to formulate what we can not know. If we believe that we come out of the universe, not it out of us, we must admit that we do not know what we are talking about when we speak of brute matter. We do know that a certain complex of energies can wag its tail and another can make syllogisms. These are among the powers of the unknown, and if, as maybe, it has still greater powers that we can not understand, as Fabre in his studies of instinct would have us believe, studies that gave Bergson one of the strongest strands for his philosophy and enabled Maeterlinck to make us fancy for a moment that we heard a clang from behind phenomena—if this be true, why should we not be content? Why should we employ the energy that is furnished to us by the cosmos to defy it and shake our fist at the sky? It seems to me silly.

That the universe has in it more than we understand, that the private soldiers have not been told the plan of campaign, or even that there is one, rather than some vaster unthinkable to which every predicate is an impertinence, has no bearing upon our conduct. We still shall fight—all of us because we want to live, some, at least, because we want to realize our spontaneity and prove our powers, for the joy of it, and we may leave to the unknown the supposed final valuation of that which in any event has value to us. It is enough for us that the universe has produced us and has within it, as less than it, all that we believe and love. If we think of our existence not as that of a little god outside, but as that of a ganglion within, we have the infinite behind us. It gives us our only but our adequate significance. A grain of sand has the same, but what competent person supposes that he understands a grain of sand? That is as much beyond our grasp as man. If our imagination is strong enough to accept the vision of ourselves as parts inseverable from the rest, and to extend our final interest beyond the boundary of our skins, it justifies the sacrifice even of our lives for ends outside of ourselves. The motive, to be sure, is the common wants and ideals that we find in man. Philosophy does not furnish motives, but it shows men that they are not fools for doing what they already want to do. It opens to the forlorn hopes on which we throw ourselves away, the vista of the farthest stretch of human thought, the chords of a harmony that breathes from the unknown.

NOTES

NATURAL LAW

[1] Suggested by reading FRANCOIS GENY, SCIENCE ET TECHNIQUE EN DROIT POSITIF PRIVE, Paris, 1915.

LAW IN SCIENCE AND SCIENCE IN LAW[1]

Reprinted from *Harvard Law Review,* volume 12, pp. 443-463, February 25, 1899.

THE law of fashion is a law of life. The crest of the wave of human interest is always moving, and it is enough to know that the depth was greatest in respect of a certain feature or style in literature or music or painting a hundred years ago to be sure that at that point it no longer is so profound. I should draw the conclusion that artists and poets, instead of troubling themselves about the eternal, had better be satisfied if they can stir the feelings of a generation, but that is not my theme. It is more to my point to mention that what I have said about art is true within the limits of the possible in matters of the intellect. What do we mean when we talk about explaining a thing? A hundred years ago men explained any part of the universe by showing its fitness for certain ends, and demonstrating what they conceived to be its final cause according to a providential scheme. In our less theological and more scientific day, we explain an object by tracing the order and process of its growth and development from a starting point assumed as given.

This process of historical explanation has been applied to the matter of our profession, especially of recent years, with great success, and with so much eagerness, and with a feeling that when you had the true historic dogma you had the last word not only in the present but for the immediate future, that I have felt warranted heretofore in throwing out the caution that continuity with the past is only a necessity and not a duty. As soon as a legislature is able to imagine abolishing the requirement of a consideration for a simple contract, it is at perfect liberty to abolish it, if it thinks it wise to do so, without the slightest regard to continuity with the past. That continuity simply limits the possibilities of our imagination, and settles the terms in which we shall be compelled to think.

Historical explanation has two directions or aspects, one practical and the other abstractly scientific. I by no means share that morality which finds in a remoter practice the justification of philosophy and science. I do not believe that we must justify our pursuits by the motive of social well-being. If we have satisfied ourselves that our pursuits are good for society, or at least not bad for it, I think that science, like art, may be pursued for the pleasure of the pursuit and of its fruits, as an end in itself. I somewhat sympathize with the Cambridge mathematician's praise of his theorem, "The best of it all is that it can never by any possibility be made of the slightest use to anybody for anything." I think it one of the glories of man that he does not sow seed, and weave cloth, and produce all the other economic means simply to sustain and multiply other sowers and weavers that they in their turn may multiply, and so *ad infinitum,* but that on the contrary he devotes a certain part of his economic means to uneconomic ends—ends, too, which he finds in himself and not elsewhere. After the production of food and cloth has gone on a certain time, he stops producing and goes to the play, or he paints a picture, or asks unanswerable questions about the universe, and thus delightfully consumes a part of the world's food and clothing while he idles away the only hours that fully account for themselves.

Thinking in this way, you readily will understand that I do not consider the student of the history of legal doctrine bound to have a practical end in view. It is perfectly proper to regard and study the law simply as a great anthropological document. It is proper to resort to it to discover what ideals of society have been strong enough to reach that final form of expression, or what have been the changes in dominant ideals from century to century. It is proper to study it as an exercise in the morphology and transformation of human ideas. The study pursued for such ends becomes science in the strictest sense. Who could fail to be interested in the transition through the priest's test of truth,[2] the miracle of the ordeal, and the soldier's, the battle of the duel, to the democratic verdict of the jury! Perhaps I might add, in view of the great increase of jury-waived cases, a later transition yet—to the commercial and rational test of the judgment of a man trained to decide.

It is still only the minority who recognize how the change of emphasis which I have called the law of fashion has prevailed even in the realm of morals. The other day I was looking over Bradford's history—the book which Mr. Bayard brought as a gift from Lambeth to the Massachusetts State House—and I was struck to see recounted the execution of a man with horrible solemnities for an offence which still, to be sure, stands on the statute book as a serious crime, but which no longer is often heard of in court, which many would regard as best punished simply by the disgust of normal men, and which a few would think of only as a physiological aberration, of interest mainly to the pathologist. I found in the same volume the ministers consulted as the final expounders of the law, and learnedly demonstrating that what now we should consider as needing no other repression than a doctor's advice, was a crime punishable with death and to be ferreted out by searching the conscience of the accused, although after discussion it was thought that torture should be reserved for state occasions.

To take a less odius as well as less violent contrast, when we read in the old books that it is the duty of one exercising a common calling to do his work upon demand and to do it with reasonable skill, we see that the gentleman is in the saddle and means to have the common people kept up to the mark for his convenience. We recognize the imperative tone which in our day has changed sides, and is oftener to be heard from the hotel clerk than from the guest.

I spoke of the scientific study of the morphology

and transformation of human ideas in the law, and perhaps the notion did not strike all of you as familiar. I am not aware that the study ever has been systematically pursued, but I have given some examples as I have come upon them in my work, and perhaps I may mention some now by way of illustration, which, so far as I know, have not been followed out by other writers. In the Lex Salica [3]—the law of the Salian Franks—you find going back to the fifth century a very mysterious person, later [4] named the salmannus—the sale-man—a third person who was called in to aid in completing the transfer of property in certain cases. The donor handed to him a symbolic staff which he in due season handed over in solemn form to the donee. If we may trust M. Dareste, and take our information at second hand, a copious source of error, it would look as if a similar use of a third person was known to the Egyptians and other early peoples. But what is certain is that we see the same form used down to modern times in England for the transfer of copyhold. I dare say that many of you were puzzled, as I was when I was a law student, at the strange handing over of a staff to the lord or steward of the manor as a first step toward conveying copyhold land to somebody else. It really is nothing but a survival of the old form of the Salic law, as M. Vinogradoff at last has noticed, in his work on Villainage in England. There you have the Salic device in its original shape. But it is the transformations which it has undergone to which I wish to call your attention. The surrender to the steward is expressed to be to the use of the purchaser or donee. Now, although Mr. Kenelm Digby in his History of the Law of Real Property warns us that this has nothing to do with the doctrine of uses, I venture to think that, helped by the work of learned Germans as to the development of the saleman on the continent, I have shown heretofore that the saleman became in England the better known feoffee to uses, and thus that the connection between him and the steward of the manor when he receives the surrender of a copyhold is clear. But the executor originally was nothing but a feoffee to uses. The heir was the man who paid his ancestor's debts and took his property. The executor did not step into the heir's shoes, and come fully to represent the person of the testator as to personal property and liabilities until after Bracton wrote his great treatise on the Laws of England. Surely a flower is not more unlike a leaf, or a segment of a skull more unlike a vertebra, than the executor as we know him is remote from his prototype, the saleman of the Salic law. I confess that such a development as that fills me with interest, not only for itself, but as an illustration of what you see all through the law—the paucity of original ideas in man, and the slow, coasting way in which he works along from rudimentary beginnings to the complex and artificial conceptions of civilized life. It is like the niggardly uninventiveness of nature in its other manifestations, with its few smells or colors or types, its short list of elements, working along in the same slow way from compound to compound until the dramatic impressiveness of the most intricate compositions, which we call organic life, makes them seem different in kind from the elements out of which they are made, when set opposite to them in direct contrast.

In a book which I printed a good many years ago I tried to establish another example of the development and transformation of ideas. The early law embodied hatred for any immediate source of hurt, which comes from the association of ideas and imperfect analysis, in the form of proceedings against animals and inanimate objects, and of the *noxae deditio* by which the owner of the offending thing surrendered it and was free from any further liability. I tried to show that from this primitive source came, in part at least, our modern responsibility of an owner for his animals and of a master for his servants acting within the scope of their employment, the limited liability of shipowners under the law which allows them to surrender their vessel and free themselves, and that curious law of deodand, under which a steam engine was declared forfeited by the Court of Exchequer in 1842.[5] I shall have to suggest later that it played a part also in the development of contract.

Examples like these lead us beyond the transformations of an idea to the broader field of the development of our more general legal conceptions. We have evolution in this sphere of conscious thought and action no less than in lower organic stages, but an evolution which must be studied in its own field. I venture to think that the study is not yet finished. Take, for instance, the origin of contract. A single view has prevailed with slight modifications since Sohm published "Das Recht der Eheschliessung" in 1875. But fashion is potent in science as well as elsewhere, and it does not follow because Sohm smashed his predecessor that there may not arise a later champion who will make some impact upon him. Sohm, following a thought first suggested, I believe, by Savigny, and made familiar by Maine in his "Ancient Law," sees the beginning of contract in an interrupted sale. This is expressed in later law by our common law Debt, founded upon a *quid pro quo* received by the debtor from the creditor. Out of this, by a process differently conceived by different writers, arises the formal contract, the *fides facta* of the Salic law, the covenant familiar to us. And this dichotomy exhausts the matter. I do not say that this may not be proved to the final and correct account, but there are some considerations which I should like to suggest in a summary way. We are not bound to assume with Sohm that his Frankish ancestors had a theory in their heads which, even if a trifle inarticulate, was the majestic peer of all that was done at Rome. The result of that assumption is to lead to the further one, tacitly made, but felt to be there, that there must have been some theory of contract from the beginning, if only you can find what it was. It seems to me well to remember that men begin with no theory at all, and with no such generalization as contract. They begin with particular cases, and even when they have generalized they are often a long way from the final generalizations of a later time. Down into this century consideration was described by enumeration, as you may see in Tidd's "Practice," or Blackstone,[6] and only of late years has it been reduced to the universal expression of detriment to the promisee. So, bailment was Bailment and nothing further than modern times. It was not contract. And so warranty was Warranty, a duty imposed by law upon the vendor, and nothing more.[7] A trust still is only a Trust, although according to the orthodox it creates merely a personal obligation.

Well, I have called attention elsewhere to the fact that giving hostages may be followed back to the beginning of our legal history, as far back as sales, that is, and that out of the hostage grew the surety, quite independently of the development of debt or formal contract. If the obligation of the surety, who, by a paradox explained by his origin, appears often in early law without a principal contractor, as the only party bound, had furnished the analogy for other undertakings, we never should have had the doctrine of consideration, If other undertakings were to be governed by the analogy of the law developed out of sales, sureties must either have received a *quid pro quo* or have made a covenant. There was a clash between the competing ideas, and just as commerce was prevailing over war the children of the sale drove the child of the hostage from the field. In the time of Edward III, it was decided that a surety was not bound without a covenant, except in certain cities where local custom maintained the ancient law. Warranty of land came to require, and thus to be, a covenant in the same way, although the warranty of title upon a sale of chattels still retains its old characteristics, except that it now is thought of as a contract.[8]

But the hostage was not the only competitor for domination. The oath also goes back as far as the history of our race.[9] It started from a different point, and, leaving the possible difference of sanction on one side, it might have been made to cover the whole field of promises. The breach of their promissory oath by witnesses still is punished as perjury, and formerly there were severe penalties for the jury if convicted of a similar offence by attaint.[10] The solemnity was used for many other purposes, and, if the church had had its way, the oath, helped by its cousin the plighting of troth, would have been very likely to succeed. In the time of Henry III, faith, oath, and writing, that is, the covenant, were the popular familiar forms of promise. The plighting of a man's faith or troth, still known to us in the marriage ceremony, was in common use, and the courts of the church claimed jurisdiction over it as well as over the oath. I have called attention elsewhere to a hint of inclination on the part of the early clerical chancellors to continue the clerical jurisdiction in another court, and to enforce the ancient form of obligation. Professor Ames has controverted my suggestion, but I cannot but think it of significance that down to later times we still find the ecclesiastical tribunals punishing breach of faith or of promissory oaths with spiritual penalties. When we know that a certain form of undertaking was in general use, and that it was enforced by the clergy in their own courts, a very little evidence is enough to make us believe that in a new court, also presided over by a clergyman and with no substantive law of its own, the idea of enforcing it well might have been entertained, especially in view of the restrictions which the civil power put upon the church. But oath and plighting of troth did not survive in the secular forum except as an occasional solemnity, and I have mentioned them only to show a lively example of the struggle for life among competing ideas, and of the ultimate victory and survival of the strongest. After victory the law of covenant and debt went on, and consolidated and developed their empire in a way that is familiar to you all, until they in their turn lost something of their power and prestige in consequence of the rise of a new rival, Assumpsit.

There were other seeds which dropped by the wayside in early law, and which were germs of relations that now might be termed contractual, such as the blood covenant, by which people bound themselves together or made themselves of one substance by drinking the blood or eating the flesh of a newly killed animal. Such was the fiction of family relationship, by which, for instance, the Aedui symbolized their alliance with the Romans.[11] I may notice in this connection that I suspect that the *mundium* or early German guardianship was the origin of our modern bail, while, as I have said, the surety came from a different source. I mention these only to bring still closer home the struggle for existence between competing ideas and forms to which I have referred. In some instances the vanquished competitor has perished. In some it has put on the livery of its conqueror, and has become in form and external appearance merely a case of covenant or assumpsit.

Another important matter is the way in which the various obligations were made binding after they were recognized. A breach of oath of course brought with it the displeasure of the gods. In other cases, as might be expected, we find hints that liabilities of a more primitive sort were extended to the new candidates for legal recognition. In the Roman law a failure to pay the price of a purchase seems to have suggested the analogy of theft. All over the world slavery for debt is found, and this seems not to have stood on the purely practical considerations which first would occur to us, but upon a notion akin to the noxal surrender of the offending body for a tort. There is a mass of evidence that various early contracts in the systems of law from which our own is descended carried with them the notion of pledging the person of the contracting party,—a notion which we see in its extreme form in the seizure or division of the dead body of the debtor,[12] and which seems to come out in the maxim *Debita inhaerent ossibus debitoris.*

I am not going to trace the development of every branch of our law in succession, but if we turn to the law of torts we find there, perhaps even more noticeably than in the law of contracts, another evolutionary process which Mr. Herbert Spencer has made familiar to us by the name of Integration. The first stage of torts embraces little if anything beyond those simple acts of violence where the appeals of death, of wounding or maiming, of arson and the like had taken the place of self-help, to be succeeded by the modification known as the action of trespass. But when the action on the case let libel and slander and all the other wrongs which are known to the modern law into the civil courts, for centuries each of the recognized torts had its special history, its own precedents, and no one dreamed, so far as I know, that the different cases of liability were, or ought to be, governed by the same principles throughout. As is said in the preface to Mr. Jaggard's book, "the use of a book on Torts, as a distinct subject, was a few years ago a matter of ridicule." You may see the change which has taken place by comparing Hilliard on Torts, which proceeds by enumeration in successive chapters through assault and battery, libel and slander, nuisance, trespass, conversion, etc., with Sir Frederick Pollock's Introduction, in which he says that the purpose of his book "is to show that there really is a Law of Torts, not merely a number of rules of law about various kinds of torts—that this is a true living branch of the Common Law, not a collection of heterogeneous instances." It would be bold, perhaps, to say that the integration was complete, that it did not rest partly in tendency. The recent much discussed case of Allen *v.* Flood, in the House of Lords, seems to me to indicate that, in the view of the older generation even of able and learned men, the foundation of liability still is somewhat in the air, and that tradition and enumeration are the best guides to this day. But I have no doubt that the generalizing principle will prevail, as generalization so often prevails, even in advance of evidence, because of the ease of mind and comfort which it brings.

Any one who thinks about the world as I do does not need proof that the scientific study of any part of it has an interest which is the same in kind as that of any other part. If the examples which I have given fail to make the interest plain, there is no use in my adding to them, and so I shall pass to another part of my subject. But first let me add a word. The man of science in the law is not merely a bookworm. To a microscopic eye for detail he must unite an insight which tells him what details are significant. Not every maker of exact investigation counts, but only he who directs his investigation to a crucial point. But I doubt if there is any more exalted form of life than that of a great abstract thinker, wrapt in the successful study of problems to which he devotes himself, for an end which is neither unselfish nor selfish in the common sense of those words, but is simply to feed the deepest hunger and to use the greatest gifts of his soul.

But after all the place for a man who is complete in all his powers is in the fight. The professor, the man of letters, gives up one-half of life that his protected talent may grow and flower in peace. But to make up your mind at your peril upon a living question, for purposes of action, calls upon your whole nature. I trust that I have shown that I appreciate what I thus far have spoken of as if it were the only form of the scientific study of law, but of course I think, as other people do, that the main ends of the subject are practical, and from a practical point of view, history, with which I have been dealing thus far, is only a means and one of the least of the means, of mastering a tool. From a practical point of view, as I have illustrated upon another occasion, its use is mainly negative and skeptical. It may help us to know the true limit of a doctrine, but its chief good is to burst inflated explanations. Every one instinctively recognizes that in these days the justification of a law for us cannot be found in the fact that our fathers always have followed it. It must be found in some help which the law brings toward reaching a social end which the governing power of the community has made up its mind that it wants. And when a lawyer sees a rule of law in force he is very apt to invent, if he does not find, some ground of policy for its base. But in fact some rules are mere survivals. Many might as well be different, and history is the means by which we measure the power which the past has had to govern the present in spite of ourselves, so to speak, by imposing traditions which no longer meet their original end. History sets us free and enables us to make up our minds dispassionately whether the survival which we are enforcing answers any new purpose when it has ceased to answer the old. Notwithstanding the contrasts which I have been making, the practical study of the law ought also to be scientific. The true science of the law does not consist mainly in a theological working out of dogma or a logical development as in mathematics, or only in a study of it as an anthropological document from the outside; an even more important part consists in the establishment of its postulates from within upon accurately measured social desires instead of tradition. It is this latter part to which I now am turning, and I begin with one or two instances of the help of history in clearing away rubbish,—instances of detail from my own experience.

Last autumn our court had to consider the grounds upon which evidence of fresh complaint by a ravished woman is admitted as part of the government's case in an indictment for rape. All agree that it is an exception to the ordinary rules of evidence to allow a witness to be corroborated by proof that he has said the same thing elsewhere when not under oath, except possibly by way of rebuttal under extraordinary circumstances. But there is the exception, almost as well settled as the rule, and courts and lawyers finding the law to be established proceed to account for it by consulting their wits. We are told that the outrage is so great that there is a natural presumption that a virtuous woman would disclose it at the first suitable opportunity. I confess that I should think this was about the last crime in which such a presumption could be made, and that it was far more likely that a man who had had his pocket picked or who had been the victim of an attempt to murder would speak of it, than that a sensitive woman would disclose such a horror. If we look into history no further than Hale's "Pleas of the Crown," where we first find the doctrine, we get the real reason and the simple truth. In an appeal of rape the first step was for the woman to raise hue and cry. Lord Hale, after stating that fact, goes on to say that upon an indictment for the same offence the woman can testify, and that her testimony will be corroborated if she made fresh complaint and pursued the offender. That is the hue and cry over again. At that time there were few rules of evidence. Later our laws of evidence were systematized and developed. But the authority of Lord Hale has caused his dictum to survive as law in the particular case, while the principle upon which it would have to be justified has been destroyed. The exception in other words is a pure survival, having nothing or very little to back it except that the practice is established.[13]

In a somewhat earlier case [14] I tried to show that the doctrine of trespass *ab initio* in like manner was the survival in a particular class of cases of a primitive rule of evidence, which established intent by a presumption of law from subsequent conduct, after the rule had gone to pieces and had been forgotten as a whole. Since that decision Professor Ames has made some suggestions which may or may not modify or enlarge the view which I took, but which equally leave the doctrine a survival, the reasons for which long have disappeared.

In Brower *v.* Fisher,[15] the defendant, a deaf and dumb person, had conveyed to the plaintiff real and personal property, and had got a judgment against the plaintiff for the price. The plaintiff brought a bill to find out whether the conveyance was legal, and got an injunction *pendente lite* to stay execution on the judgment. On the plaintiff's petition a commission of lunacy was issued to inquire whether the defendant was *compos mentis*. It was found that he was so unless the fact that he was born deaf and dumb made him otherwise. Thereupon Chancellor Kent dismissed the bill but held the inquiry so reasonable that he imposed no costs. The old books of England fully justified his view; and why? History again gives us the true reason. The Roman law held very properly that the dumb, and by extension the deaf, could not make the contract called *stipulatio* because the essence of that contract was a formal question and answer which the dumb could not utter and the deaf could not hear. Bracton copies the Roman law and repeats the true reason, that they could not express assent, *consentire;* but shows that he had missed the meaning of *stipulari* by suggesting that perhaps it might be done by gestures or writing. Fleta copied Bracton, but seemed to think that the trouble was inability to bring the consenting mind, and whereas the Roman law explained that the rule did not apply to one who was only hard of hearing — *qui tardius exaudit* — Fleta seems to have supposed that this pointed to a difference between a man born deaf and dumb and one who became so later in life.[16] In Perkin's "Profitable Book," this is improved upon by requiring that the man should be born blind, deaf, and dumb, and then the reason is developed that "a man that is born blind, deaf, and dumb can have no understanding, so that he cannot make a gift or a grant." [17] In a case before Vice-Chancellor Wood [18] good sense prevailed, and it was laid down that there is no exception to the presumption of sanity in the case of a deaf and dumb person.

Other cases of what I have called inflated and unreal explanations, which collapse at the touch of history, are the liability of a master for the torts of his servant in the course of his employment, to which I have referred earlier, and which thus far never, in my opinion, has been put upon a rational footing; and the liability of a common carrier, which, as I conceive, is another distorted survival from the absolute responsibility of bailees in early law, crossed with the liability of those exercising a common calling to which I have referred. These examples are sufficient, I hope, to illustrate my meaning, and to point out the danger of inventing reasons offhand for whatever we find established in the law. They lead me to some other general considerations in which history plays no part, or a minor part, but in which my object is to show the true process of law-making, and the real meaning of a decision upon a doubtful case and thus, as in what I have said before, to help in substituting a scientific foundation for empty words.

I pass from unreal explanations to unreal formulas and inadequate generalizations, and I will take up one or two with especial reference to the problems with which we have to deal at the present time. The first illustration which occurs to me, especially in view of what I have been saying, is suggested by another example of the power of fashion. I am immensely struck with the blind imitativeness of man when I see how a doctrine, a discrimination, even a phrase, will run in a year or two over the whole English-speaking world. Lately have we not all been bored to death with *volenti non fit injuria,* and with Lord Justice Bowen's remark that it is *volenti* and not *scienti*? I congratulate any State in whose reports you do not see the maxim and its qualification repeated. I blush to say that I have been as guilty as the rest. Do we not hear every day of taking the risk—an expression which we never heard used as it now is until within a very few years? Do we not hear constantly of invitation and trap—which came into vogue within the memory of many, if not most of those who are here? Heaven forbid that I should find fault with an expression because it is new, or with the last mentioned expressions on any ground! Judges commonly are elderly men, and we are more likely to hate at sight any analysis to which they are not accustomed, and which disturbs repose of mind, than to fall in love with novelties. Every living sentence which shows a mind at work for itself is to be welcomed. It is not the first use but the tiresome repetition of inadequate catch words upon which I am observing,—phrases which originally were contributions, but which, by their very felicity, delay further analysis for fifty years. That comes from the same source as dislike of novelty,—intellectual indolence or weakness,—a slackening in the eternal pursuit of the more exact.

The growth of education is an increase in the knowledge of measure. To use words familiar to logic and to science, it is a substitution of quantitative for qualitative judgments. The difference between the criticism of a work of art by a man of perception without technical training and that by a critic of the studio will illustrate what I mean. The first, on seeing a statue, will say, "It is grotesque," a judgment of quality merely; the second will say, "That statute is so many heads high, instead of the normal so many heads." His judgment is one of quantity. On hearing a passage of Beethoven's Ninth Symphony the first will say, "What a gorgeous sudden outburst of sunshine!"—the second, "Yes, great idea to bring in his major third just there, wasn't it?" Well, in the law we only occasionally can reach an absolutely final and quantitative determination, because the worth of the competing social ends which respectively solicit a judgment for the plaintiff or the defendant cannot be reduced to number and accurately fixed. The worth, that is, the intensity of the competing desires, varies with the varying ideals of the time, and, if the desires were constant, we could not get beyond a relative decision that one was greater and one was less. But it is of the essence of improvement that we should be as accurate as we can. Now to recur to such expressions as taking the risk and *volenti non fit injuria,* which are very well for once in the sprightly mouth which first applies them, the objection to the repetition of them as accepted legal formulas is that they do not represent a final analysis, but dodge difficulty and responsibility with a rhetorical phrase. When we say that a workman takes a certain risk as incident to his employment, we mean that on some general grounds of policy blindly felt or articulately present to our mind, we read into his contract a term of which he never thought; and the real question in every case is, What are the grounds, and how far do they extend? The question put in that form becomes at once and plainly a question for scientific determination, that is, for quantitative comparison by means of whatever measure we command. When we speak of taking the risk apart from contract, I believe that we merely are expressing what the law means by negligence, when for some reason or other we wish to express it in a conciliatory form.

In our approach towards exactness we constantly tend to work out definite lines or equators to mark distinctions which we first notice as a difference of poles. It is evident in the beginning that there must be differences in the legal position of infants and adults. In the end we establish twenty-one as the dividing point. There is a difference manifest at the outset between night and day. The statutes of Massachusetts fix the dividing points at one hour after sunset and one hour before sunrise, ascertained according to mean time. When he has discovered that a difference is a difference of degree, that distinguished extremes have between them a penumbra in which on gradually shades into the other, a tyro thinks to puzzle you by asking where you are going to draw the line, and an advocate of more experience will show the arbitrariness of the line proposed by putting cases very near to it on one side or the other. But the theory of the law is that such lines exist, because the theory of the law as to any possible conduct is that it is either lawful or unlawful. As that difference has no gradation about it, when applied to shades of conduct that are very near each other it has an arbitrary look. We like to disguise the arbitrariness, we like to save ourselves the trouble of nice and doubtful discriminations. In some regions of conduct of a special sort we have to be informed of facts which we do not know before we can draw our lines intelligently, and so, as we get near the dividing point, we call in the jury. From saying that we will leave a question to the jury to saying that it is a question of fact is but a step, and the result is that at this day it has come to be a widespread doctrine that negligence not only is a question for the jury but is a question of fact. I have heard it urged with great vehemence by counsel, and calmly maintained by professors that, in addition to their wrongs to labor, courts were encroaching upon the province of the jury when they directed a verdict in a negligence case, even in the unobstrusive form of a ruling that there was no evidence of neglect.

I venture to think, on the other hand, now, as I thought twenty years ago, before I went upon the bench, that every time that a judge declines to rule whether certain conduct is negligent or not he avows his inability to state the law, and that the meaning of leaving nice questions to the jury is that while if a question of law is pretty clear we can decide it, as it is our duty to do, if it is difficult it can be decided better by twelve men taken at random from the street. If a man fires a gun over a prairie that looks empty to the horizon, or crosses a railroad which he can see is clear for a thousand yards each way, he is not negligent, that is, he is free from legal liability in the first case, he has not prevented his recovery by his own conduct, if he is run over, in the second, as matter of law. If he fires a gun into a crowded street, or tries to cross a track ten feet in front of an express train in full sight running sixty miles an hour, he is liable, or he cannot recover, again as matter of law, supposing these to be all the facts in the case. What new question of fact is introduced if the place of firing is something half way between a prairie and a crowded street, or if the express train is two hundred, one hundred, or fifty yards away? I do not wish to repeat arguments which I published long ago, and which have been more or less quoted in leading text-books. I only wish to insist that false reasons and false analogies shall not be relied upon for daily practice. It is so easy to accept the phrase "there is no evidence of negligence," and thence to infer, as the English House of Lords has inferred, as Professor Thayer infers in his admirable Preliminary Treatise on Evidence which has appeared since these words were written, that the question is the same in kind as any other question whether there is evidence of a fact.

When we rule on evidence of negligence we are ruling on a standard of conduct, a standard which we hold the parties bound to know beforehand, and which in theory is always the same upon the same facts and not a matter dependent upon the whim of the particular jury or the eloquence of the particular advocate. And I may be permitted to observe that, referring once more to history, similar questions originally were, and to some extent still are, dealt with as questions of law. It was and is so on the question of probable cause in malicious prosecution. It was so on the question of necessaries for an infant,[20] It was so in questions of what is reasonable,[21] as—a reasonable fine,[22] convenient time,[23] seasonable time,[24] reasonable time,[25] reasonable notice of dishonor.[26] It is so in regard to the remoteness of damage in an action of contract.[27] Originally in malicious prosecution, probable cause, instead of being negatived in the declaration, was pleaded by the defendant, and the court passed upon the sufficiency of the cause alleged. In the famous case of Weaver v. Ward,[28] the same course was suggested as proper for negligence. I quote: "as if the defendant had said that the plaintiff ran across his piece when it was discharging, or had set forth the case with the circumstances, so as it had appeared to the court that it had been inevitable, and that the defendant had committed no negligence to give occasion to the hurt." But about the middle of the last century, when the rule of conduct was complicated with practical details the court began to leave some of these questions to the jury. Neverthedess, Mr. starkie, a man of intellect, who was not imposed upon by phrases, very nearly saw the ground upon which it was done, and puts it on the purely practical distinction that when the circumstances are too special and complicated for a general rule to be laid down the jury may be called in. But it is obvious that a standard of conduct does not cease to be law because the facts to which that standard applies are not likely often to be repeated.

I do not believe that the jury have any historic or *a priori* right to decide any standard of conduct. I think that the logic of the contrary view would be that every decision upon such a question by the court is an invasion of their province, and that all the law properly is in their breasts. I refer to the subject, however, merely as another matter in which phrases have taken the place of real reasons, and to do my part toward asserting a certain freedom of approach in dealing with negligence cases, not because I wish to quarrel with the existing and settled practice. I think that practice may be a good one, as it certainly is convenient, for Mr. Starkie's reason. There are many cases where no one could lay down a standard of conduct intelligently without hearing evidence upon that, as well as concerning what the conduct was. And although it does not follow that such evidence is for the jury, any more than the question of fact whether a legislature passed a certain statute, still they are a convenient tribunal, and if the evidence to establish a rule of law is to be left to them, it seems natural to leave the conclusion from the evidence to them as well. I confess that in my experience I have not found juries specially inspired for the discovery of truth. I have not noticed that they could see further into things or form a saner judgment than a sensible and well trained judge. I have not found them freer from prejudice than an ordinary judge would be. Indeed one reason why I believe in our practice of leaving questions of negligence to them is what is precisely one of their gravest defects from the point of view of their theoretical function: that they will introduce into their verdict a certain amount—a very large amount, so far as I have observed—of popular prejudice, and thus keep the administration of the law in accord with the wishes and feelings of the community. Possibly such a justification is a little like that which an eminent English barrister gave me many years ago for the distinction between barristers and solicitors. It was in substance that if law was to be practised somebody had to be damned, and he preferred that it should be somebody else.

My object is not so much to point out what seem to me to be fallacies in particular cases as to enforce by various examples and in various applications the need of scrutinizing the reasons for the rules which we follow, and of not being contented with hollow forms of words merely because they have been used very often and have been repeated from one end of the union to the other. We must think things not words, or at least we must constantly translate our words into facts for which they stand, if we are to keep to the real and the true. I sometimes tell students that the law schools pursue an inspirational combined with a logical method, that is, the postulates are taken for granted upon authority without inquiry into their worth, and then logic is used as the only tool to develop the results. It is a necessary method for the purpose of teaching dogma. But inasmuch as the real justification of a rule of law, if there be one, is that it helps to bring about a social end which we desire, it is no less necessary that those who make and develop the law should have those ends articulately in their minds. I do not expect or think it desirable that the judges should undertake to renovate the law. That is not their province. Indeed, precisely because I believe that the world would be just as well off if it lived under laws that differed from ours in many ways, and because I believe that the claim of our especial code to respect is simply that it exists, that it is the one to which we have become accustomed, and not that it represents an eternal principle, I am slow to consent to overruling a precedent, and think that our most important duty is to see that the judicial duel shall be fought out in the accustomed way. But I think it most important to remember whenever a doubtful case arises, with certain analogies on one side and other analogies on the other, that what really is before us is a conflict between two social desires, each of which seeks to extend its dominion over the case, and which cannot both have their way. The social question is which desire is strongest at the point of conflict. The judicial one may be narrower, because one or the other desire may have been expressed in previous decisions to such an extent that logic requires us to assume it to preponderate in the one before us. But if that be clearly so, the case is not a doubtful one. Where there is doubt the simple tool of logic does not suffice, and even if it is disguised and unconscious the judges are called on to exercise the sovereign prerogative of choice.

I have given an example of what seems to me the uninstructive and indolent use of phrases to save the trouble of thinking closely, in the expression "taking the risk," and of what I think a misleading use in calling every question left to the jury a question of fact. Let me give one of over-generalization, or rather of the danger of reasoning from generalizations unless you have the particulars which they embrace in mind. A generalization is empty so far as it is general. Its value depends on the number of particulars which it calls up to the speaker and the hearer. Hence the futility of arguments on economic questions by any one whose memory is not stored with economic facts. Allen *v.* Flood was decided lately by the English House of Lords upon a case of maliciously inducing workmen to leave the plaintiff's employ. It is made harder to say what the precise issue before the House was, by the fact that except in fragmentary quotations it does not appear what the jury were told would amount to a malicious interference. I infer that they were instructed as in Temperton v. Russell,[29] in such a way that their finding meant little more than that the defendant had acted with knowledge and understanding of the harm which he would inflict if successful. Or if I should add an intent to harm the plaintiff without reference to any immediate advantage to the defendant, still I do not understand that finding meant that the defendant's act was done from disinterestedly malevolent motives, and not from a wish to better the defendant's union in a battle of the market. Taking the point decided to be what I suppose it to be, this case confirms opinions which I have had occasion to express judicially, and commands my hearty assent. But in the elaborate, although to my notion inadequate, discussion which took place, eminent judges intimated that anything which a man has a right to do he has a right to do whatever his motives, and this has been hailed as a triumph of the principle of external standards in the law, a principle which I have done my best to advocate as well as to name. Now here the reasoning starts from the vague generalization Right, and one asks himself at once whether it is definite enough to stand the strain. If the scope of the right is already determined as absolute and irrespective of motive, *cadit quaestio,* there is nothing to argue about. So if all rights have that scope. But if different rights are of different extent, if they stand on different grounds of policy and have different histories, it does not follow that because one right is absolute another is,—and if you simply say all rights shall be so, that is only a pontifical or imperial way of forbidding discussion. The right to sell property is about as absolute as any I can think of, although, under statutes at least, even that may be affected by motive, as in the case of an intent to prefer creditors. But the privilege of a master to state his servant's character to one who is thinking of employing him is also a right within its limits. Is it equally extensive? I suppose it would extend to mistaken statements volunteered in good faith out of love for the possible employer. Would it extend to such statements volunteered simply out of hate for the man? To my mind here, again, generalities are worse than useless, and the only way to solve the problem presented is to weigh the reasons for the particular right claimed and those for the competing right to be free from slander as well as one can, and to decide which set preponderates. Any solution in general terms seems to me to mark a want of analytic power.

Gentlemen, I have tried to show by examples something of the interest of science as applied to the law, and to point out some possible improvement in our way of approaching practical questions in the same sphere. To the latter attempt, no doubt, many will hardly be ready to yield me their assent. But in that field, as in the other, I have had in mind an ultimate dependence upon science because it is finally for science to determine, so far as it can, the relative worth of our different social ends, and, as I have tried to hint, it is our estimate of the proportion between these, now often blind and unconscious, that leads us to insist upon and to enlarge the sphere of one principle and to allow another gradually to dwindle into atrophy. Very likely it may be that with all the help that statistics and every modern appliance can bring us there never will be a commonwealth in which science is everywhere supreme. But it is an ideal, and without ideals what is life worth? They furnish us our perspectives and open glimpses of the infinite. It often is a merit of an ideal to be unattainable. Its being so keeps forever before us something more to be done, and saves us from the ennui of a monotonous perfection. At the least it glorifies dull details, and uplifts and sustains weary years of toil with George Herbert's often quoted but ever inspiring verse:

"Who sweeps a room as in Thy cause,
Makes that and the action fine."

NOTES

LAW IN SCIENCE AND SCIENCE IN LAW

1 An Address delivered by Mr. Justice Holmes before the New York State Bar Association on January 17, 1899. — Ed.

2 I do not forget that the church abolished the ordeal.

3 Merkel, c. 46.

4 A. D. 1108, Beseler, 263, n.

5 Regina v. Eastern Counties Railway Co., 10 M. & W. 59.

6 1 Tidd, ch. 1; 2 Bl. Comm. 444, 445.

7 Glanv. x, ch. 15; Bracton, 151; 1 Löning, Vertragsbruch, § 14, p. 103; cf. Sohm, Inst. Rom. Law, § 46, § 11, n. 7.

8 Y. B., 13 & 14 Ed. III, 80.

9 Cæsar, B. G., iv, 11; Ammianus Marcellinus, xvii, 1, 13, jurantes concepts *ria patrio* verbis.

10 Bracton, 292 *b*.

11 Strabo, iv, 32.

12 See, e. g., Three Metrical Romances, Camden Soc. 1842, introd. page xxvi and cantos xii & xxii; Boccaccio, Bohn's tr. page 444 n., referring to an old English ballad.

13 Commonwealth v. Cleary, 172 Mass. 172.

14 Commonwealth v. Rubin, 165 Mass. 453.

15 4 Johns. Ch. 441.

16 Pl. 25; Co. Lit. 42 *b*.

17 But see C. 6, 22, 10.

18 Harrod v. Harrod, 1 K. & J. 4, 9.

19 Knight v. Jermin, Cro. Eliz. 134; s. c. *nom.* Knight v. German, Cro. Eliz. 70; Paine v. Rochester, Cro. Eliz. 871; Chambers v. Taylor, Cro. Eliz. 900.

20 Mackarell v. Bachelor, Cro. Eliz. 583. As to married women see Manby v. Scott, 1 Siderfin, 109, 2 Sm. L. C.

21 Caterall v. Marshall, 1 Mod. 70.

22 Hobart v. Hammond, 4 Co. Rep. 27 b.

23 Stodder v. Harvey, Cro. Jac. 204.

24 Bell v. Wardell, Willes, 202, A. D. 1740 .

25 Butler v. Play, 1 Mod. 27.

26 Tindal v. Brown, 1 T. R. 167, A. D. 1786. In this case an exact line has been worked out for commercial paper, and an arbitrary rule established.

27 Hobbs v. London & Southwestern Railway, L. R. 10 Q. B. 111, 122; Hammond & Co. v. Bussey, 20 Q. B. D. 79, 89; Johnson v. Faxon, Mass. Jan. 9, 1899.

28 Hobart, 134.

29 [1893] 1 Q. B. 715.

THE SOLDIERS' FAITH

An address delivered on Memorial Day, May 30, 1895, at a meeting called by the Graduating Class of Harvard University.

Reprinted from Speeches by Oliver Wendel Holmes, Boston, Little, Brown & Co., 1913. pp. 56-66.

ANY day in Washington Street, when the throng is greatest and busiest, you may see a blind man playing a flute. I suppose that some one hears him. Perhaps also my pipe may reach the heart of some passer in the crowd.

I once heard a man say, "Where Vanderbilt sits, there is the head of the table. I teach my son to be rich." He said what many think. For although the generation born about 1890 and now governing the world, has fought two at least of the greatest wars in history, and has witnessed others, war is out of fashion, and the man who commands the attention of his fellows is the man of wealth. Commerce is the great power. The aspirations of the world are those of commerce. Moralists and philosophers, following its lead, declare that war is wicked, foolish and soon to disappear.

The society for which many philanthropists, labor reformers and men of fashion unite in longing is one in which they may be comfortable and may shine without much trouble or any danger. The unfortunately growing hatred of the poor for the rich seems to me to rest on the belief that money is the main thing (a belief in which the poor have been encouraged by the rich), more than on any grievance. Most of my readers would rather that their daughters or their sisters should marry a son of one of the great rich families than a regular army officer, were he as beautiful, brave, and gifted as Sir William Napier. I have heard the question asked whether our war was worth fighting, after all. There are many, poor and rich, who think that love of country is an old wife's tale, to be replaced by interest in a labor union, or, under the name of cosmopolitanism, by a rootless self-seeking search for a place where the most enjoyment may be had at the least cost.

Meantime we have learned the doctrine that evil means pain, and the revolt against pain in all its forms has grown more and more marked. From societies for the prevention of cruelty to animals up to socialism, we express in numberless ways the notion that suffering is a wrong which can be and ought to be prevented, and a whole literature of sympathy has sprung into being which points out in story and in verse how hard it is to be wounded in the battle of life, how terrible, how unjust it is that any one should fail.

Even science has had its part in the tendencies which we observe. It has shaken established religion in the minds of very many. It has pursued analysis until at last this thrilling world of colors and sounds and passions has seemed fatally to resolve itself into one vast network of vibrations endlessly weaving an aimless web, and the rainbow flush of cathedral windows, which once to enraptured eyes appeared the very smile of God, fades slowly out into the pale irony of the void.

And yet from vast orchestras still comes the music of mighty symphonies. Our painters even now are spreading along the walls of our Library glowing symbols of mysteries still real, and the hardly silenced cannon of the East proclaim once more that combat and pain still are the portion of men. For my own part, I believe that the struggle for life is the order of the world, at which it is vain to repine. I can imagine the burden changed in the way in which it is to be borne, but I cannot imagine that it ever will be lifted from men's backs. I can imagine a future in which science shall have passed from the combative to the dogmatic stage, and shall have gained such catholic acceptance that it shall take control of life, and condemn at once with instant execution what now is left for nature to destroy. But we are far from such a future, and we cannot stop to amuse or to terrify ourselves with dreams. Now, at least, and perhaps as long as man dwells upon the globe, his destiny is battle, and he has to take the chances of war. If it is our business to fight, the book for the army is a war-song, not a hospital-sketch. It is not well for soldiers to think much about wounds. Sooner or later we shall fall; but meantime it is for us to fix our eyes upon the point to be stormed, and to get there if we can.

Behind every scheme to make the world over, lies the question, What kind of a world do you want? The ideals of the past for men have been drawn from war, as those for women have been drawn from motherhood. For all our prophecies, I doubt if we are ready to give up our inheritance. Who is there who would not like to be thought a gentleman? Yet what has that name been built on but the soldier's choice of honor rather than life? To be a soldier or descended from soldiers, in time of peace to be ready to give one's life rather than to suffer disgrace, that is what the word has meant; and if we try to claim it at less cost than a splendid carelessness for life, we are trying to steal the good will without the responsibilities of the place. We will not dispute about tastes. The man of the future may want something different. But who of us could endure a world, although cut up into five-acre lots and having no man upon it who was not well fed and well housed, without the divine folly of honor, without the senseless passion for knowledge out-reaching the flaming bounds of the possible, without ideals the essence of which is that they never can be achieved? I do not know what is true. I do not know the meaning of the universe. But in the midst of doubt, in the collapse of creeds, there is one thing I do not doubt, that no man who lives in the same world with most of us can doubt, and that is that the faith is true and adorable which leads a soldier to throw away his life in obedience to a blindly accepted duty, in a cause which he little understands, in a plan of campaign of which he has no notion, under tactics of which he does not see the use.

Most men who know battle know the cynic force with which the thoughts of common-sense will assail them in times of stress; but they know that in their greatest moments faith has trampled those thoughts under foot. If you have been in line, suppose on Tremont Street Mall, ordered simply to wait and to do nothing, and have watched the enemy bring their guns to bear upon you down a gentle slope like that from Beacon Street, have seen the puff of the firing, have felt the burst of the spherical case-shot as it came toward you, have heard and seen the shrieking fragments go tearing through your company, and have known that the next or the next shot carries your fate; if you have advanced in line and have seen ahead of you the spot which you must pass where the rifle bullets are striking; if you have ridden by night at a walk toward the blue line of fire at the dead angle of Spottsylvania, where for twenty-four hours the soldiers were fighting on the two sides of an earthwork, and in the morning the dead and dying lay piled in a row six deep, and as you rode have heard the bullets splashing in the mud and earth about you; if you have been on the picketline at night in a black and unknown wood, have heard the spat of the bullets upon the trees, and as you moved have felt your foot slip upon a dead man's body; if you have had a blind fierce gallop against the enemy, with your blood up and a pace that left no time for fear,—if, in short, as some, I hope many, who hear me, have known, you have known the vicissitudes of terror and of triumph in war, you know that there is such a thing as the faith I spoke of. You know your own weakness and are modest; but you know that man has in him that unspeakable somewhat which makes him capable of miracle, able to lift himself by the might of his own soul, unaided, able to face annihilation for a blind belief.

From the beginning, to us, children of the North, life has seemed a place hung about by dark mists, out of which come the pale shine of dragon's scales, and the cry of fighting men, and the sound of swords. Beowulf, Milton, Durer, Rembrandt, Schopenhauer, Turner, Tennyson, from the first war-song of our race to the stall-fed poetry of modern English drawing-rooms, all have had the same vision, and all have had a glimpse of a light to be followed. "The end of worldly life awaits us all. Let him who may, gain honor ere death. That is best for a warrior when he is dead." So spoke Beowulf a thousand years ago.

"Not of the sunlight,
Not of the moonlight,
Not of the starlight!
O young Mariner,
Down to the haven,
Call your companions,
Launch your vessel,
And crowd your canvas,
And, ere it vanishes
Over the margin,
After it, follow it,
Follow The Gleam."

So sang Tennyson in the voice of the dying Merlin.

When I went to the war I thought that soldiers were old men. I remembered a picture of the revolutionary soldier which some of you may have seen, representing a white-haired man with his flint-lock slung across his back. I remembered one or two living examples of revolutionary soldiers whom I had met, and I took no account of the lapse of time. It was not until long after, in winter quarters, as I was listening to some of the sentimental songs in vogue, such as—

"Farewell, Mother, you may never
See your darling boy again."

that it came over me that the army was made up of what I now should call very young men. I dare say that my illusion has been shared by some of those now present, as they have looked at us upon whose heads the white shadows have begun to fall. But the truth is that war is the business of youth and early middle age. You who called this assemblage together, not we, would be the soldiers of another war, if we should have one, and we speak to you as the dying Merlin did in the verse which I just quoted. Would that the blind man's pipe might be transfigured by Merlin's magic, to make you hear the bugles as once we heard them beneath the morning stars! For you it is that now is sung the Song of the Sword:—

"The War-Thing, the Comrade,
Father of honor
And giver of kingship,
The fame-smith, the song master.
. . . .
Priest (saith the Lord)
Of his marriage with victory.
. . . .
Clear singing; clean slicing;
Sweet spoken, soft finishing;
Making death beautiful.
Life but a coin
To be staked in the pastime
Whose playing is more
Than the transfer of being;
Arch-anarch, chief builder,
Prince and evangelist,
I am the Will of God:
I am the Sword."

War, when you are at it, is horrible and dull. It is only when time has passed that you see that its message was divine. I hope it may be long before we are called again to sit at that master's feet. But some teacher of the kind we all need. In this snug, over-safe corner of the world we need it, that we may realize that our comfortable routine is no eternal necessity of things, but merely a little space of calm in the midst of the tempestuous untamed streaming of the world, and in order that we may be ready for danger. We need it in this time of individualist negations, wtih its literature of French and American humor, revolting at discipline, loving flesh-pots, and denying that anything is worthy of reverence,—in order that we may remember all that buffoons forget. We need it everywhere and at all times. For high and dangerous action teaches us to believe as right beyond dispute things for which our doubting minds are slow to find words of proof. Out of heroism grows faith in the worth of heroism. The proof comes later, and even may never come. Therefore, I rejoice at every dangerous sport which I see pursued. The students at Heidelberg, with their sword-slashed faces, inspire me with sincere respect. I gaze with delight upon our polo players. If once in a while in our rough riding a neck is broken, I regard it, not as a waste, but as a price well paid for the breeding of a race fit for headship and command.

We do not save our traditions, in this country. The regiments whose battle-flags were not large enough to hold the names of the battles they had fought, vanished with the surrender of Lee, although their memories inherited would have made heroes for a century. It is the more necessary to learn the lesson afresh from perils newly sought, and perhaps it is not vain for us to tell the new generation what we learned in our day, and what we still believe. That the joy of life is living, is to put out all one's powers as far as they will go; that the measure of power is obstacles overcome, to ride boldly at what is in front of you, be it fence or enemy; to pray, not for comfort, but for combat; to keep the soldier's faith against the doubts of civil life, more besetting and harder to overcome than all the misgivings of the battle-field, and to remember that duty is not to be proved in the evil day, but then to be obeyed unquestioning; to love glory more than the temptations of wallowing ease, but to know that one's final judge and only rival is oneself; with all our failures in act and thought, these things we learned from noble enemies in Virginia or Georgia or on the Mississippi, thirty years ago; these things we believe to be true.

> "'Life is not lost,' said she, 'for which is bought
> Endless renown.'"

We learned also, and we still believe, that love of country is not yet an idle name.

> "Deare countrey! O how dearely deare,
> Ought thy remembrance, and perpetuall band
> Be to thy foster-child, that from thy hand
> Did commun breath and nouriture receave!
> How brutish is it not to understand
> How much to her we owe, that all us gave;
> That gave unto us all, whatever good we have!"

As for us, our days of combat are over. Our swords are rust. Our guns will thunder no more. The vultures that once wheeled over our heads are buried with their prey. Whatever of glory yet remains for us to win must be won in the council or the closet, never again in the field. I do not repine. We have shared the incommunicable experience of war; we have felt, we still feel, the passion of life to its top.

Three years ago died the old colonel of my regiment, the Twentieth Massachusetts. He gave our regiment its soul. No man could falter who heard his "Forward, Twentieth!" I went to his funeral. From a side door of the church a body of little choir-boys came in like a flight of careless doves. At the same time the doors opened at the front, and up the main aisle advanced his coffin followed by the few gray heads who stood for the men of the Twentieth, the rank and file whom he had loved, and whom he led for the last time. The church was empty. No one remembered the old man whom we were burying, no one save those next to him, and us. And I said to myself, The Twentieth has shrunk to a skeleton, a ghost, a memory, a forgotten name which we other old men alone keep in our hearts. And then I thought: It is right. It is as the colonel would have had it. This also is part of the soldier's faith: Having known great things, to be content with silence. Just then there fell into my hands a little song sung by a warlike people on the Danube, which seemed to me fit for a soldier's last word, another song of the sword, but a song of the sword in its scabbard, a song of oblivion and peace.

A soldier has been buried on the battle-field.

"And when the wind in the tree-tops roared,
The soldier asked from the deep dark grave:
'Did the banner flutter then?'
'Not so, my hero,' the wind replied,
'The fight is done, but the banner won,
Thy comrades of old have borne it hence,
Have borne it in triumph hence.'
Then the soldier spake from the deep dark grave:
'I am content.'

. . . .

"Then he heareth the lovers laughing pass,
And the soldier asks once more:
'Are these not the voices of them that love,
That love—and remember me?'
'Not so, my hero,' the lovers say,
'We are those that remember not
For the spring has come and the earth has smiled,
And the dead must be forgot.'
Then the soldier spake from the deep dark grave:
'I am content.'

RADIO ADDRESS ON THE 90TH BIRTHDAY

According to the New York Times, March 9, 1931, this address was broadcast from his home in Washington, D. C. Justice Holmes had been felicitated by Chief Justice Hughes and the bar of the nation, and this was his response. Incidentally, Justice Holmes never again made a radio address and this was the first time he had ever spoken on the radio.

IN THIS symposium my part is only to sit in silence. To express one's feelings as the end draws near is too intimate a task.

But I may mention one thought that comes to me as a listener-in. The riders in a race do not stop short when they reach the goal. There is a little finishing canter before coming to a standstill. There is time to hear the kind voice of friends and to say to one's self: "The work is done."

But just as one says that, the answer comes: "The race is over, but the work never is done while the power to work remains."

The canter that brings you to a standstill need not be only coming to rest. It cannot be while you still live. For to live is to function. That is all there is in living.

And so I end with a line from a Latin poet who uttered the message more than fifteen hundred years ago:

"Death plucks my ears and says, Live—I am coming."

PART III.

LETTERS
OF
MR. JUSTICE HOLMES

LETTERS

OF MR. JUSTICE HOLMES

Justice Holmes' letters reflect the intense and cosmopolitan interest Justice Holmes had in the many facets of literature, current events, political science, etc., as well as his philosophy of life. It would be impossible to include them all in this collection. Set forth here are merely a few letters for the purpose of indicating his literary style and tremendous and variegated interest and curiosity. Written to his old friend Sir Frederick Pollock, who had corresponded with him from 1874 to practically the day of his death in 1934, these letters are reprinted from the *Holmes-Pollock Letters, the Correspondence of Mr. Justice Holmes and Sir Frederick Pollock,* 1872-1932, *edited by Mark de Wolfe Howe. Cambridge, Harvard University Press,* 1941. 2 v.

Holmes was a prolific letter writer and corresponded with many interesting personalities of his day. See: The Holmes-Cohen correspondence (In Journal of the History of Ideas. 1948, vol. 9, p. 52); Justice Oliver Wendell Holmes; his book notices and uncollected letters and papers, edited and annotated by Harry S. Shriver . . . N. Y. 1936, 280 p.; Justice Holmes to Doctor Wu; an intimate correspondence, 1921-1932. N. Y., [1947?] 58 p.; Touched with fire – civil war letters and diary of Oliver Wendell Holmes, Jr. 1801-1864, edited by Mark de Wolfe Howe, Cambridge, 1946, 158 p.; Holmes-Laski letters . . . 1916-1935, edited by Mark de Wolfe Howe, Cambridge, 1953, 2 v.

WASHINGTON, April 23, 1910

Dear F. P.:

I am just too late to get the return mail in answer to yours but I hasten to reply, partly because I have just received a semi-request to send you the accompanying paper. I know the writer only by correspondence. He seems to me half crank, and yet I am told that he has done things in former days in connection with news, and he seems to me to have ideas. My trouble is that while he has been sending in things for two or three years I don't seem to get any forrader with what he has to say. He thinks himself that he has done more than Darwin. His contempt for government interference with rates etc., and his belief in the validity of the outside organizations I confess I share to a great extent. Of course I enforce whatever constitutional laws Congress or anybody else sees fit to pass— and do it in good faith to the best of my ability—but I don't disguise my belief that the Sherman Act is a humbug based on economic ignorance and incompetence, and my disbelief that the Interstate Commerce Commission is a fit body to be entrusted with rate-making, even in the qualified way in which it is entrusted. The Commission naturally is always trying to extend its power and I have written some decisions limiting it (by construction of statutes only). However, I am so sceptical as to our knowledge about the goodness or badness of laws that I have no practical criticism except what the crowd wants. Personally I bet that the crow if it knew more wouldn't want what it does—but that is immaterial. I have been working madly to keep my cases written as soon as given to me, but my share this year has not been of remarkable interest. The term draws to a close—one week more of argument and final adjournment as usual at the end of May. Now I must rush to a Conference. My love to Lady Pollock, to whom I will write soon.

Yours, ever,
O.W.H.

WASHINGTON, December 29, 1915

Dear F. P.:

. . . We are getting through the two weeks Xmas adjournment. The time has been so broken up that I have little to show for them. I read a little book, *The Freudian Wish,* by Holt, Harvard College, who seems to think that psychology is reborn between Freud and him but from whose work I derived less nourishment than Walter Lippmann who sent it to me seemed to have done. Monstrous clever lad, W. L., and only 26 and he has done much. But these young men are so damned solemn that I have been philosophising anew on emotional weather and its independence of what might be expected to be the causes, *e. g.*, workingmen oppressed before the French Revolution, yet seemingly gay (Restif de la Bretonne), workingmen now in the saddle, yet groaning and grunting and seeming to be having a worse time than ever.

The first half of the 19th Century was unhygienic but jovial.

We now have improved hygiene and all manner of intelligent isms but don't seem to get a good time out of it.

At times I think the men in the trenches are the gayest people left. Possibly gaiety is the miasmic mist of misery. I was rather gay in the army when certainly I was unhappy enough. *Que sçay je?*

Apropos of Pound perhaps I said before that I keep all his essays. I have one volume bound and the stuff for another. I admire his learning and his command of it, but as yet have not perceived a very strong personal reaction upon his knowledge—as one does in Wigmore—whom I hope to see here on January 1. . . .

Yours ever,

O. W. Holmes

I didn't remember what a lambkin you were—only just 70! Welcome to the higher story and may you live on it many years. I shall be 75 March 8.

Beverly Farms, July 18, 1924

Dear Pollock:

The hatching of pigeons in your chambers needs explanation. "How—How—How—the Devil got the apple in?" I . . . should be in repose but for Oswald Spengler, *Der Untergang des Abendlandes* that I have been toiling through with a dictionary. The book is pretty thick with suggestion, and the writer seemingly at home in the higher mathematics, music and art, but I suspect less so in the physical sciences. His thesis that every *Kult,* the Greek, the Arabian, the Egyptian, the Chinese, that of the *Abendland,* is the incommunicable result of a special way of seeing and feeling life, that there is no eternal truth, no universal morality, no ever abiding questions, but that each *Kult* has its day and, being an organism, its end. Ours reached its climax in the calculus and the music of Parsifal. I don't value his conclusion, but do his *aperçus.* Isn't that so of all theorists and system makers? He not only suggests new things but makes me realize more fully what I believed before, *e. g.,* how little we understand the Greeks, their drama, their philosophy, the meaning of their key words. But, oh, to have unloaded upon one as a job—a duty—a task of which you count the pages! Yet when one suspects that a man knows something about life that one hasn't heard before one is uneasy until one has found out what he has to say. It is long since I have got so much from a book as this, and if I heard that the swine were dead I should thank God. However only 53 pages more. My love to Lady Pollock.

Yours ever,
O. W. H.

BEVERLY FARMS, June 20, 1928

My dear young Frederick:

It is good to see your handwriting again and to welcome you back from your youthful tasks—my time for them has gone by. The fatigue of Washington to Boston and Boston to Washington is enough for me, and I walk very little. I am interested by what you tell of Charybdis and the truant Scylla. I dissented in the case of tapping telephone wires. The C. J. who wrote the prevailing opinion, perhaps as a rhetorical device to obscure the difficulty, perhaps merely because he did not note the difference, which perhaps

I should have emphasized more, spoke of the objection to the evidence as based on its being obtained by "unethical" means (horrid phrase), although he adds & by a misdemeanor under the laws of Washington.[1] I said that the State of Washington had made it a crime and that Government could not put itself in the position of offering to pay for a crime in order to get evidence of another crime. Brandeis wrote much more elaborately, but I didn't agree with all that he said.[2] I should not have printed what I wrote, however, if he had not asked me to. I am reading an able book: Parrington, *Main Currents in American Thought,* which gives a very interesting picture, or rather analysis, of the elements at work from the beginning. But I shall not easily believe the thesis running through it and started by earlier works of Beard (*An Economic Interpretation of the Constitution,* etc.) to the effect that the Constitution primarily represents the triumph of the money power over democratic agrarianism & individualism. Beard, I thought years ago when I read him, went into rather ignoble though most painstaking investigation of the investments of the leaders, with an innuendo even if disclaimed. I shall believe until compelled to think otherwise that they wanted to make a nation and invested (bet) on the belief that they would make one, not that they wanted a powerful government because they had invested. Belittling arguments always have a force of their own, but you and I believe that high-mindedness is not impossible to man. The result is that I am not taking unmixed pleasure in one of the ablest and most instructive books that I have read for a long time. I have brought with me Bertrand Russell's *Philosophy,* but that must wait till I have finished Parrington's second volume. I have let in a little sweetness and light by reading *en passant, But Gentlemen Marry Brunettes,* a sequel to *Gentlemen Prefer Blondes,* with which perhaps you improved your mind. But sexual talk or innuendo is displeasing from a woman, I think. Perhaps because we know, though the older literary tradition is the other way, that they take less interest in the business than we do. We have been here a week and a half and are settling into our routine, the main event a motor drive of two hours, which is about my limit. (I interrupted myself here to write to the Clerk to send you the opinion and dissents in the above mentioned case if he still has copies.) Please give my love to Lady Pollock. I rarely see anyone but am happy in solitude. Most of the places here now to me are sockets from which the occupants that I knew have been extracted by the final dentist.

Yours ever,
O. W. H.

. . . The Prayer Book is a mystery that I do not touch.

BEVERLY FARMS, August 16, 1931

My dear Pollock:

Will this letter hit you as you sink to shore from the billows of the Baltic, or how otherwise? I know not. It is hard to deal with such sports as you two. But I owe a line to both of you. I have read nothing of Dickens except *Our Mutual Friend* for many years. I have given *Vanity Fair* my first adequate reading. It seems to me to be a great novel—very great. The greatest drawback to me in this and *The Newcomes* is that mundane motives and interests seem to be Thackeray's own ultimates, *non obstant* pious ejaculations when he talks of Amelia. Of course I am not talking religion but of the scale of intellectual preoccupations. I admit that the bias is more natural in London than elsewhere. The prizes are greater—and there was splendor in Thackeray's time—and even in mine.

I don't think Plato's *Laws* is dull, except as all antiquity is, and I don't see why it should be thought to have been a compromise. Perhaps what seems queerest to us in his infinitesimal state is that the citizens never have to think about making a living. That is left to the slaves and foreigners. I think one likes the old fellow as he drools on (I speak as a modern). I await your address about the Inns of Court with interest. The last few days my secretary has been away and I have taken the opportunity to read some detective stories for which I have an ignoble liking. I have read four running. My wife used to remark that many could begin a novel well but few could end one well. That struck me that with all these—the conclusion generally impotent and one that one didn't like.

I also have read Strachey, *Portraits in Miniature.* For the most part (one or two exceptions) they did not seem to me up to his earlier work. Also I didn't care much for his *Elizabeth* & *Essex.* The only moment that I remember when Essex interested me was when he spoke ill of the figure of his Mistress. A minor work by Willa Cather [3] (American). She seemed to me really great in *My Antonia.* Except for the interjection of slumber I really should have had some of those longed for hours when I wondered what to do, but such hours are very rare. Apart from all else more people come than I want, though each individual is welcome. Perhaps I make a mistake in not trying to walk but it is an effort and I doubt if it is wise to try even an eighth of a mile. Time is slowly taking down the house. I suppose next month the American Bar Association intends to give me a medal and I am expected to say a few words by radio —details not yet settled—at any rate, not a very exciting occasion.[4]

In view of uncertainties I will write no more. My love to my dear Lady Pollock. . . .

Yours ever,
O. W. H.

I have been accompanying Remy de Gourmont in some of his *Promenades philosophiques.* He is so clever that he ought to have been a little bigger.

WASHINGTON, May 15, 1932

My dear Pollock:

It is less than a month before I go to Beverly Farms, if nothing turns out wrong. It is wonderful and incredible to have no duties. I can't tell you how much I like it. I ought to be getting cultivated, for my secretary calculates that, roughly, we have read 4,500,000 words since we got here, but I am afraid that a good deal buzzes through my head without much profit to me. I forget if I have mentioned the accursed Spengler, *Decline of the West,* whom I now have read in translation (vol. 1 years ago in German with a dictionary). He has as swelled a head as man can have and live, but the beast has ideas, many of which I don't know enough to criticise. I wish he was dead. On the other side is that dear delightful Wodehouse, whom I read and even reread with guffaws. I accept with humility your criticism of my writing. I don't know why it has become so small & I suppose it is old age makes me get my letters wrong at times. We began today a book by Sir A. Salter, *Recovery,* which I like very much, though the criticisms on *Laissez Faire,* mentioned by him and now generally prevalent, leave me not fully convinced. There has been a lot of rain and the Potomac is high, but falling. I must take my lad up to Great Falls—which I have not seen this year. . . . Is this enough of my gossip?

Yours ever,
O. W. H.

My love to Lady Pollock.

NOTES

MR. JUSTICE HOLMES by Sir Frederick Pollock

[1] Olmstead v. U. S., 277 U. S. at p. 466.

[2] In his dissenting opinion Justice Brandeis stated that the tapping of telephone wires and the use of evidence so obtained violated the constitutional provisions against unreasonable searches and seizures (4th Amendment), and against compelling a person in a criminal case to become a witness against himself (5th Amendment). Holmes in his dissent said: "While I do not deny it, I am not prepared to say that the penumbra of the 4th and 5th amendments cover the defendant, although I fully agree that Courts are apt to err by sticking too closely to the words of a law where those words import a policy that goes beyond them." *Id.* at 469.

[3] Shadows on the Rock (1931).

[4] The American Bar Association, at its thirty-fourth annual meeting, in September 1931, conferred on Holmes a medal "for conspicuous service in the cause of American jurisprudence." Prevented by ill health from responding by radio, Holmes sent a letter of thanks to the Association which is published in 56 *Am. Bar Asso. Report* 136-137 (1931).

PART IV.

COURT DECISIONS OF MR. JUSTICE HOLMES

MR. JUSTICE HOLMES AND THE CONSTITUTION

A review of his twenty-five years on the Supreme Court

By Felix Frankfurter

Reprinted from the *Harvard Law Review,* volume 41, pp. 121-173, December 1929. See footnote 48 to article by A. D. Hill on Justice Holmes, p. 37, *ante.*

This article contains important excerpts from the majority and minority opinions of Justice Holmes as well as a critical evaluation of his contribution as a jurist. It was written by a famous American jurist and legal scholar, who is now an associate justice of the U. S. Supreme Court.

I

When the present Chief Justice * was appointed, a leading New York newspaper gave utterance to a wide-spread public appreciation of his "tact and good humor" by remarking that "with Justice Taft as moderator, it is probable that not a few asperities that mar the harmony of the celestial chamber, the consulting room, will be softened, and that not quite so often in the future will the Court divide five and four." Such an exaggerated view of the power of *camaraderie* neglects the deeper influences behind constitutional adjudications. Divisions of the Court in decisive issues are not due to want of "tact and good humor" in the "moderator," nor is accord secured through genial and irenic personalities. A more lubricating humor and accommodating mind probably never presided over the Supreme Court than during the incumbency of Chief Justice Fuller. Yet divided opinions in cases involving public issues were plentiful during his time, as they were during the time of Chief Justice White, as they have been, and will continue to be, during the successive terms of Chief Justice Taft. The key to an understanding of the Court's attitude in cases of great public moment is not to be found in the temperamental felicities of the judges, but in a candid analysis of the operation of the judicial process in constitutional controversies. In the nature of Supreme Court litigation must be sought the explanation for the large incidence of dissent.[1]

The stuff of constitutional law, it cannot be too often recalled, differs profoundly from ordinary law. The dominant issues of Supreme Court litigation and the consequences of their adjudications are not those of the familiar lawsuits between John Doe and Richard Roe. The Supreme Court marks the boundaries between state and national action; it mediates between citizen and government. This tribunal is the final authority in adjusting the relationship of the individual to the separate states, of the individual to the United States, of the forty-eight states to one another, of the states to the Union, and of the three departments of government to each other. The Court thus exercises essentially political functions. It escapes the rough and tumble of politics partly through the restraint of traditional mental habits and the scrutiny of professional opinion, but largely because the Court moves only when invoked, and then only under the guise of settling a lawsuit.[2]

II

The complex process involved in these political adjustments by the Supreme Bench we call, compendiously, American Constitutional Law. Its operations to date are to be gathered from the decisions and doctrines, the rules and refinements, recorded in the two hundred and seventy-five volumes of United States Reports.

Broadly classified, two types of constitutional claims come before the Court:

First. Specific provisions of the Constitution guarding against the recurrence of well-defined, historic grievances, or embodying a specific limitation of power either upon the states or the central government, in the explicit distribution of authority under our federalism.

Second. Broad standards of fair dealing, and divisions of power as between states and nation not spelt out in the Constitution, but derived from political conceptions regarding its purposes and their achievement.

From these two categories of constitutional issues flow two different series of adjudications which require different materials for judgment and in which reason has different scope.

First. Certain constitutional provisions are so definite in their terms and their history that they canalize judicial review within narrow limits. They are seldom tested and still more rarely is the Supreme Court troubled with doubt about their meaning. Whether "a fact tried by a jury" has been "re-examined in any Court of the United States" otherwise than "according to the rules of the common law," [3] whether a tax is laid upon articles exported from any state,[4] whether a crime is "infamous," [5] even whether the prohibition against "unreasonable searches and seizures" [6] is violated, are neither frequent nor fighting issues before the Court. Constitutional law here allows comparatively meager play for individual judgment as to policy.

Second. The broad, undefined clauses of the Constitution and the general theories which underlie it give rise to very different problems for adjudication. Words like "liberty" and "property," phrases like "regulate Commerce . . . among the several States," "due process of law," and "equal protection of the laws" are the foundations for judgment upon the whole appalling domain of social and economic facts. But, as the late Judge Hough reminded us, phrases like "due process of law" are of "convenient vagueness." [7] Their content is derived from without, not revealed within the Constitution. Because of them the Court is compelled to put meaning into the Constitution, not take it out. For such features of the Constitution a favorite quotation of John Chipman Gray is peculiarly pertinent: "Whoever hath an *absolue authority* to *interpret* any written or spoken laws, it is he who is truly the law-giver to all intents and purposes, and not the person who first wrote or spoke them." [8] The scope for interpretation of the Constitution is here relatively unrestricted, and the room for exercise of individual notions of policy correspondingly wide. The judges are cartographers who give temporary definiteness but not definitiveness to the undefined and ever-shifting boundaries between state and nation, between freedom and authority. This is, therefore, the most active and the most controversial sphere of Supreme Court litigation.

Even in considering the application of these broad powers, important distinctions must be observed. In a federated nation, especially one as vast in its territory and varied in its interests as ours, the authority must be lodged somewhere to make necessary accommodations between states and the central government. The Supreme Court is that ultimate arbiter, and it relies largely on the commerce clause for its control. But to believe that this power is exercised by distilling meaning out of the words of the Constitution would be sheer illusion. Decisions under the commerce clause, whether allowing or confining state action, whether sanctioning or denying federal power, are inevitably exercises in judgment. The Stock Yards Act,[9] the Grain Futures Act,[10] the West Virginia Natural Gas Act,[11] the recapture clause of the Transportation Act,[12] the first Child Labor Law,[13] all involved "interpretation" of the commerce clause; but the fate of these laws depended on the Supreme Court's judgment upon the economic and industrial data which underlay this legislation.

The "due process of law" and "equal protection of the laws" clauses serve purposes very different from those of the commerce clause. They do not express a necessary adjustment in the distribution of powers in a federal system. These broad guarantees in favor of the individual, with resulting limitations upon both state and federal governments, seek to embody "immutable principles of liberty and justice." [14] Clearly they open the door to the widest differences of opinion. The words of these provisions are so unrestrained by their intrinsic meaning as well as by their history and traditions, that each Justice is impelled to depend upon his own controlling conceptions, which are in turn bound by his experience and imagination, his hopes and fears, his faith and doubts.

III

Freed of its enveloping fog of ambiguities constitutional law is neither mystery nor metaphysics—nor revelation. Probably no large branch of private law is easier to state in terms of legal formulas than the law of the Constitution. The formulated precepts of judgment are few; the instances which call for their application are as shifting and as intricate as the complexities and conflicts of society. Hence, with the great men of the Supreme Court, constitutional adjudication has always been statecraft. As mere lawyers, at least two members of his Court were abler than Marshall. His supremacy lay in his recognition of the practical needs of government. Those of his successors whose labors history has validated have been men who brought to their task insight into the problems of their generation. Taney's judicial performance has unfortunately been obscured by the tragic dicta of the *Dred Scott* case.[15] His decision in the *Charles*

River Bridge case [16] shows the quality of his statesmanship; Story's dissent proves that even vast erudition is no substitute for creative imagination.[17] Though Chief Justice Waite be not on the calendar of our great names, is there any doubt today that on crucial issues such as were raised by *Munn v. Illinois*,[18] Waite had prophetic insight, while Field, despite his powerful mind, was mastered by the philosophy and experience of a frontier community? [19] Mr. Justice Moody served, unhappily, less than three full terms on the Court. But his opinions [20] have left a notable impress upon its history, because therein he reflected an understanding of governmental problems, gained from his wide experience as a prosecutor, Congressman, Secretary of the Navy, and Attorney-General. Not anointed priests, but men with proved grasp of affairs, who have developed resilience and spaciousness of mind through seasoned and diversified experience in a work-a-day world, usually in public life, are the judges who have wrought abidingly on the Supreme Court.[21]

Mr. Justice Holmes is the great exception. Though he did not bring to the Court the training of a lawyer accustomed to great affairs, his work is yet in the school of statesmanship. Where others are guided through experience of life, he is led by the divination of the philosopher and the imagination of the poet. He is, indeed, philosopher become king.

Taking his seat on December 8, 1902, Mr. Justice Holmes came to the Supreme Court at the high tide of the Roosevelt era.[22] Politics reflected vigorously the clash of the great political and economic forces which the Civil War had released and the Spanish War intensified. Government extended its activities widely. It was a period of legislative exuberance, both at Washington and in the states. This political ferment brought to the Court problems of state and national powers in greater volume and in subtler forms than ever before. "We are very quiet there," said Mr. Justice Holmes of the Supreme Court in 1913, "but it is the quiet of a storm center, as we all know." [23]

Questions whose decision touched the life of men widely and intimately became the staple business of the Court. To an extent unparalleled in the country's and the Court's history, the Supreme Court became the arbiter of political controversies. With such problems, Mr. Justice Holmes had had little concern before coming to Washington. During his preceding twenty years on the Massachusetts Supreme Judicial Court (whose Chief Justice he was when appointed to the Supreme Bench), constitutional issues rarely came before him. Insofar as they did, however, he left no doubt about his mode of approach to their solution, and foreshadowed his constitutional philosophy of the last twenty-five years.[24] This period covers a fifth of the active history of the Court, for, with less than a handful of exceptions, its significant decisions began with Marshall in 1801.[25] In volume, Mr. Justice Holmes has participated in more than a third of the adjudications of the Court.[26] His own opinions form an imposing and coherent body of constitutional law.[27]

IV

In our days, as in Marshall's, the issues before the Court have necessitated not merely an interpretation of this or that clause of the Constitution, but a comprehensive attitude toward the Constitution and a conscious conception of the functions of the Court as its interpreter. Marshall's great major premise was "that it is *a constitution* we are expounding." [28] That was the background against which he projected every inquiry as to specific power or specific limitation. Taking as his starting point, not as a mere intellectual concept only, a recognition that the Constitution deals with great governmental powers to be exercised to great public ends, he went far towards erecting the structure within which the national spirit could freely move and flourish. Like all truths, Marshall's canons of construction had to be revivified for new demands made upon them by a new generation. Constant resort to the reviewing power of the Court, based on claims that acts of legislatures or Congress transcended constitutional limitations, called for reconsideration of the nature of the instrument which the Court must construe and of the role of the Court in its interpretation. There always *is* a starting point in such questions, however inarticulate or unconscious. What the pressure of new legislation demanded was an inquiry as to meaning—a vigorous realization of the scope and theory of constitutional law, an analysis of the concrete issues in a constitutional controversy. In a time of legislative activity and deep stirring in the law, signifying the impact of new facts and changng social conceptions, the starting point must be a conscious one, lest power and policy be unconsciously confused.

Mr. Justice Holmes recalls us to the tradition of Marshall, that it *is* a Constitution we are applying. Its framers intentionally did not bound it with outlines sharp and contemporary, but flexible and prophetic. In the undefined domain of constitutional law it is preeminently true that exercise of judgment is screened by formal "principles." That is the significance of Mr. Justice Holmes' aphorism that "general propositions do not decide concrete cases." [29] But the intensity with which "general propositions" are felt, and the flexibility with which they are enforced, do decide cases. For, behind divisions of opinion lie varying recognitions of competing "general propositions" and of the necessity of mediating between them or of leaving their accommodations to the legislature. In law, also, the emphasis makes the song. Whether the Constitution is treated primarily as a text for interpretation or as an instrument of government may make all the difference in the world. The fate of cases, and thereby of legislation, will turn on whether the meaning of the document is derived from itself or from one's conception of the country, its development, its needs, its place in a civilized society.

To Mr. Justice Holmes the Constitution is not a document for fastidious dialectics but the means of ordering the life of a people. It had its roots in the past—"continuity with the past is only a necessity and not a duty" [30]—but not less so was it intended for the unknown future.

> ". . . the provisions of the Constitution are not mathematical formulas having their essence in their form; they are organic living institutions transplanted from English soil. Their significance is vital not formal; it is to be gathered not simply by taking the words and a dictionary, but by considering their origin and the line of their growth." [31]
>
> ". . . when we are dealing with words that also are a constituent act, like the Constitution of the United States, we must realize that they have called into life a being the development of which could not have been foreseen completely by the most gifted of its begetters. It was enough for them to realize or to hope that they had created an organism; it has taken a century and has cost their successors much sweat and blood to prove that they created a nation. The case before us must be considered in the light of our whole experience and not merely in that of what was said a hundred years ago." [32]

While the Supreme Court is thus in the perilous realm of government, it is itself freed from the terrible burdens of governing wisely. The Court is merely the brake on other men's conduct, the judge of other men's decisions. Responsibility for action rests with legislators. Mr. Justice Holmes has always been keenly sensitive to the subtle forces involved in the process of reviewing other men's judgment, not as to its wisdom but as to their right to believe in the reasonableness of its wisdom. The nature of the Court's task raises the crucial problem in our constitutional system: that its successful working calls for rare intellectual disinterestedness and penetration, lest limitations in personal experiences and imaginaton operate as limitations of the Constitution.[33] In view of the complexities of modern society and of the inevitable narrowness of individual experience, tolerance and humility in passing judgment on the validity of the experience and beliefs of others become the chief dynamic factors in the disposition of cases.

"It is a misfortune if a judge reads his conscious or unconscious sympathy with one side or the other prematurely into the law, and forgets that what seem to him to be first principles are believed by half his fellow men to be wrong. I think that we have suffered from this misfortune, in State courts at least, and that this is another and very important truth to be extracted from the popular discontent. When twenty years ago a vague terror went over the earth and the word socialism began to be heard, I thought and still think that fear was translated into doctrines that had no proper place in the Constitution or the common law. Judges are apt to be naif, simple-minded men, and they need something of Mephistopheles. We too need education in the obvious—to learn to transcend our own convictions and to leave room for much that we hold dear to be done away with short of revolution by the orderly change of law." [34]

"While the courts must exercise a judgment of their own, it by no means is true that every law is void which may seem to the judges who pass upon it excessive, unsuited to its ostensible end, or based upon conceptions of morality with which they disagree. Considerable latitude must be allowed for differences of view as for possible peculiar conditions which this court can know but imperfectly, if at all. Otherwise a constitution, instead of embodying only relatively fundamental rules of right, as generally understood by all English-speaking communities, would become the partisan of a particular set of ethical or economical opinions, which by no means are held *semper ubique et ab omnibus.*" [35]

For Mr. Justice Holmes, "principles" are rarely absolute. Usually they are sententious expressions of conflicting or at least overlapping policies. The vital issue is their accommodation. Decisions thus become a matter of more or less, of drawing lines. Law "as soon as it is civilized" generally depends on differences of degree,[36] but especially constitutional law. This by no means implies a crude empiricism. True, judgment enters; choice must be exercised. But the choice is not capricious. It involves judgment between defined claims, each of recognized validity and with a pedigree of its own, but all of which necessarily cannot be completely satisfied. Primarily this process of adjustment is legislation. To legislative determinations, therefore, great deference must be shown in the exercise of the revisory process called adjudication.

"All rights tend to declare themselves absolute to their logical extreme. Yet all in fact are limited by the neighborhood of principles of policy which are other than those on which the particular right is founded, and which become strong enough to hold their own when a certain point is reached. The limits set to property by other public interests present themselves as a branch of what is called the police power of the State. The boundary at which the conflicting interests balance cannot be determined by any general formula in advance, but points in the line, or helping it, are fixed by decisions that this or that concrete case falls on the nearer or farther side. For instance, the police power may limit the height of buildings, in a city, without compensation. To that extent it cuts down what otherwise would be the rights of property. But if it should attempt to limit the height so far as to make an ordinary building

> lot wholly useless, the rights of property would prevail over the other public interest, and the police power would fail. To set such a limit would need compensation and the power of eminent domain." [37]
>
> "Great constitutional provisions must be administered with caution. Some play must be allowed for the joints of the machine, and it must be remembered that legislatures are ultimate guardians of the liberties and welfare of the people in quite as great a degree as the courts." [38]
>
> " . . . in dealing with state legislation upon matters of substantive law we should avoid with great caution attempts to substitute our judgment for that of the body whose business it is in the first place, with regard to questions of domestic policy that fairly are open to debate . . . and while I should not dream of asking where the line can be drawn, since the great body of the law consists in drawing such lines, yet when you realize that you are dealing with a matter of degree you must realize that reasonable men may differ widely as to the place where the line should fall." [39]

These *apercus* give the clues to his constitutional philosophy and his judicial technique. So guided, Mr. Justice Holmes has resolved the eternal conflict between nation and states, between freedom and restraint, in the thousand instances in which, with infinite variety and ever-new detail, it has solicited his judgment.

V

In its relations to other countries, the American Union is a nation capable of asserting its authority like other nations on behalf of the civilized needs of the world.

"It is said that a treaty cannot be valid if it infringes

the Constitution, that there are limits, therefore, to the treaty-making power, and that one such limit is that what an act of Congress could not do unaided, in derogation of the powers reserved to the States, a treaty cannot do.

"Acts of Congress are the supreme law of the land only when made in pursuance of the Constitution, while treaties are declared to be so when made the authority of the United States. It is open to question whether the authority of the United States means more than the formal acts prescribed to make the convention. We do not mean to imply that there are no qualifications to the treaty-making power; but they must be ascertained in a different way. It is obvious that there may be matters of the sharpest exigency for the national well being that an act of Congress could not deal with but that a treaty followed by such an act could, and it is not lightly to be assumed that, in matters requiring national action, 'a power which must belong to and somewhere reside in every civilized government' is not to be found. . . The treaty in question does not contravene any prohibitory words to be found in the Constitution. The only question is whether it is forbidden by some invisible radiation from the general terms of the Tenth Amendment. We must consider what this country has become in deciding what that Amendment has reserved. . . .

"Here a national interest of very nearly the first magnitude is involved. It can be protected only by national action in concert with that of another power. The subject-matter is only transitory within the State and has no permanent habitat therein. But for the treaty and the statute there soon might be no birds for any powers to deal with. We see nothing in the Constitution that compels the Government to sit by while a food supply is cut off and the protectors of our forests and our crops are destroyed. It is not sufficient to rely upon the States. The reliance is vain, and were it otherwise, the question is whether the United States is forbidden to act."[40]

Similarly, the United States has full control over activities of commerce which cross state boundaries. The needs of commerce among the several states furnished the great centripetal force in the establishment of the nation; barring the war powers, the commerce clause has become the most powerful instrument of the national government. By no means reflecting a bias towards centralization, Mr. Justice Holmes has reaffirmed the profound justification of the commerce clause.

"I do not think the United States would come to an end if we lost our power to declare an Act of Congress void. I do think the Union would be imperiled if we could not make that declaration as to the laws of the several States. For one in my place sees how often a local policy prevails with those who are not trained to national views and how often action is taken that embodies what the Commerce Clause was meant to end."[41]

Regulations of commerce by Congress raises some of the thorniest problems that can confront a federal government ruling a continent. The wisdom of a particular exertion of this power is for the judgment of Congress. But its judgment must satisfy the Supreme Court's judgment. The legal question is formulated in terms of passing on the power of Congress, and the subject is a constant temptation to logomhacy. The national power is denied or mutilated by distinctions that do not respond to the actualities of modern industry. Shrewd compromises among competing interests are clouded by illusory generalities. Here, as elsewhere, Mr. Justice Holmes insists on the need "to think things instead of words." To him "commerce is not a technical legal conception, but a practical one, drawn from the course of business."[42] From this practical conception he has drawn its practical implications. Against the majority of the Court, he has found no hindrance in the Constitution to legislation seeking industrial peace on railroads, or promoting civilized social standards through interstate commerce.

"It cannot be doubted that to prevent strikes, and, so far as possible, to foster its scheme of arbitration, might be deemed by Congress an important point of policy, and I think it impossible to say that Congress might not reasonably think that the provision in question would help a good deal to carry its policy along. But suppose the only effect really were to tend to bring about the complete unionizing of such railroad laborers as Congress can deal with, I think that object alone would justify the act. I quite agree that the question what and how much good labor unions do, is one on which intelligent people may differ,— I think that laboring men sometimes attribute to them advantatges, as many attribute to combinations of capital disadvantages, that really are due to economic conditions of a far wider and deeper kind—but I could not pronounce it unwarranted if Congress should decide that to foster a strong union was for the best interest, not only of the men, but of the railroads and the country at large." [43]

"The objection urged against the power [to prohibit the shipment in interstate commerce of the products of cotton mills employing child labor] is that the States have exclusive control over their methods of production and that Congress cannot meddle with them, and taking the proposition in the sense of direct intermeddling I agree to it and suppose that no one denies it. But if an act is within the powers specifically conferred upon Congress, it seems to me that it is not made any less constitutional because of the indirect effects that it may have, however obvious it may be that it will have those effects, and that we are not at liberty upon such grounds to hold it void. . . . I should have thought that that matter had been disposed of so fully as to leave no room for doubt. I should have thought that the most conspicuous decisions of this Court had made it clear that the power to regulate commerce and other constitutional powers could not be cut down or qualified by the fact that it might interfere with the carrying out of the domestic policy of any State. . . .

"The notion that prohibition is any less prohibition when applied to things now thought evil I do not understand. But if there is any matter upon which civilized countries have agreed—far more unanimously than they have with regard to intoxicants and some other matters over which this country is now emotionally aroused—it is the evil of premature and excessive child labor. I should have thought that if we were to introduce our own moral conceptions where in my opinion they do not belong, this was preeminently a case for upholding the exercise of all its powers by the United States.

"But I had thought that the propriety of the exercise of a power admitted to exist in some cases was for the consideration of Congress alone and that this Court always had disavowed the right to intrude its judgment upon questions of policy or morals. It is not for this Court to pronounce when prohibition is necessary to regulation if it ever may be necessary—to say that it is permissible as against strong drink but not as against the product of ruined lives.

"The act does not meddle with anything belonging to the States. They may regulate their internal affairs and their domestic commerce as they like. But when they seek to send their products across the State line they are no longer within their rights. If there were no Constitution and no Congress their power to cross the line would depend upon their neighbors. Under the Constitution such commerce belongs not to the States but to Congress to regulate. It may carry out its views of public policy whatever indirect effect they may have upon the activities of the States. Instead of being encountered by a prohibitive tariff at her boundaries the State encounters the public policy of the United States which it is for Congress to express. The public policy of the United States is shaped with a view to the benefit of the nation as a whole. If, as has been the case within the memory of men still living, a State should take a different view of the propriety of sustaining a lottery from that which generally prevails, I cannot believe that the fact would require a different decision from that reached in *Champion v. Ames.* Yet in that case it would be said with quite as much force as in this that Congress was attempting to intermeddle with the State's domestic affairs. The national welfare as understood by Congress may require a different attitude within its sphere from that of some self-seeking State. It seems to me entirely constitutional for Congress to enforce its understanding by all the means at its command."[44]

The Nation that was called into being by the Constitution was adequately endowed to meet growth and change, and to maintain its dignity among the peoples of the world. But the Constitution was also the product of great historic conflicts. It sought to guard against the recurrence of historic grievances by preferring the risks of tolerance to the dangers of tyranny. Mr. Justice Holmes has been faithful to this tradition, and his dissenting opinion in the *Abrams* case will live as long as English prose has power to thrill.

"I do not doubt for a moment that by the same reasoning that would justify punishing persuasion to murder, the United States constitutionally may punish speech that produces or is intended to produce a clear and imminent danger that it will bring about forthwith certain substantive evils that the United States constitutionally may seek to prevent. The power undoubtedly is greater in time of war than in time of peace because war opens dangers that do not exist at other times.

"But as against dangers peculiar to war, as against others, the principle of the right to free speech is always the same. It is only the present danger of immediate evil or an intent to bring it about that warrants Congress in setting a limit to the expression of opinion where private rights are not concerned. Congress certainly cannot forbid all effort to change the mind of the country. . . .

"In this case sentences of twenty years imprisonment have been imposed for the publishing of two leaflets that I believe the defendants had as much right to publish as the Government has to publish the Constitution of the United States now vainly invoked by them. Even if I am technically wrong and enough can be squeezed from these poor and puny anonymities to turn the color of legal litmus paper; I will add, even if what I think the necessary intent were shown; the most nominal punishment seems to me all that possibly could be inflicted, unless the defendants are to be made to suffer not for what the indictment alleges but for the creed that they avow—a creed that I believe to be the creed of ignorance and immaturity when honestly held, as I see no reason to doubt that it was held here, but which, although made the subject of examination at the trial, no one has a right to consider in dealing with the charges before the Court.

"Persecution for the expression of opinions seems to me perfectly logical. If you have no doubt of your premises or your power and want a certain result with all your heart you naturally express your wishes in law and sweep away all opposition. To allow opposition by speech seems to indicate that you think the speech impotent, as when a man says that he has squared the circle, or that you do not care wholeheartedly for the result, or that you doubt either your power or your premises. But when men have realized that time has upset many fighting faiths, they may come to believe even more than they believe the very foundations of their own conduct that the ultimate good desired is better reached by free trade in ideas—that the best test of truth is the power of the thought to get itself accepted in the competition of the market, and that truth is the only ground upon which their wishes safely can be carried out. That at any rate is the theory of our Constitution. It is an experiment, as all life is an experiment. Every year if not every day we have to wager our salvation upon some prophecy based upon imperfect knowledge. While that experiment is part of our system I think that we should be eternally vigilant against attempts to check the expression of opinions that we loathe and believe to be fraught with death, unless they so imminently threaten immediate interference with the lawful and pressing purposes of the law that an immediate check is required to save the country. I wholly disagree with the argument of the Government that the First Amendment left the common law as to seditious libel in force. History seems to me against the notion. I had conceived that the United States through many years had shown its repentance for the Sedition Act of 1798, by repaying fines that it imposed. Only the emergency that makes it immediately dangerous to leave the correction of evil counsels to time warrants making any exception to the sweeping command, 'Congress shall make no law . . . abridging the freedom of speech.' Of course I am speaking only of expressions of opinion and exhortations, which were all that were uttered here, but I regret that I cannot put into more impressive words my belief that in their conviction upon this indictment the defendants were deprived of their rights under the Constitution of the United States." [45]

VI

Nowhere is Mr. Justice Holmes' statesmanship more manifest than in his lively realization that in domestic affairs the nation is a union of states. Modern inventions have extended enormously the scope of federal control, and as an exercise in ratiocination the commerce clause could dry up the local areas of regulation. Logically there is no limit to the interrelation of national commerce and the activities of men in the separate states. But the purposes of our federalism must be observed and adjustments struck between states and nation.

"In modern societies every part is related so organically to every other, that what affects any portion must be felt more or less by all the rest. Therefore, unless everything is to be forbidden and legislation is to come to a stop, it is not enough to show that, in the working of a statute, there is some tendency, logically discernible, to interfere with commerce or existing contracts." [46]

"I see nothing in the commerce clause to prevent a State from giving a preference to its inhabitants in the enjoyment of its natural advantages. If the gas were used only by private persons for their own purposes I know of no power in Congress to require them to devote it to public use or to transport it across state lines. It is the law of West Virginia and of West Virginia alone that makes the West Virginia gas what is called a public utility, and how far it shall be such is a matter that that law alone decides. I am aware that there is some general language in *Oklahoma v. Kansas Natural Gas Co.,* 221 U. S. 229, 255, a decision that I thought wrong, implying that Pennsylvania might not keep its coal, or the north-

> west its timber, &c. But I confess I do not see what is to hinder. Certainly if the owners of the mines or the forests saw fit not to export their products the Constitution would not make them do it. I see nothing in that instrument that would produce a different result if the State gave the owners motives for their conduct, as by offering a bonus. However far the decision in the case referred to goes it cannot outweigh the consensus of the other decisions to which I have referred and that seem to me to confirm what I should think plain without them, that the Constitution does not prohibit a State from securing a reasonable preference for its own inhabitants in the enjoyment of its products even when the effect of its law is to keep property within its boundaries that otherwise would have passed outside." [47]

Not the commerce clause, but the Fourteenth Amendment now furnishes the most far-reaching obstacles to state legislation. When that Amendment first came before the Supreme Court in the *Slaughter-House Cases,*[49] four dissenting Justices, under the lead of Mr. Justice Field, sought to encrust upon the undefined language of the due process clause the eighteen century "law-of-nature" doctrines. As the new protection of the Fourteenth Amendment was persistently invoked by counsel against the growing efforts of the states to regulate economic enterprise, the rejected dissents of Mr. Justice Field gradually established themselves as the views of the Court. Though speaking the language of abstractions, the opinions of Mr. Justice Field reflected adequately enough the vital elements of the social and economic order in which he grew up.[99] But his society was in process of drastic transformation, and indeed had largely passed, certainly when Mr. Justice Peckham wrote Mr. Justice Field's dissents into the opinions of the Court.[50] Between the dictum, in 1876, of Chief Justice Waite, in *Munn v. Illinois* that "for protection against abuses by legislatures [in fixing utility rates] the people must resort to the polls, not to the courts,"[51] and the decision in the *Lochner* case,[52] in 1905, striking down a ten-hour law for bakers, lies the history of the emergence of modern large-scale industry, of the consequent public control of business, and of judicial review of such regulation. The doctrinal process by which the Court came to its present pervasive control of state action, though in no wise impinging on the national interests safeguarded by the commerce clause, has been explained by Mr. Justice Holmes:

> ". . . the only objection that can be urged [against a minimum wage law for women passed by Congress for the District of Columbia] is found within the vague contours of the Fifth Amendment, prohibiting the depriving any person of liberty or property without due process of law. To that I turn.
>
> "The earlier decisions upon the same words in the Fourteenth Amendment began within our memory and went no farther than an unpretentious assertion of the liberty to follow the ordinary callings. Later that innocuous generality was expanded into the dogma, Liberty of Contract. Contract is not specially mentioned in the text that we have to construe. It is merely an example of doing what you want to do, embodied in the word liberty. But pretty much all law consists in forbidding men to do some things that they want to do, and contract is no more exempt from law than other acts." [53]

The meaning of this operation of judicial review was put by Judge Hough with characteristic pungency: "No man has seen more plainly that the court was measuring the legislature's reasons by its own intellectual yardstick than has Justice Holmes; none more keenly perceived that the notations thereupon marked those results of environment and education which many men seem to regard as the will of God or the decrees of fate." [54] Against this subtle danger of the unconscious identification of personal views with constitutional sanction Mr. Justice Holmes has battled incessantly. His influence was powerful in arresting the tide which reached its crest in the *Lochner* case. There followed a period of judicial recession, of greater tolerance towards the exercise of legislative discretion. Between 1908 and the World War, the Court allowed legislation to prevail which in various aspects curbed freedom of enterprise and withdrew phases of industrial relations from the area of individula bargaining. In the period between *Muller v. Oregon*,[55] in 1908, and *Bunting v. Oregon*,[56] in 1917, Mr. Justice Holmes' views prevailed. But those who had assumed a permanent change in the Court's outlook were to be disappointed. The philosophy of Mr. Justice Field is obdurate. Change in the Court's personnel, and pressure of post-war economic and social views soon reflected themselves in decisions. *Adkins v. Children's Hospital* [57] (a minimum wage law for women in industry), *Burns Baking Co. v. Bryan* [58] (a standard-weight bread law to protect buyers from short weights and honest bakers from unfair competition), *Tyson v. Banton* [59] (a law fixing the re-sale price of theatre tickets by ticket-scalpers in New York) show a reversion to the Field-Peckham period. In truth, *Burns Baking Co. v. Bryan* allows less scope to the legislature than any decision in the period that culminated in the *Lochner* case.

We are, then, where we were in 1905. Mr. Justice Holmes' classic dissent in the *Lochner* case, therefore, still needs to be quoted:

> "This case is decided upon an economic theory which a large part of the country does not entertain. If it were a question whether I agreed with that theory, I should desire to study it further and long before making up my mind. But I do not conceive that to be my duty, because I strongly believe that my agreement or disagree-

> ment has nothing to do with the right of a majority to embody their opinions in law. It is settled by various decisions of this court that state constitutions and state laws may regulate life in many ways which we as legislators might think as injudicious or if you like as tyrannical as this, and which equally with this intrefere with the liberty of contract. Sunday laws and usury laws are ancient examples. A more modern one is the prohibition of lotteries. The liberty of the citizen to do as he likes so long as he does not interfere with the liberty of others to do the same, which has been a shibboleth for some well-known writers, is interfered with by school laws, by the Post Office, by every state or municipal institution which takes his money for purposes thought desirable, whether he likes it or not. The Fourteenth Amendment does not enact Mr. Herbert Spencer's Social Statics. . . . Some of these laws embody convictions or prejudices which judges are likely to share. Some may not. But a constitution is not intended to embody a particular economic theory, whether of paternalism and the organic relation of the citizen to the State or of *laissez faire*. It is made for people of fundamentally differing views, and the accident of our finding certain opinions natural and familiar or novel and even shocking ought not to conclude our judgment upon the question whether statutes embodying them conflict with the Constitution of the United States."[60]

In the hundreds of instances in which legislation has been challenged in the name of the Fourteenth Amendment, Mr. Justice Holmes has been loyal to his philosophy. Government means experimentation. To be sure, constitutional limitations confine the area of experiment. But these limitations are not self-defining and were intended to permit government. The door was left open to trial and error—"constitutional law like other mortal contrivances has to take some chances. . . ."[61] Opportunity must be allowed for vindicating reasonable belief by experience. Above all, Mr. Justice Holmes has sturdily resisted every tendency to impose upon the forty-eight states the Court's views or assumptions on social policy. He has given meaning to our federalism, satisfying the requirements of national uniformity as well as of local diversity.

". . . we must be cautious about pressing the broad words of the Fourteenth Amendment to a drily logical extreme. Many laws which it would be vain to ask the court to overthrow could be shown, easily enough, to transgress a scholastic interpretation of one or another of the great guarantees in the Bill of Rights. They more or less limit the liberty of the individual or they diminish property to a certain extent. We have few scientifically certain criteria of legislation, and as it often is difficult to mark the line where what is called the police power of the States is limited by the Constitution of the United States, judges should be slow to read into the latter a *nolumus mutare* as against the law-making power."[62]

"Again, we cannot wholly neglect the long settled law and common understanding of a particular state in considering the plaintiff's rights. We are bound to be very cautious in coming to the conclusion that the Fourteenth Amendment has upset what thus has been established and accepted for a long time. Even the incidents of ownership may be cut down by the peculiar laws and usages of a State."[63]

"Obviously the question so stated is one of local experience on which this court ought to be very slow to declare that the State Legislature was wrong in its facts. . . . If we might trust popular speech in some States it was right—but it is enough that this court has no such knowledge of local conditions as to be able to say that it was manifestly wrong."[64]

"If the Fourteenth Amendment is not to be a greater

hamper upon the established practices of the States in common with other governments than I think was intended, they must be allowed a certain latitude in the minor adjustments of life, even though by their action the burdens of a part of the community are somewhat increased. The traditions and habits of centuries were not intended to be overthrown when that amendment was passed."[65]

"There is nothing that I more deprecate than the use of the Fourteenth Amendment beyond the absolute compulsion of its words to prevent the making of social experiments that an important part of the community desires, in the insulated chambers afforded by the several States, even though the experiments may seem futile or even noxious to me and to those whose judgment I most respect."[66]

These are the generalizations which Mr. Justice Holmes has applied again and again to the solution of problems arising under different governmental powers, one or two illustrations of which will have to suffice. To consider Mr. Justice Holmes' opinions is to string pearls.

In all the varieties of state action evoked by a complex industrial civilization, he permits the states ample scope for energy and individuality. In the struggle which has centered around the conception of "liberty," he has resisted doctrinaire interpretation, disclosing with acuteness when a claim is doctrinaire and translating large words into the realities of existence.

"If Montana deems it advisable to put a lighter burden upon women than upon men with regard to an employment that our people commonly regard as more appropriate for the former, the Fourteenth Amendment does not interfere by creating a fictitious equality where there is a real difference. The particular points at which that difference shall be emphasized by legislation are largely in the power of the state."[67]

"In present conditions a workman not unnaturally may believe that only by belonging to a union can he secure a contract that shall be fair to him. . . . If that belief, whether right or wrong, may be held by a reasonable man, it seems to me that it may be enforced by law in order to establish the equality of position between the parties in which liberty of contract begins. Whether in the long run it is wise for the workingmen to enact legislation of this sort is not my concern, but I am strongly of opinion that there is nothing in the Constitution of the United States to prevent it, and that *Adair* v. *United States*, 208 U. S. 161, and *Lochner* v. *New York*, 198 U. S. 45, should be overruled."[68]

"If the legislature shares the now prevailing belief as to what is public policy and finds that a particular instrument of trade war is being used against that policy in certain cases, it may direct its law against what it deems the evil as it actually exists without covering the whole field of possible abuses, and it may do so none the less that the forbidden act does not differ in kind from those that are allowed. . . .

"It might have been argued to the legislature with more force than it can be to us that recoupment in one place of losses in another is merely an instance of financial ability to compete. If the legislature thought that that particular manifestation of ability usually came from great corporations whose power it deemed excessive and for that reason did more harm than good in their State, and that there was no other case of frequent occurrence where the same could be said, we cannot review their economics or their facts."[69]

Equally adequate is the scope permitted the states in devising ways and means for paying the bills of society, or in using taxation as an instrument of social policy. Mr. Justice Holmes allows no finicky or textual arguments to interpose the Constitution as a barrier to the states' taxing power. His opinions reveal an amiable appreciation of the tantalizing difficulty of statesmen to make taxation palatable in any form.

"There is a look of logic when it is said that special assessments are founded on special benefits and that a law which makes it possible to assess beyond the amount of the special benefit attempts to rise above its source. But that mode of argument assumes an exactness in the premises which does not exist. The foundation of this familiar form of taxation is a question of theory. The amount of benefit which an improvement will confer upon particular land, indeed whether it is a benefit at all, is a matter of forecast and estimate. In its general aspects at least it is peculiarly a thing to be decided by those who make the law. The result of the supposed constitutional principle is simply to shift the burden to a somewhat large taxing district, the municipality, and to disguise rather than to answer the theoretic doubt. It is dangerous to tie down legislatures too closely by judicial constructions not necessarily arising from the words of the Constitution. Particularly, as was intimated in *Spencer* v. *Merchant,* 125 U. S. 345, it is important for this court to avoid extracting from the very general language of the Fourteenth Amendment a system of delusive exactness in order to destroy methods of taxation which were well known when that Amendment was adopted and which it is safe to say that no one then supposed would be disturbed. . . ." [70]

"The objection to the taxation as double may be laid on one side. That is a matter of state law alone. The Fourteenth Amendment no more forbids double taxation than it does doubling the amount of a tax; short of confiscation or proceedings unconstitutional on other grounds. . . . We are of opinion that it also is within the power of a State, so far as the Constitution of the United States is concerned, to tax its own corporations in respect of the stock held by them in other domestic corporations, although unincorporated stockholders are exempt. A State may have a policy in taxation. *Quong Wing* v. *Kirkendall*, 223 U. S. 59, 63. If the State of Arkansas wished to discourage but not to forbid the holding of stock in one corporation by another and sought to attain the result by this tax, or if it simply saw fit to make corporations pay for the privilege, there would be nothing in the Constitution to hinder. A discrimination between corporations and individuals with regard to a tax like this cannot be pronounced arbitrarily, although we may not know the precise ground of policy that led the State to insert the distinction in the law." [71]

Judicial review of utility regulations transfers to courts the accommodation of clashing interests. No amount of constitutional metaphysics about "valuation" can conceal the downright exercise of practical judgment. Mr. Justice Holmes has laid down the real considerations in these cases and the restraint which judges should exercise in their application.

"An adjustment of this sort under a power to regulate rates has to steer between Scylla and Charybdis. On the one side if the franchise is taken to mean that the most profitable return that could be got, free from competition, is protected by the Fourteenth Amendment, then the power to regulate withdraws the protection of the Amendment altogether, then the property is naught. This is not a matter of economic theory, but of fair interpretation of a bargain. Neither extreme can have been meant. A midway between them must be hit." [72]

"We express no opinion whether to cut this telephone company down to six per cent by leigslation would or would not be confiscatory. But when it is remembered what clear evidence the court requires before it declares legislation otherwise valid void on this ground, and when it is considered how speculative every figure is that we have set down with delusive exactness, we are of opinion that the result is too near the dividing line not to make actual experiment necessary. The Master thought that the probable net income for the year would suffer the greatest decrease would be 8.60 per cent, on the values estimated by him. The Judge on assumptions to which we have stated our disagreement makes the present earnings 5-10/17 per cent, with a reduction by the ordinance to 3-8/17 per cent. The whole question is too much in the air for us to feel authorized to let the injunction stand."[73]

The cases arising under the power of eminent domain give strong proof of the element of relativity in constitutional law. A state can take private property, even though paying for it, only for "public purposes." When is a purpose "public"? High-sounding generalities only cover up the process of specific judgment. Time and place and local needs must govern. These are essentially the concern of the local legislature. Behind legal issues phrased as "the power of eminent domain" or "the police power," Mr. Justice Holmes has seen the state's well-being through a wise disposition of its limited natural resources.

. . . it appears to us that few public interests are more obvious, indisputable and independent of particular theory than the interest of the public of a State to maintain the rivers that are wholly within it substantially undiminished, except by such drafts upon them as the guardian of the public welfare may permit for the purpose of turning them to a more perfect use. This public interest is omnipresent wherever there is a state, and grows more pressing as population grows. It is fundamental, and we are of opinion that the private property of riparian proprietors cannot be supposed to have deeper roots. Whether it be said that such an interest justifies the cutting down by statute, without compensation, in the exercise of police power, of what otherwise would be private rights of property, or that apart from statute those rights do not go to the height of what the defendant seeks to do, the result is the same. But we agree with the New Jersey courts, and think it quite beyond any rational view of riparian rights that an agreement, of no matter what private owners, could sanction the diversion of an important stream outside the boundaries of the state in which it flows. The private right to appropriate is subject not only to the rights of lower owners but to the initial limitation that it may not substantially diminish one of the great foundations of public welfare and health.

"We are of opinion, further, that the constitutional power of the State to insist that its natural advantages shall remain unimpaired by its citizens is not dependent upon any nice estimate of the extent of present use or speculation as to future needs. The legal conception of the necessary is apt to be confined to somewhat rudimentary wants, and there are benefits from a great river that might escape a lawyer's view. But the State is not required to submit even to an easthetic analysis. Any analysis may be inadequate. It finds itself in possession of what all admit to be a great public good, and what it has it may keep and give no one a reason for its will." [74]

"In the organic relations of modern society it may sometimes be hard to draw the line that is supposed to limit the authority of the legislature to exercise or delegate the power of eminent domain. But to gather the streams from waste and to draw from them energy, labor without brains, and so to save mankind from toil that it can be spared, is to supply what, next to intellect, is the very foundation of all our achievements and all our welfare. If that purpose is not public we should be at a loss to say what is. The inadequacy of use by the general public as a universal test is established." [75]

Grade-crossings and automobiles have created baffling problems for a crowded population. Mr. Justice Holmes has not increased the difficulties of legislators by finding in the Constitution rigid limitations to their regulation.

"Grade crossings call for a necessary adjustment of two conflicting interests—that of the public using the streets and that of the railroads and the public using them. Generically the streets represent the more important interest of the two. There can be no doubt that they did when these railroads were laid out, or that the advent of automobiles has given them an additional claim to consideration. . . . Being places to which the public is invited and that it necessarily frequents, the State, in the care of which this interest is and from which, ultimately, the railroads derive their right to occupy the land, has a constitutional right to insist that they shall not be made dangerous to the public, whatever may be the cost to the parties introducing the danger. . . . It is said that if the same requirement were made for the other grade crossings of the road it would soon be bankrupt. That the States might be so foolish as to kill a goose that lays golden eggs for them, has no bearing on their constitutional rights. If it reasonably can be said that safety requires the change it is for them to say whether they will insist upon it, and neither prospective bankruptcy nor engagement in interstate commerce can take away this fundamental right of the sovereign of the soil. . . . Intelligent self-interest should lead to a careful consideration of what the road is able to do without ruin, but this is not a constitutional duty." [76]

"The question is whether a State may require all corporations or persons . . . who operate automobiles, &c., for the transportation of persons or property over a regular route and between fixed termini on the public highways of the State, for compensation, to obtain a certificate from the railroad commission that public necessity and convenience require such operation. . . .

"The point before us seems to me well within the legislative power. We all know what serious problems the automobile has introduced. The difficulties of keeping the streets reasonably clear for travel and for traffic are very great. If a State speaking through its legislature should think that, in order to make its highways most useful, the business traffic upon them must be controlled, I suppose that no one would doubt that it constitutionally could, as, I presume, most States or cities do, exercise some such control. The only question is how far it can go. I see nothing to prevent its going to the point of requiring a license and bringing the whole business under the control of a railroad commission so far as to determine the number, character and conduct of transportation companies and so to prevent the streets from being made useless and dangerous by the number and lawlessness of those who seek to use them." [77]

Again and again, and in various forms, he has repelled effort to spell pedantic perfection into the Fourteenth Amendment. Especially ominous is the recent tendency to defeat legislation in vindication of fictitious equalities, supposedly demanded by the guaranty of "equal protection of the laws." Undoubtedly distinctions have to be made, and "even nice distinctions are to be expected," [78] particularly when determining who shall bear the loss in destroying existing contract rights.[79] "It often is a delicate matter to decide which interest preponderates and how far the State may go without making compensation." [80] But the emphasis of Mr. Justice Holmes has been on the necessity for allowing ample freedom to the states in making decisions which, howsoever made, will hurt.

"The dangers of a delusive exactness in the application of the Fourteenth Amendment have been adverted to before now. . . . I cannot understand the notion that it would be unconstitutional to authorize boycotts and the like in aid of the employees' or the employers' interest by statute when the same result has been reached constitutionally without statute by Courts with whom I agree. . . .

"I think further that the selection of the class of employers and employees for special treatment, dealing with both sides alike, is beyond criticism on principles often asserted by this Court. And especially I think that without legalizing the conduct complained of the extraordinary relief by injunction may be denied to the class. Legislation may begin where an evil begins. If, as many intelligent people believe, there is more danger that the injunction will be abused in labor cases than elsewhere I can feel no doubt of the power of the legislature to deny it in such cases." [81]

"If the Legislature of Pennsylvania was of opinion that disease is likely to be spread by the use of unsterilized shoddy in comfortables I do not suppose that this Court would pronounce the opinion so manifestly absurd that it could not be acted upon. If we should not, then I think that we ought to assume the opinion to be right for the purpose of testing the law. The Legislature may have been of opinion further that the actual practice of filling comfortables with unsterilized shoddy gathered from filthy floors was wide spread, and this again we must assume to be true. It is admitted to be impossible to distinguish the innocent from the infected product in any practicable way, when it is made up into the comfortables.

On these premises, if the Legislature regarded the danger as very great and inspection and tagging as inadequate remedies, it seems to me that in order to prevent the spread of disease it constitutionally could forbid any use of shoddy for bedding and upholstery. . . .

"It is said that there was unjustifiable discrimination. A classification is not to be pronounced arbitrarily because it goes on practical grounds and attacks only those objects that exhibit or foster an evil on a large scale. It is not required to be mathematically precise and to embrace every case that theoretically is capable of doing the same harm." [82]

"We have seen more than once that the public welfare may call upon the best citizens for their lives. It would be strange if it could not call upon those who already sap the strength of the State for these lesser sacrifices, often not felt to be such by those concerned, in order to prevent our being swamped with incompetence. It is better for all the world, if instead of waiting to execute degenerate offspring for crime, or to let them starve for their imbecility, society can prevent those who are manifestly unfit from continuing their kind. The principle that sustains compulsory vaccination is broad enough to cover cutting the Fallopian tubes. . . . Three generations of imbeciles are enough.

"But, it is said, however it might be if this reasoning were applied generally, it fails when it is confined to the small number who are in the insituations named and is not applied to the multitudes outside. It is the usual last resort of constitutional arguments to point out shortcomings of this sort. But the answer is that the law does all that is needed when it does all that it can, indicates a policy, applies it to all within the lines, and seeks to bring within the lines all similarly situated so far and so fast as its means allow." [83]

These opinions are the more significant in that, not infrequently, they come from a man who, as judge, enforces statutes based upon economic and political theories which he does not share and of whose efficacy in action he is sceptical.[84] The judicial function here reaches its highest exercise.

But there are limits to state action, derived from the fact of Union and from the traditions of fair play. The problems raised by "big business" baffled the wisdom of a Roosevelt and a Wilson. Their intricacies are not likely to lessen with time. The widest scope must therefore be permitted the inventions and the bunglings of legislatures. However, they must not outrage decency nor disregard those procedural safeguards which are so largely the assurance of political liberty. Again, the difficulties of adjusting the powers of taxation between states and nation will more and more challenge the skill of statesmen. But a state cannot levy upon the agencies of the United States though operating within its borders; nor, in tapping common sources of revenue, like a transcontinental railroad system, can a state under guise of a financial formula project itself beyond its boundaries.

> "The statute bristles with severities that touch the plaintiff alone, and raises many questions that would have to be answered before it could be sustained. We deem it sufficient to refer to those that were mentioned by the District Court; a classification which, if it does not confine itself to the American Sugar Refinery, at least is arbitrary beyond possible justice,—and a creation of presumptions and special powers against it that can have no foundation except the intent to destroy. . . .
>
> "As to the presumptions, of course the legislature may go a good way in raising one or in changing the burden of proof, but there are limits. . . . The presumption created here has no relation in experience to general facts. It has no foundation except with tacit reference to the plaintiff. But it is

not within the province of a legislature to declare an individual guilty or presumptively guilty of a crime." [85]

"The State claims the right to tax on the ground that taxation of the agency may be taxation of the means employed by the government and invalid upon admitted grounds, but that taxation of the property of the agent is not taxation of the means. We agree that it 'is not always, or generally, taxation of the means,' as said by Chief Justice Chase in *Thomson* v. *Pacific Railroad*, 9 Wall. 579, 591. But it may be, and in our opinion clearly is when as here not only the agent was created but all the agent's property was acquired and used, for the sole purpose of producing a weapon for the war. This is not like the case of a corporation having its own purposes as well as those of the United States and interested in profit on its own account. The incorporation and formal erection of a new personality was only for the convenience of the United States to carry out its end." [86]

"As the law is administered, the tax commissioner fixes the value of the total property of each railroad by the total value of its stocks and bonds and assesses the proportion of this value that the main track mileage in North Dakota bears to the main track of the whole line. But on the allegations of the bill, which is all that we have before us, the circumstances are such as to make that mode of assessment indefensible. North Dakota is a State of plains, very different from the other States, and the cost of the roads there was much less than it was in mountainous regions that the roads had ot traverse. The State is mainly agricultural. Its markets are outside its boundaries and most of the distributing centers from which it purchases also are outside. It naturally follows that the great and very valuable terminals of the roads are in other States. So looking only to the physical track the injustice of assuming the value to be evenly distributed according to main track mileage is plain. But that is not all.

"The only reason for allowing a State to look beyond its borders when it taxes the property of foreign corporations is that it may get the true value of the things within it, when they are part of an organic system of wide extent, that gives them a value above what they otherwise would possess. The purpose is not to expose the heel of the system to a mortal dart—not, in other words, to open to taxation what is not within the State." [87]

Very recently, Mr. Justice Holmes has summed up his philosophy on these great issues of state power and judicial control. His dissent in the New York ticket-scalping case reveals his mind with luminous candor; it also gives a glimpse of the gracious hold beauty has on his outlook. Nothing less than the whole of this opinion will adequately convey it.

"We fear to grant power and are unwilling to recognize it when it exists. The States very generally have stripped jury trials of one of their most important characteristics by forbidding the judges to advise the jury upon the facts (*Graham* v. *United States,* 231 U. S. 474, 480), and when legislatures are held to be authorized to do anything considerably affecting public welfare it is covered by apologetic phrases like the police power, or the statement that the business concerned has been dedicated to a public use. The former expression is convenient, to be sure, to conciliate the mind to something that needs explanation: the fact that the constitutional requirement of compensation when property is taken cannot be pressed to its grammatical extreme; that property rights may be taken for public purposes without pay if you do not take too much; that some play must be allowed to the joints if the machine is to work. But police power is often used in a wide sense to cover and, as I said, to apologize for the general power of the legislature to make a part of the community uncomfortable by a change.

"I do not believe in such apologies. I think the proper course is to recognize that a state legislature can do whatever it sees fit to do unless it is restrained by some express prohibition in the Constitution of the United States or of the State, and that Courts should be careful not to extend such prohibitions beyond their obvious meaning by reading into them conceptions of public policy that the particular Court may happen to entertain. Coming down to the case before us I think, as I intimated in *Adkins* v. *Children's Hospital*, 261 U. S. 525, 569, that the notion that a business is clothed with a public interest and has been devoted to the public use is little more than a fiction intended to beautify what is disagreeable to the sufferers. The truth seems to me to be that, subject to compensation when compensation is due, the legislature may forbid or restrict any business when it has a sufficient force of public opinion behind it. Lotteries were thought useful adjuncts of the State a century or so ago; now they are believed to be immoral and they have been stopped. Wine has been thought good for man from the time of the Apostles until recent years. But when public opinion changed it did not need the Eighteenth Amendment, notwithstanding the Fourteenth, to enable a State to say that the business should end. *Mugler* v. *Kansas*, 123 U. S. 623. What has happened to lotteries and wine might happen to theatres in some moral storm of the future, not because theatres were devoted to public use, but because people had come to think that way.

"But if we are to yield to fashionable conventions, it seems to me that theatres are as much devoted to public use as anything well can be. We have not that respect for art that is one of the glories of France. But to many people the superfluous is the necessary, and it seems to me that Government does not go beyond its sphere in attempting to make life livable for them. I am far from saying that I think this particular law a wise and rational provision. That is not my affair. But if the people of the State of New York speaking by their authorized voice say that they want it, I see nothing in the Constitution of the United States to prevent their having their will."[88]

VII

The judicial process in Mr. Justice Holmes is a fertile interplay between generalization and particular. The particular in isolation is meaningless; the generalization without concreteness, sterile. At the core of his decisions is the realization that words are only symbols of things and feelings and relations. He does not delude himself with phrases, and saves us, if we have the wit to see, from verbal mirages. And so his constitutional opinions are but applications of his candid insight into the realities of law and the share which courts have in its making. Jurisdiction rests ultmately on power, but there may be moral restraints upon its abstract scope. Law has the mandate of man's striving for reason and justice; but explicitly it is the voice of some defined organ of government.

"But the word 'right' is one of the most deceptive of pitfalls; it is so easy to slip from a qualified meaning in the premise to an unqualified one in the conclusion. Most rights are qualified."[89]

"Delusive exactness is a source of fallacy throughout the law. By calling a business 'property' you make it seem like land, and lead up to the conclusion that a statute cannot substantially cut down the advantages of ownership existing before the statute was passed. An established business no doubt may have pecuniary value and commonly is protected by law against various unjustified injuries. But you cannot give it definiteness of contour by calling it a thing. It is a course of conduct and like other conduct is subject to substantial modification according to time and circumstances both in itself and in regard to what shall justify doing it a harm." [90]

"The foundation of jurisdiction is physical power, although in civilized times it is not necessary to maintain that power throughout proceedings properly begun, and although submission to the jurisdiction by appearance may take the place of service upon the person. . . . No doubt there may be some extension of the means of acquiring jurisdiction beyond service or appearance, but the foundation should be borne in mind. . . . And in States bound together by a Constitution and subject to the Fourteenth Amendment, great caution should be used not to let fiction deny the fair play that can be secured only by a pretty close adhesion to fact." [91]

"The appellants, starting from the sound proposition that jurisdiction is founded upon power, overwork the argument drawn from the power of the United States over the Steel Corporation. Taking the United States in this connection to mean the total powers of the Central and the State Governments, no doubt theoretically it could draw a line of fire around its boundaries and recognize nothing concerning the corporation or any interest in it that happened outside. But it prefers to consider itself civilized and to act accordingly. Therefore New Jersey having authorized this corporation like others to issue certificates that so far represent the stock that ordinarily at least no one can get the benefits of ownership except through and by means of the paper, it recognizes as owner anyone to whom the person declared by the paper to be owner has transferred it by the indorsement provided for, wherever it takes place." [92]

"If we suppose for the moment that the Government's contention is so far correct that the Crown of Spain in form asserted a title to this land at the date of the Treaty of Paris, to which the United States succeeded, it is not to be assumed without argument that the plaintiff's case is at an end. It is true that Spain in its earlier decrees embodied the universal feudal theory that all lands were held from the Crown, and perhaps the general attitude of conquering nations toward people not recognized as entitled to the treatment accorded to those in the same zone of civilization with themselves. It is true also that in legal theory sovereignty is absolute, and that as against foreign nations, the United States may assert, as Spain asserted, absolute power. But it does not follow that as against the inhabitants of the Philippines the United States asserts that Spain had such power. When theory is left on one side sovereignty is a question of strength and may vary in degree. How far a new sovereign shall insist upon the theoretical relation of the subjects to the head in the past and how far it shall recognize actual facts are matters for it to decide. . . .

"No one, we suppose, would deny that, so far as consistent with paramount necessities, our first object in the internal administration of the islands is to do justice to the natives, not to exploit their country for private gain. By the organic act of July 1, 1902, c. 1369, § 12, 32 Stat. 691, all the property and rights acquired there by the United States are to be administered 'for the benefit of the inhabitants thereof.' It is reasonable to suppose that the attitude thus assumed by the United States with regard to what was unquestionably its own is also its attitude in deciding what it will claim for its own. The same statute made a bill of rights embodying the safeguards of the Constitution, and like the Constitution, extends those safeguards to all. It provides that 'no law shall be enacted in said islands which shall de-prive any person of life, liberty, or property without due process of law, or deny to any person therein the equal protection of the laws.' § 5. In the light of the declaration that we have quoted from § 12, it is hard to believe that the United States was ready to declare in the next breath that 'any person' did not embrace the inhabitants of Benguet, or that it meant by 'property' only that which had become such by ceremonies of which presumably a large part of the inhabitants never had heard, and that it proposed to treat as public land what they, by native custom and by long association, one of the profoundest factors in human thought, regarded as their own." [93]

"The common law is not a brooding omnipresence in the sky but the articulate voice of some sovereign or quasi-sovereign that can be identified; although some decisions with which I have disagreed seem to me to have forgotten the fact. It always is the law of some State, and if the District Courts adopt the common law of torts, as they have shown a tendency to do, they thereby assume that a law not of maritime origin and deriving its authority in that territory only from some particular State of this Union also governs maritime torts in that territory—and if the common law, the statute law has at least equal force, as the discussion in *The Osceola* assumes. On the other hand the refusal of the District Courts to give remedies coextensive with the common law would prove no more than that they regarded their jurisdiction as limited by the ancient lines —not that they doubted that the common law might and would be enforced in the courts of the States as it always has been." [94]

"I do not suppose that anyone would say that the words, 'The judicial power shall extend . . . to all cases of admiralty and maritime jurisdiction,' Const. Art. III, § 3, by implication enacted a whole code for master and servant at sea, that could be modified only by a constitutional amendment. But somehow or other the ordinary common-law rules of liability as between master and servant have come to be applied to a considerable extent in the admiralty. If my explanation, that the source is the common law of the several States, is not accepted, I can only say, I do not know how, unless by the fiat of the judges. But surely the power that imposed the liability can change it, and I suppose that Congress can do as much as the judges who introduced the rules. For we know that they were introduced and cannot have been elicited by logic alone from the mediaeval sea laws."[95]

The eternal struggle in the law between constancy and change is largely a struggle between history and reason, between past reason and present needs. The valid claims of both, with varying weight in different aspects of legal control, find frequent expression in Mr. Justice Holmes' opinions. The essential difficulty of these adjustments lies in the impossibility of making quantitative determinations.[96] Specific cases gradually work out approximate directions. A neat application of the claims of history and of reason was strikingly indicated by two of his opinions rendered the same day. In determining the present attitude of the law towards a man standing his ground when attacked with a deadly weapon, ancient history has very little pertinence:

"It is useless to go into the developments of the law from the time when a man who had killed another no matter how innocently had to get his pardon, whether of grace or of course. Concrete cases or illustrations stated in the early law in conditions very different from the present, like the reference to retreat in Coke, Third Inst. 55, and elsewhere, have had a tendency to ossify into specific rules without much regard for reason. . . . The law has grown, and even if historical mistakes have contributed to its growth it has tended in the direction of rules consistent with human nature." [97]

But when the technical restriction of the Constitution as to laying a "direct tax" is invoked against the modern device of succession taxes, "a page of history is worth a volume of logic." [98] And whether the past has controlling claims or its wisdom be outworn can be ascertained only by the critical pursuit of reason.

"Most of the things we do, we do for no better reason than that our fathers have done them or that our neighbors do them, and the same is true of a larger part than we suspect of what we think. The reason is a good one, because our short life gives us no time for a better, but it is not the best. It does not follow, because we all are compelled to take on faith at second hand most of the rules on which we base our action and our thought, that each of us may not try to set some corner of his world in the order of reason, or that all of us collectively should not aspire to carry reason as far as it will go throughout the whole domain. In regard to the law, it is true, no doubt, that an evolutionist will hesitate to affirm universal validity for his social ideals, or for the principles which he thinks should be embodied in legislation. He is content if he can prove them best for here and now. He may be ready to admit that he knows nothing about an absolute best in the cosmos, and even that he knows next to nothing about a permanent best for men. Still it is true that a body of law is more rational and more civilized when every rule it contains is referred articulately and definitely to an end which it subserves, and when the grounds for desiring that end are stated or are ready to be stated in words." [99]

VIII

From the constitutional opinions of Mr. Justice Holmes there emerges the conception of a nation adequate to its national and international duties, consisting of federated states in their turn possessed of ample power for the diverse uses of a civilized people. He has been mindful of the Union for which he fought at Balls Bluff, Antietam, and Fredericksburg; he has been equally watchful to assure scope for the states upon which the Union rests. Federated power over commerce beyond state lines has not been paralyzed by sterile abstractions; nor are the states hampered in grappling with their local problems by a partisan or provincial application of the Fourteenth Amendment. He has found the Constitution equal to the needs of a great nation at war. But according to the same Constitution the individual must not be sacrificed to the Moloch of fear.

To be sure, some of his weightiest utterances are dissenting opinions—but they are dissents that record prophecy and shape history.[100] In their impact and sweep and freshness, his opinions have been a superb vehicle for the views which they employ. It all seems so easy—brilliant birds pulled from the magician's sleeve—but it is the delusive ease of great effort as well as great art. He has told us that in deciding cases "one has to try to strike the jugular." "The eternal effort of art, even the art of writing legal decisions, is to omit all but the essentials. 'The point of contact' is the formula, the place where the boy got his finger pinched; the rest of the machinery doesn't matter." So we see nothing of the draftsmanship, but get, like Corot's pictures, "magisterial summaries." We see more. Back of his approach to an obscure statute or a knotty point of legal history, we catch a glimpse of his own approach to life. Unawares Santayana has given the clue:

"Why is there a limited authority in institutions? Why are compromise and partial cooperation practicable in society? Why is there sometimes a right to revolution? Why is there sometimes a duty to loyalty? Because the whole transcendental philosophy, if made ultimate, is false, and nothing but a selfish perspective hypostasized; because the will is absolute neither in the individual nor in humanity; because nature is not a product of the mind, but on the contrary there is an external world, ages prior to any *a priori* idea of it, which the mind recognizes and feeds upon; because there is a steady human nature within us, which our moods and passions may wrong, but cannot annul; because there is no absolute imperative, but only the operation of instincts and interests more or less subject to discipline and mutual adjustment; and finally because life is a compromise, an incipient loose harmony between the passions of the soul and the forces of nature, forces which likewise generate and protect the souls of other creatures, endowing them with powers of expression and self-assertion comparable to our own and with aims not less sweet and worthy in their own eyes; so that the quick and honest mind can not but practice courtesy in the universe, exercising its will without vehemence or forced assurance, judging with serenity, and in everything discarding the word absolute as the most false and the most odious of words." [101]

Serenely dwelling above the sound of passing shibboleths, Mr. Justice Holmes has steadfastly refused to hearken to the murmur of the moment. But his humility is too deep to make him regard even the highest tribunal as a Grand Lama. Like all human institutions, the Supreme Court must earn reverence through the test of truth.[102]

He has built himself into the structure of our national life. He has written himself into the slender volume of the literature of all time.

NOTES

MR. JUSTICE HOLMES AND THE CONSTITUTION

* William Howard Taft.

1 In the quinquennium of 1910-1914, according to a rough classification between cases involving constitutional and kindred issues of public law on the one hand, and all other cases on the other, there were dissents in about thirteen per cent of the constitutional cases, and in only eight per cent of the non-constitutional cases. According to a similar classification for the 1921-1925 quinquennium, dissents were recorded in twenty-seven per cent of the constitutional cases and in only four per cent of the non-constitutional cases. For this analysis, I am indebted to Mr. Harry Shulman, research fellow of the Harvard Law School.

From time to time it is suggested that dissents should be suppressed. Such a proposal does violence to the whole history of the Supreme Court. The practice of expressing dissents in constitutional litigation has always been vigorously exercised because conceived to be rooted in judicial duty. "I am of opinion," wrote Mr. Justice Story, "that upon constitutional questions, the public have a right to know the opinion of every judge who dissents from the opinion of the court, and the reasons of his dissent." Briscoe v. Bank of Kentucky, 11 Pet. 257, 349, 350 (U. S. 1837). And so Chief Justice Taney, "It has, I find, been the uniform practice in this Court, for the justices who differed from the Court on constitutional questions, to express their dissent." Rhode Island v. Massachusetts, 12 Pet. 657, 752 (U. S. 1838). Again Mr. Justice Moody: ". . . where the judgment is a judicial condemnation of an act of a coordinate branch of our Government it is so grave a step that no member of the court can escape his own responsibility, or be justified in suppressing his own views, if unhappily they have not found expression in those of his associates." Employers' Liability Cases, 207 U. S. 463, 505 (1908). The extent to which some of the strongest members of the Court have discharged this duty is illustrated by the record of Mr. Justice Miller. During his twenty-eight years on the Court, he wrote 783 opinions of which 169 were dissents. GREGORY, SAMUEL FREEMAN MILLER (1907) c. VIII.

2 The orthodox theory of judicial review in constitutional controversies was admirably stated by Mr. John W. Davis in his presidential address before the American Bar Association in 1923: "There is a curious misconception underlying much that is said and written on this subject as to the duties that the court is called upon to discharge. One might suppose from some of these outgivings that the court sat at the outer gate of Congress waiting to visit a jealous censorship on the laws that issue from that portal; and that over them it had a general power of life and death, of approval or of veto. But august as are the functions of the court, surely they do not go one

step beyond the administration of justice to individual litigants. . . .

"Shall we say that when an American stands before the court demanding rights given him by the supreme law of the land, the court shall be deaf to his appeal? Shall wrongs visited upon him by the illegal excesses of Congress or legislatures be less open to redress than those which he may suffer from courts, or sheriffs, or military tyrants or civilian enemies? If this be so, if in any such case the ears of the court are to be closed against him, it is not the power of the court that has been reduced but the dearly-bought right of the citizen that is taken away." (1923) 48 A. B. A. REP. 193, 204.

How the American doctrine strikes a distinguished English legal mind, Lord Birkenhead made clear at the same meeting of the American Bar Association in his comment on Mr. Davis' remarks: "Your President is one for whom intellectually I have a great admiration; and personally a deep affection. His masterly address today carried me entirely with him. But surely one refinement was a little subtle. He said that the Supreme Court had not the right *in abstracto* to construe your fundamental constitutional document; but only in relation to the issues presented by an individual litigation. But is this in ultimate analysis a very serious derogation? When an issue challenged by an individual raises the question whether a law is constitutional or not, the decision of the Supreme Court decides this question for all time; and if the decision is against the legislature, the attempted law is stripped of its attempted authority." (1923) 48 A. B. A. REP. 224, 226.

[3] Slocum v. New York Life Ins. Co., 228 U. S. 364 (1913).

[4] Spalding & Bros. v. Edwards, 262 U. S. 66 (1923).

[5] United States v. Moreland, 258 U. S. 433 (1922); Brede v. Powers, 263 U. S. 4 (1923).

[6] Boyd v. United States, 116 U. S. 616 (1886); Gouled v. United States, 255 U. S. 298 (1921); Carroll v. United States, 267 U. S. 132 (1925); Byars v. United States, 273 U. S. 28 (1927). Most of these cases have arisen in recent years in connection with prohibition, which has, from time to time, been a provocative subject of Supreme Court litigation.

See also a recent application of the provision of the Fourth Amendment providing that "no Warrants shall issue, but upon probable cause, supported by Oath or affirmation" in Albrecht v. United States, 273 U. S. 1 (1927).

[7] Hough, *Due Process of Law — Today* (1919) 32 HARV. L. REV. 218.

[8] From sermon by Bishop Hoadley, quoted in GRAY, NATURE AND SOURCES OF THE LAW (2d ed. 1921) 102, 125, 172.

[9] Stafford v. Wallace, 258 U. S. 495 (1922).

[10] Chicago Board of Trade v. Olsen, 262 U. S. 1 (1923). *Cf.* Hill v. Wallace, 259 U. S. 44 (1922).

[11] Pennsylvania v. West Virginia, 262 U. S. 553 (1923).

[12] Dayton-Goose Creek Ry. v. United States, 263 U. S. 456 (1924).

[13] Hammer v. Dagenhart, 247 U. S. 251 (1918). *Cf.* Child Labor Tax Case, 259 U. S. 20 (1922).

[14] Holden v. Hardy, 169 U. S. 366, 389 (1898).

[15] Dred Scott v. Sandford, 19 How. 393, 407 (U. S. 1857). The late Gerard C. Henderson, in his POSITION OF FOREIGN CORPORATIONS IN AMERICAN CONSTITUTIONAL LAW (1918) *passim,* particularly c. 10, and Mr. Warren in his SUPREME COURT IN UNITED STATES HISTORY (1922) cc. 22 and 24, have helped to bring into perspective the constructive labors of Taney. But Taney in relation to his time still awaits an adequate history.

[16] Proprietors of The Charles River Bridge v. Proprietors of The Warren Bridge, 11 Pet. 420 (U. S. 1837).

[17] Story, to be sure, powerfully influenced American legal development, but his great talents found their best scope in private law. See Pound, *The Place of Judge Story in the Making of American Law* (1914) 7 PROC. CAMB. HIST. SOC. 33, (1914) 48 AM. L. REV. 676, the remarks in HOLMES, COLLECTED LEGAL PAPERS (1920) 35, 41, and the comments on Story by that shrewd judge of men, John C. Gray, in his NATURE AND SOURCES OF THE LAW (2d ed. 1921) 129, 253.

[18] 94 U. S. 113 (1876).

[19] See Pound, *Liberty of Contract* (1909) 18 YALE L. J. 454, 470.

[20] See, *e. g.*, The Employers' Liability Cases, 207 U. S. 463, 504 (1908) (dissent); Twining v. New Jersey, 211 U. S. 78 (1908); Knoxville v. Knoxville Water Co., 212 U. S. 1 (1909).

[21] See the very significant observations of Chief Justice Taft, in his response to the resolutions of the Bar in commemoration of Chief Justice White: "The Interstate Commerce Commission was authorized to exercise powers the conferring of which by Congress would have been, perhaps, thought in the earlier years of the Republic to violate the rule that no legislative power can be delegated. But the inevitable progress and exigencies of government and the utter inability of Congress to give the time and attention indispensable to the exercise of those powers in detail forced the modification of the rule. Similar necessity caused Congress to create other bodies with analogous relations to the existing legislative, executive, and judicial machinery of the Federal Government, and these in due course came under the examination of this court. Here was a new field of administrative law which needed a knowledge of government and an experienced understanding of our institutions safely to define and declare. The pioneer work of Chief Justice White in this field entitles him to the gratitude of his countrymen." 257 U. S. xxv-vi (1922).

[22] ". . . Roosevelt was the first President of the United States who openly proposed to use the powers of political government for the purpose of affecting the distribution of wealth in the interest of the golden mean." 2 BEARD, RISE OF AMERICAN CIVILIZATION (1927) 596. And see 2 MORISON, THE OXFORD HISTORY OF THE UNITED STATES (1927) c. LXII.

[23] HOLMES, COLLECTED LEGAL PAPERS (1920) 292.

It is noteworthy that Presidents so unlike as Lincoln and Roosevelt should have deemed relevant the views on pressing public issues of prospective members of the Supreme Court. See Lincoln's comments on Chase's "soundness on the general issues of the war," 9 NICOLAY AND HAY, ABRAHAM LINCOLN (1917) 394, and Roosevelt's inquiry through Senator Lodge whether "Judge Holmes was in entire sympathy with our views." 1 SELECTIONS FROM THE CORRESPONDENCE OF THEODORE ROOSEVELT AND HENRY CABOT LODGE (1925) 517. Chase's opinion declaring the Legal Tender Acts unconstitutional (Hepburn v. Griswold, 8 Wall. 603 (U. S. 1870) and Mr. Justice Holmes' dissent in Northern Securities Co. v. United States, 193 U. S. 197, 400 (1904), are fine instances of judicial independence.

[24] See, *e. g.*, Commonwealth v. Perry, 155 Mass. 117, 123, 28 N. E. 1126, 1127 (1891) (dissent); Opinions of the Justices, 155 Mass. 598, 607, 30 N. E. 1142, 1146 (1892) (dissent); Opinions of the Justices, 160 Mass. 586, 593; 36 N. E. 488, 491 (1894) (dissent); Vegelahn v. Guhtner, 167 Mass. 92, 104, 44 N. E. 1077, 1079 (1896) (dissent).

[25] Only 61 cases are recorded prior to Marshall's time and of these not a few are decisions on minor motions. How little constitutional law was formulated prior to 1801 is illustrated by the fact that the leading case books on constitutional law, Hall's, Thayer's, and Wambaugh's, contain less than half a dozen decided before that period.

[26] Mr. Justice Holmes has shared in the decisions recorded in eighty-nine volumes of the United States Reports (from 187 U. S. to 275 U. S.). In recent times the amount of litigation has been much heavier than in the earlier days, and the last eighty-nine volumes of the Court's opinions register much more than a third of the total volume of the Court's litigation throughout its history.

[27] . . . Of these opinions, Mr. Justice Holmes himself, doubtless, would say what he said of his work on the Massachusetts Court:

"I look into my book in which I keep a docket of the decisions of the full court which fall to me to write, and find about a thousand cases. A thousand cases, many of them upon trifling or transitory matters, to represent nearly half a lifetime. A thousand cases, when one would have liked to study to the bottom and to say his say on every question which the law ever has presented, and then to go on and invent new problems which should be the test of doctrine, and then to generalize it all and write it in continuous, logical, philosophic exposition, setting forth the whole corpus with its roots in history and its justifications of experience real or supposed!

"Alas, gentlemen, that is life. I often imagine Shakespeare or Napoleon summing himself up and thinking: "Yes, I have written five thousand lines of solid gold and a good deal of padding — I, who have covered the milky way with words that outshone the stars!' 'Yes, I beat the Austrians in Italy and elsewhere: I made a few brilliant campaigns, and I ended in middle life in a *cul-de-sac* — I, who had dreamed of a world monarchy and Asiatic power.' We cannot live our dreams. We are lucky enough if we can give a sample of our best, and if in our hearts we can feel that it has been nobly done." *Speech at a dinner given to Chief Justice Holmes by the Bar Association of Boston on March* 7, 1900, HOLMES, COLLECTED LEGAL PAPERS (1920) 245-46.

[28] McCulloch v. Maryland, 4 Wheat. 316, 407 (U. S. 1819).

[29] Lochner v. New York, 198 U. S. 45, 76 (1905).

[30] HOLMES, COLLECTED LEGAL PAPERS (1920) 211.

[31] Gompers v. United States, 233 U. S. 604, 610 (1914).

[32] Missouri v. Holland, 252 U. S. 416, 433 (1920).

[33] "Under the guise of interpreting the Constitution we must take care that we do not import into the discussion our own personal views of what would be wise, just and fitting rules of government to be adopted by a free people and confound them with constitutional limitations." Moody, J., dissenting in Twining v. New Jersey, 211 U. S. 78, 106-07 (1908).

The familiar and unconscious play an enormous role in the exercise of the judicial process, particularly where it closely touches contemporary economic and social problems. The difficulty has been penetratingly put by Lord Justice Scrutton, one of the powerful and conservative present-day English judges:

"The habits you are trained in, the people with whom you mix, lead to your having a certain class of ideas of such a nature that, when you have to deal with other ideas, you do not give as sound and accurate a judgment as you would wish. This is one of the great difficulties at present with Labour. Labour says: 'Where are your impartial Judges? They all move in the same circle as the employers, and they are all educated and nursed in the same ideas as the employers. How can a labour man or a trade unionist get impartial justice?" It is very difficult sometimes to be sure that you have put yourself into a thoroughly impartial position between two disputants, one of your own class and one not of your class." Scrutton, *The Work of the Commercial Courts* (1921) 1 CAMB. L. J. 6, 8. This psychological factor is, of course, of infinitely greater significance where a court possesses the powers of our Supreme Court.

[34] HOLMES, COLLECTED LEGAL PAPERS (1920) 295. Compare the recent observations of Professor Whitehead:

"It is the first step in sociological wisdom, to recognize that the major advances in civilization are processes which all but wreck the societies in which they occur: — like unto an arrow in the hand of a child. The art of free society consists first in the maintenance of the symbolic code; and secondly in fearlessness of revision, to secure that the code serves those purposes which satisfy an enlightened reason. Those societies which cannot combine reverence to their symbols with freedom of revision, must ultimately decay either from anarchy, or from the slow atrophy of a life stifled by useless shadows." WHITEHEAD, SYMBOLISM (1927) 88.

[35] Otis v. Parker, 187 U. S. 606, 608-09 (1903).

[36] "I do not think we need trouble ourselves with the thought that my view depends upon differences of degree. The whole law does so as soon as it is civilized. See *Nash* v. *United States,* 229 U. S. 373, 376, 377. Negligence is all degree—that of the defendant here degree of the nicest sort; and between the variations according to distance that I suppose to exist and the simple universality of the rules in the Twelve Tables or the Leges Barbarorum, there lies the culture of two thousand years." LeRoy Fibre Co. v. St. Paul Ry., 232 U. S. 340, 354 (1914).

[37] Hudson County Water Co. v. McCarter, 209 U. S. 349, 355-56 (1908).

[38] Missouri, Kansas & Texas Ry. v. May, 194 U. S. 267, 270 (1904).

[39] Schlesinger v. Wisconsin, 270 U. S. 230, 241 (1926) (dissent).

[40] Missouri v. Holland, 252 U. S. 416, 432, 433, 434, 435 (1920).

[41] HOLMES, COLLECTED LEGAL PAPERS (1920) 295-96.

[42] Swift v. United States, 196 U. S. 375, 398 (1905).

[43] Adair v. United States, 208 U. S. 161, 191-92 (1908) (dissent).

[44] Hammer v. Dagenhart, 247 U. S. 251, 277, 278, 280, 281 (1918) (dissent).

[45] Abrams v. United States, 250 U. S. 616, 627-28, 629-31 (1919) (dissent). For a discussion of Mr. Justice Holmes' interpretation of the freedom of speech guaranteed by the Constitution, see CHAFEE, FREEDOM OF SPEECH (1920) c. 2, and the comments upon the Abrams case by Sir Frederick Pollock, in (1920) 36 L. Q. REV. 334. See also Gitlow v. New York, 268 U. S. 652, 672 (1925) (dissent).

[46] Diamond Glue Co. v. United States Glue Co., 187 U. S. 611, 616 (1903).

[47] Pennsylvania v. West Virginia, 262 U. S. 553, 602-03 (1923) (Dissent).

[48] 16 Wall. 36 (U. S. 1873).

Mr. Justice Holmes had recent occasion to apply the Fourteenth Amendment on behalf of the blacks for whom it was primarily intended. "We find it unnecessary to consider the Fifteenth Amendment, because it seems to us hard to imagine a more direct and obvious infringement of the Fourteenth. That Amendment, while it applies to all, was passed, as we know, with a special intent to protect the blacks from discrimination against them. . . . The statute of Texas in the teeth of the prohibitions referred to assumes to forbid negroes to take part in a primary election the importance of which we have indicated, discriminating against them by the distinction of color alone. States may do a good deal of classifying that it is difficult to believe rational, but there are limits, and it is too clear for extended argument that color cannot be made the basis of a statutory classification affecting the right set up in this case." Nixon v. Herndon, 273 U. S. 536, 540-41 (1927).

49 Pound, *supra* note 19, at 470.

50 The broad language of Mr. Justice Peckham in Allgeyer v. Louisiana, 165 U. S. 578, 589 (1897), which led to the decision in Locher v. New York, 198 U. S. 45 (1905), is directly traceable to the dissenting opinions of Mr. Justice Field in the Slaughter-House Cases, 16 Wall. 36, 83 (U. S. 1873), and Munn v. Illinois, 94 U. S. 113, 136 (1876). As a judge of the New York Court of Appeals, Mr. Justice Peckham had already expressed the dissenting views of Mr. Justice Field in the Munn case as his own views. People v. Budd, 117 N. Y. 1, 34, 43, 22 N. E. 670, 680, 684 (1889).

51 94 U. S. 113, 134 (1876).

52 198 U. S. 45 (1905).

53 Adkins v. Children's Hospital, 261 U. S. 525, 568 (1923) (dissent).

The psychologic forces that were rationalized into legal doctrines were explained by Mr. Justice Holmes thirty years ago: "When socialism first began to be talked about, the comfortable classes of the community were a good deal frightened. I suspect that this fear has influenced judicial action both here and in England, yet it is certain that it is not a conscious factor in the decisions to which I refer. I think that something similar has led people who no longer hope to control the legislatures to look to the courts as expounders of the Constitutions, and that in some courts new principles have been discovered outside the bodies of those instruments, which may be generalized into acceptance of the economic doctrines which prevailed about fifty years ago, and a wholesale prohibition of what a tribunal of lawyers does not think about right. I cannot but believe that if the training of lawyers led them habitually to consider more definitely and explicitly the social advantage on which the rule they lay down must be justified, they sometimes would hesitate where now they are confident, and see that really they were taking sides upon debatable and often burning questions." Holmes, *The Path of the Law* (1897) (10 HARV. L. REV. 457, 467-68, COLLECTED LEGAL PAPERS (1920) 167, 184.

54 Hough, *supra* note 7, at 232.

55 208 U. S. 412 (1908).

56 243 U. S. 426 (1917).

57 261 U. S. 525 (1923).

58 264 U. S. 504 (1924).

59 273 U. S. 418 (1927).

60 Lochner v. New York, 198 U. S. 45, 75-76 (1905).

61 Blinn v. Nelson, 222 U. S. 1, 7 (1911).

62 Noble State Bank v. Haskell, 219 U. S. 104, 110 (1911).

63 Otis Co. v. Ludlow Co., 201 U. S. 140, 154 (1906).

64 Patsone v. Pennsylvania, 232 U. S. 138, 144-45 (1914).

65 Interstate Ry. v. Massachusetts, 207 U. S. 79, 87 (1907).

66 Truax v. Corrigan, 257 U. S. 312, 344 (1921) (dissent).

67 Quong Wing v. Kirkendall, 223 U. S. 59, 63 (1912).

68 Coppage v. Kansas, 236 U. S. 1, 26-27 (1915).

69 Central Lumber Co. v. South Dakota, 226 U. S. 157, 160, 161 (1912).

70 Louisville & Nashville R. R. v. Barber Asphalt Co., 197 U. S. 430, 433-34 (1905).

71 Ft. Smith Lumber Co. v. Arkansas, 251 U. S. 532, 533-34 (1920).

72 Cedar Rapids Gas Co. v. Cedar Rapids, 223 U. S. 655, 669-70 (1912).

73 Louisville v. Cumberland Tel. & Tel. Co., 225 U. S. 430, 436 (1912).

74 Hudson County Water Co. v. McCarter, 209 U. S. 349, 356-57 (1908).

75 Mt. Vernon Cotton Co. v. Alabama Power Co., 240 U. S. 30, 32 (1916).

76 Erie R. R. v. Pub. Util. Comm'rs, 254 U. S. 394, 410, 411 (1921).

77 Frost v. R. R. Comm., 271 U. S. 583, 600, 601 (1926) (dissent).

78 Galveston, etc. Ry. v. Texas, 210 U. S. 217, 225 (1908).

79 "The line cannot be drawn by generalities, but successive points in it must be fixed by weighing the particular facts. Extreme cases on the one side and on the other are *Edgar A. Levy Leasing Co.* v. *Siegel,* 258 U. S. 242, and *Pennsylvania Coal Co.* v. *Mahon,* 260 U. S. 393." Frost v. R. R. Comm., 271 U. S. 583, 601 (1926) (dissent). In the Levy case, drastic inroads upon the rights of landlords under existing leases were sustained under the "police power," as a means of relieving post-war housing shortage in New York. In the Mahon case the Supreme Court, through Mr. Justice Holmes, decided that restrictions upon the right to mine coal, even though in the interest of safety, upon land granted by deeds which conveyed that right could not be made without providing compensation. The nature of the issues involved in drawing the line in these cases is strikingly illustrated by comparing the opinion of Mr. Justice Holmes in the Mahon case with the dissent of Mr. Justice Brandeis in the same case.

80 Frost v. R. R. Comm., 271 U. S. 583, 601 (1926) (dissent).

81 Truax v. Corrigan, 257 U. S. 312, 342, 343 (1921) (dissent).

82 Weaver v. Palmer Bros. Co., 270 U. S. 402, 415-16 (1926).

83 Buck v. Bell, 274 U. S. 200, 207, 208 (1927).

84 See HOLMES, COLLECTED LEGAL PAPERS (1920) 279 *et seq.*, 293-94. Compare, *e. g.*, his decision in Central Lumber Co. v. South Dakota, 226 U. S. 157 (1912), sustaining the regulation of competition, with his economic views expressed in Dr. Miles Medical Co. v. Park & Sons Co., 220 U. S. 373, 409, 411, 412 (1911) (dissent).

A striking illustration of Mr. Justice Holmes' deference to legislation with which he has no sympathy appears in his dissent in Bartels v. Iowa, 262 U. S. 404, 412 (1923). "It is with hesitation and unwillingness that I differ from my brethren with regard to a law like this but I cannot bring my mind to believe that in some circumstances, and circumstances existing it is said in Nebraska, the statute might not be regarded as a reasonable or even necessary method of reaching the desired result. The part of the act with which we are concerned deals with the teaching of young children. Youth is the time when familiarity with a language is established and if there are sections in the State where a child would hear only Polish or French or German spoken at home I am not prepared to say that it is unreasonable to provide that in his early years he shall hear and speak only English at school. But if it is reasonable it is not an undue restriction of the liberty either of teacher or scholar. . . . I think I appreciate the objection to the law but it appears to me to present a question upon which men reasonably might differ and therefore I am unable to say that the Constitution of the United States prevents the experiment being tried."

[85] McFarland v. Am. Sugar Co., 241 U. S. 79, 86 (1916).

[86] Clallan County v. United States, 263 U. S. 341, 344-45 (1923).

[87] Wallace v. Hines, 253 U. S. 66, 69 (1920).

[88] Tyson v. Banton, 273 U. S. 418, 445-47 (1927) (dissent).

[89] Am. Bank & Trust Co. v. Federal Bank, 256 U. S. 350, 358 (1921).

[90] Truax v. Corrigan, 257 U. S. 312, 342-43 (1921) (dissent).

[91] McDonald v. Mabee, 243 U. S. 90, 91 (1917).

[92] Disconto-Gessellschaft v. U. S. Steel Co., 267 U. S. 22, 28 (1925).

[93] Carino v. Insular Government, 212 U. S. 449, 457-59 (1909).

[94] Southern Pac. Co. v. Jensen, 244 U. S. 205, 222 (1917) (dissent).

[95] Knickerbocker Ice Co. v. Stuart, 253 U. S. 149, 167 (1920) (dissent).

[96] ". . . in the law we only occasionally can reach an absolutely final and quantitative determination, because the worth of the competing social ends which respectively solicit a judgment for the plaintiff or the defendant cannot be reduced to number and accurately fixed. The worth, that is, the intensity of the competing desires, varies with the varying ideals of the time, and, if the desires were constant, we could not get beyond a relative decision that one was greater and one was less. But it is of the essence of improvement that we should be as accurate as we can." Holmes, *Law in Science and Science in Law* (1899) 12 HARV. L. REV. 443, 456; COLLECTED LEGAL PAPERS (1920) 210, 231.

[97] Brown v. United States, 256 U. S. 335, 343 (1921). See also Holmes, *Law in Science and Science in Law* (1899) 12 HARV. L. REV. 443, *et seq.*, COLLECTED LEGAL PAPERS (1920) 210 *et seq.*

98 New York Trust Co. v. Eisner, 256 U. S. 345, 349 (1921).

99 Holmes, *The Path of the Law* (1897) 10 HARV. L. REV. 457, 468-69; COLLECTED LEGAL PAPERS (1920) 167, 185-86.

A fine illustration of his critical rigor is furnished by Mr. Justice Holmes' dissent in the litigation which settled the historic controversy between the President and the Senate in regard to the President's power of removal. In two paragraphs he gives the pith of arguments which, with the details of elaborate research, are set forth in 190 pages of opinions by the majority and the minority:

"The arguments [for the President's power of removal] drawn from the executive power of the President, and from his duty to appoint officers of the United States (when Congress does not vest the appointment elsewhere), to take care that the laws be faithfully executed, and to commission all officers of the United States, seem to me spider's webs inadequate to control the dominant facts.

"We have to deal with an office that owes its existence to Congress and that Congress may abolish tomorrow. Its duration and the pay attached to it while it lasts depend on Congress alone. Congress alone confers on the President the power to appoint to it and at any time may transfer the power to other hands. With such power over its own creation, I have no more trouble in believing that Congress has power to prescribe a term of life for it free from any interference than I have in accepting the undoubted power of Congress to decree its end. I have equally little trouble in accepting its power to prolong the tenure of an incumbent until Congress or the Senate shall have assented to his removal. The duty of the President to see that the laws be executed is a duty that does not go beyond the laws or require him to achieve more than Congress sees fit to leave within his power." Myers v. United States, 272 U. S. 52, 177 (1926) (dissent).

100 "In a court not subject to sudden change, able and continued dissent delimits and accentuates decision; it reveals far more than does the majority opinion the intellectual differences of the council table; and the present status of police power is to me more clearly revealed by the dissents of Justice Holmes than by the syllabi of digests." Hough, *supra* note 7, at 231. The extent to which dissents in course of time establish themselves as doctrines of the Court is illustrated in Terral v. Burke Constr. Co., 257 U. S. 529 (1922), and Sonneborn Bros. v. Cureton, 262 U. S. 506 (1923).

"*Stare decisis* is ordinarily a wise rule of action. But it is not a universal, inexorable command. The instances in which the Court has disregarded its admonition are many. The existing admiralty jurisdiction rests, in large part, upon like action of the Court in *The Genesee Chief*, 12 How. 443, 456. In that case the Court overruled *The Thomas Jefferson*, 10 Wheat. 428, and *The Steamboat Orleans* v. *Phoebus*, 11 Pet. 175; and a doctrine declared by Mr. Justice Story with the concurrence of Chief Justice Marshall, and approved by Chancellor Kent, was abandoned when found to be erroneous, although it had been acted on for twenty-six years." Brandeis, J., dissenting in Washington v. Dawson & Co., 264 U. S. 219, 228, 238-39 (1924). See also Mr. Justice Brandeis' dissent in Jaybird Mining Co. v. Weir, 271 U. S. 609, 615, 619-20 (1926), and cases therein cited.

[101] Santayana, *German Philosophy and Politics* (1915) 12 J. OF PHIL., PSYCHOL., ETC., 645, 649.

[102] See the Lincoln Day, 1898, address of Mr. Justice Brewer, *Government by Injunction* (1898) 15 NAT. CORP. REP. 849: "It is a mistake to suppose that the Supreme Court is either honored or helped by being spoken of as beyond criticism. On the contrary, the life and character of its justices should be the objects of constant watchfulness by all, and its judgments subject to the freest criticism. The time is past in the history of the world when any living man or body of men can be set on a pedestal and decorated with a halo. True, many criticisms may be, like their authors, devoid of good taste, but better all sorts of criticism than no criticism at all. The moving waters are full of life and health; only in the still waters is stagnation and death."

PART V.

MR. JUSTICE HOLMES EVALUATED

THE SECRET OF MR. JUSTICE HOLMES: AN ANALYSIS

By Harold R. McKinnon

Characteristic of the American democratic tradition is the right to evaluate and criticize the thoughts of others, no matter how important they may be. Despite the venerable esteem in which Justice Holmes is held in American society today, he too has not escaped criticism. Current attacks on his philosophy have branded him as totalitarian, sceptical and unconcerned with the influence of morality on law. These attacks have been met by many defenders of Justice Holmes.

The following two articles represent both schools of thought. The article by Harold R. McKinnon, of the California bar, is reprinted from the *American Bar Association Journal,* vol. 36, pp. 261-264, 342-346 (April 1950). The article by Judge Charles E. Wyzanski, Jr., is reprinted from the *Vanderbilt Law Review,* vol. 7, pp. 311-324 (April 1954).

Other articles that can be read with profit on this controversy are: H. B. Davis, End of the Holmes Tradition. *University of Kansas City Law Review,* vol. 19, pp. 53-65 (Dec. 1950-Feb. 1951); W. Mendelson, Mr. Justice Holmes — humility, skepticism and democracy. *Minnesota Law Review,* vo. 36, pp. 343-363 (March 1952); B. V. Palmer, Totalitarianism of Mr. Justice Holmes. *American Bar Association Journal,* vol. 37, pp. 809-811 (Nov. 1951); F. Rodell, Justice Holmes and his hecklers. *Yale Law Journal,* vol. 60, pp. 620-624 (April 1951); B. Palmer, Hobbes, Holmes & Hitler. *American Bar Association Journal,* vol. 31, pp. 569-573 (November 1945); L. B. Boudin, Justice Holmes and his world. *Lawyers Guild Review,* vol. 3, pp. 24-41 (July-August 1943); J. C. Ford, the fundamental of Holmes' juristic philosophy. *Fordham Law Review,* vol. 11, pp. 255-278 (November 1942); C. W. Briggs, Justice Holmes was not a ladder to Hitler. *American Bar Association Journal,* vol. 32, pp. 631-634 (October 1946); F. F. Lucey, Holmes — Liberal — humanitarian — believer in democracy. *Georgetown Law Journal,* vol. 39, pp. 523-562 (May 1951); M. DeW. Howe, The positivism of Mr. Justice

Holmes. *Harvard Law Review,* vol. 64, pp. 529-546 1951); Hart, Holmes' Positivism — An addendum. *Harvard Law Review,* vol. 64, pp. 929-937 (1951); Howe, Holmes' Positivism — A brief rejoinder. *Harvard Law Review,* vol. 64, pp. 937-939 (1951); E. Cahn, Jurisprudence. *Annual Survey of American Law* 1951, pp. 861-864.

Two things about Justice Oliver Wendell Holmes need reconciliation. He had a very bad philosophy. Yet he ranks among the greatest men of our time.

His philosophy was agnostic, materialistic, hopeless of the attainment of any ultimate truth, meaning or standard of value. As a result, it is fundamentally indistinguishable from the amoral realism of those regimes of force and power that are the scandal of the century.

Nevertheless his rank is preëminent. Devotion to him has become a cult. Max Lerner, for example, says of him that "during the last quarter-century of his life he emerged as easily the most important legal philosopher of America," and that he is "perhaps the most complete personality in the history of American thought." Judge Jerome Frank commends him for having put away "childish longings for a father-controlled world," and says that in consequence "whatever clear vision of legal realities we have attained in this country in the past twenty-five years is in large measure due to him". Mr. Justice Frankfurter says that he is Plato's "philosopher become king," and that, "He, above all others, has given the directions of contemporary jurisprudence." Mr. Justice Frankfurter further says, "He has built himself into the structure of our national life. He has written himself into the slender volume of the literature of all times." The late Justice Benjamin N. Cardozo regarded Holmes in similar fashion, for he called him "the great overlord of the law and its philosophy," and said that, "He is today for all students of the law and for all students of human society the philosopher and the seer, the greatest of our age in the domain of jurisprudence, and one of the greatest of the ages."

Admiration of him is not limited to legal circles. His Olympian quality has made him the hero of a successful play and biography; his letters are read and quoted throughout the country; and his very name has become a symbol of what is implicitly felt to be something characteristic of American life.

To the critic, therefore, Mr. Justice Holmes is a riddle for solution: a thinker who in his cosmic appraisals rejected what are the very foundations of our society but who is nevertheless honored as few other men of his time.

What is the secret of the riddle?

HOLMES' PHILOSOPHY WAS NOT CONSISTENT

Holmes was not a systematic philosopher. He scanned the universe and he looked for what is ultimate, and in that sense he philosophized. But he made no effort to place conclusions in rational and systematic order. He made intellectual thrusts here and there, like the essayist or poet; but there was no overall pattern in his thinking. The results are an incompleteness and inconsistency that make it difficult to describe his convictions with accuracy. A mental attitude is clearly discernible, however. It is the attitude of positive science utilized as the only valid method of knowledge. In other words, it is antimetaphysical, skeptical and disdainful of any constants or universals beneath the flux of change.

His concept of man is an instance in point. When thinking coldly, he said, he saw "no reason for attributing to man a significance different in kind from that which belongs to a baboon or to a grain of sand." Such a creature, of course, could not be the subject of moral rights or obligations. Thus Holmes said, "Our morality seems to me only a check on the ultimate domination of force, just as our politeness is a check on the impulse of every pig to put his feet in the trough." At another time he called ethics "a body of imperfect social generalizations expressed in terms of emotion." Therefore Holmes says, "I don't believe that it is an absolute principle or even a human ultimate that man always is an end in himself—that his dignity must be respected, etc. We march up a conscript with bayonets behind to die for a cause he doesn't believe in. And I feel no scruples about it."

HUMAN RIGHTS ARE PRODUCTS OF LAW

From this it follows that man has no rights that are antecedent to the authority of the state. Human rights are inventions to account for the legal rules imposed upon us by society. That is, society decrees that we do certain things and abstain from certain things if we would remain free. Believing this, Holmes said, "I not only accept the rules but come in time to accept them with sympathy and emotional affirmation and begin to talk about duties and rights." But a "right" itself is an "empty substratum" by which we pretend to account for the fact of legal coercion. It is "only the hypostasis of a prohphecy—the imagination of a substance supporting the fact that the public force will be brought to bear upon those who do things said to contravene it." Holmes conceded that a man will fight for his rights, but, he said, "that does not seem to me the same thing as the supposed *a priori* discernment of a duty or the assertion of a pre-existing right. A dog will fight for his bone." Commenting upon this, Mr. Lerner says, "We have here the behavioristic definition of law, squeezing it dry of all morality and sentiment. . . ." And in describing Holmes' doctrine on rights, Professor Harold Laski says, "Man may be an end to himself; to society, he is but a means likely enough to be used for purposes he may passionately deny."

ULTIMATE REALITY IS FORCE

In such a regime, the ultimate reality is force. Thus Holmes said, "I believe that force, mitigated so far as may be by good manners, is the *ultima ratio*, and between two groups that want to make inconsistent kinds of world I see no remedy except force."

This leaves no room for moral judgment or indignation, and human contests are like dog fights. Consistently, therefore, Holmes said (of World War I), "When the Germans in the late war disregarded what we called the rules of the game, I don't see there was anything to be said except: we don't like it and shall kill you if we can."

In Holmes' philosophy, truth fares no better than morals. First, it is the child of force. Thus he said, "Truth is the majority vote of that nation that can lick all the others." Next, it is essentially subjective and identifiable with the transient opinion of the crowd. Therefore he said that "the best test of truth is the power of the thought to get itself accepted in the competition of the market." Finally, since our convictions have no objective basis, we must accord the convictions of our opponents the same credit as our own. Accordingly, to Holmes both sides were right in the Civil War; and speaking about the fight for the kind of world we believe in, he said, "Deep-seated preferences can not be argued about—you can not argue a man into liking a glass of beer—and therefore, when differences are sufficiently far reaching, we try to kill the other man rather than let him have his way. But that is perfectly consistent with admitting that, so far as appears, his grounds are just as good as ours." So with the secrets of philosophy; for he said that if a man should ask him whether there was any use trying to unravel the history of civilization that is woven in the tissue of our jurisprudence, or trying to do any great work, either of speculation or of practical affairs, he would have to say, "I cannot answer him; or at least my answer is as little worth making for any effect it will have upon his wishes as if he asked why should I eat this, or drink that. You must begin by wanting to."

Negations such as these are suggestive of a thorough-going skepticism. And it was true of Holmes. ". . . we begin," he said, "with an act of faith, with deciding that we are not God, for if we were dreaming the universe we should be God so far as we knew." Moreover, "You never can prove that you are awake. By an act of faith I assume that you exist in the same sense that I do and by the same act assume that I am in the universe and not it in me." There were some things which he held, and which he called "can't helps," but these were but his own preferences, because he said, "I regard myself as a cosmic ganglion—a part of an unimaginable and don't venture to assume that my *can't helps* which I call reason and truth are cosmic *can't helps.*" "To have doubted one's own first principles," he said, "is the mark of a civilized man."

HOLMES' PHILOSOPHY MADE HIM AGNOSTIC

With such tenets, it scarcely needs saying that Holmes lacked religious faith. His approach to religion was rationalist, with a deep bias against affirmation. As the dramatist Emmet Lavery puts it in the play, *The Magnificent Yankee,* Holmes shouted "Not proved," at the universe, and the universe echoed "not proved." A clue to his antireligious attitude is to be found in his criticism of William James. Holmes said he suspected James' philosophy was a wishful construction and "that the aim and end of the whole business is religious." And on James' death, Holmes wrote of him, "His reason made him skeptical and his wishes led him to turn down the lights so as to give miracle a chance."

A touching instance of his lack of faith is reënacted in the play *The Magnificent Yankee.* After half a century of marriage, Holmes' wife is approaching death. She shrinks from the idea of eternal separation from her husband, but his frequently expressed agnosticism has disqualified him from comforting her now. Justice Brandeis calls and Holmes leaves the two alone. But the substitute comforter is no better than his colleague. Mrs. Holmes asks him for some assurance of survival, to which Brandeis replies that, "the memory of virtue is immortal." "But," replies the invalid, "the memory of virtue isn't enough." Brandeis acknowledges defeat in a dumb silence, and Holmes reappears, substituting an artificial gaiety for the missing faith.

In respect of religion, the late Morris R. Cohen said that Holmes remained essentially an agnostic; but he added that instead of a personal God, Holmes substituted the "unimaginable whole of realty, which served equally well to teach the great lesson of humility." Apart from the incongruity of applying the term "humility" to the state of being crushed by an overwhelming universe bereft of personality, the portrait is correct. Holmes felt resigned to fate, not called to surpass it.

The climax of Holmes' agnosticism is revealed in a letter written by him near the end of his life to a Chinese law student, J. C. H. Wu, in which Holmes said, caricaturing the words of Simeon when the infant Jesus was presented to him in the temple, "I bow my head, I think serenely, and say as I told some one the other day, O Cosmos—Now lettest thou thy ganglion dissolve in peace."

HOLMES' PHILOSOPHY EXALTED COURAGE

The question then remains, what is life worth? For lack of convictions, for lack of truth, for lack of morals, and of faith, what supplies the meaning of life, what gives a motive for going on?

In his answer to this question, Holmes touches the nethermost depth of unreality and inconsistency. In general, his doctrine proposes an iron cage of action for the sake of action, with a romantic exaltation of courage in the pursuit of unknown goals combined with a hedonist enjoyment of such creature comforts as chance affords. In a speech before the Bar Association of Boston, he declared himself "The joy of life is to put out one's power in some natural and useful or harmless way. There is no other. . . . With all humility, I think 'Whatsoever they hand findeth to do, do it with thy might' infinitely more important than the vain attempt to love one's neighbor as one's self. . . . Life is action, the use of ones' powers. As to use them to their height is our joy and duty, so it is the one end that justifies itself. . . . When it is said that we are too much occupied with the means of living to life, I answer that the chief worth of civilization is just that it makes the means of living more complex; that it calls for great and combined intellectual efforts, instead of simple, uncoordinated ones, in order that the crowd may be fed and clothed and housed and moved from place to place. Because more complex and intense intellectual efforts mean a fuller and richer life. They mean more life. Life is an end in itself, and the only question as to whether it is worth living is whether you have enough of it."

This speech drew strong criticism from William James, who said that Holmes seemed "unable to make any other than that one set speech which comes out on every occasion," and he added that to make the joy of life systematic and to oppose it to other duties was to pervert it, "especially when one is a Chief Justice."

The same theme occurs in the conclusion of Holmes' radio speech on his ninetieth birthday. In this speech he made his often quoted reference to the canter of the race horse after it passes the finish line. He then said, "The canter that brings you to a standstill need not be only coming to rest. It cannot be while you still live. For to live is to function. That is all there is in living.

"And so I end with a line from a Latin poet . . . 'Death plucks my ears and says, Live—I am coming'."

"THE STRUGGLE FOR LIFE IS THE ORDER OF THE WORLD"

The "action" theme occurs also in his exaltation of war and the fighting courage of the soldier. He said that moralists and philosophers declare that war is "wicked, foolish and soon to disappear," but that for his own part he believed "that the struggle for life is the order of the world, at which it is vain to repine," that man's destiny is battle, and he has to take the chances of war," and that "The ideals of the past for men have been drawn from war, as those for women have been drawn from motherhood." Regarding the soldier, he said, "I do not know what is true. I do not know the meaning of the universe. But in the midst of doubt, in the collapse of creeds, there is one thing I do not doubt, that no man who lives in the same world with most of us can doubt, and that is that the faith is true and adorable which leads a soldier to throw away his life in obedience to a blindly accepted duty, in a cause which he little understands, in a plan of campaign of which he has no notion, under tactics of which he does not see the use." While war is horrible, he said, its message is "divine," because it leads us to discipline. Some such teacher we need, "that we may realize that our comfortable routine is no eternal necessity of things, but merely a little space of calm in the midst of the tempestuous untamed streaming of the world . . ." And so he says, "Out of heroism grows faith in the worth of heroism. The proof comes later, and even may never come. Therefore I rejoice at every dangerous sport . . . The students at Heidelberg, with their sword-slashed faces, inspire me with sincere respect. I gaze with delight upon our poloplayers. If once in a while in our riding a neck is broken, I regard it, not as a waste, but as a price well paid for the breeding of a race fit for headship and command."

But, as I have said, Holmes was not consistent. In his search for the meaning of life, he could descend, in another mood, from the romantic idealization of the soldier's sacrifice to lower levels of satisfaction. Thus, in a letter to Pollock, he wrote, "I was repining at the thought of my slow progress—how few new ideas I had or picked up—when it occurred to me to think of the total of life and how the greater part was wholly absorbed in living and continuing life—victuals—procreation—rest and eternal terror. And I bid myself accept the common lot; an adequate vitality would say daily: 'God—what a good sleep I've had.'

'My eye, that was dinner.' 'Now for a rattling walk—' in short, realize life as an end in itself. Functioning is all there is—only our keenest pleasure is in what we might call the higher sort. I wonder if cosmically an idea is any more important than the bowels."

LAW IS THE PRODUCT OF IRRESPONSIBLE WILL AND FORCE

If we pass from Holmes' philosophy of life to his idea of law, the portrait changes somewhat. Viewing law from the standpoint of its ultimate foundations, he regarded it as a product of irresponsible will and force,—a conclusion which necessarily followed from the philosophy above indicated. Yet, on occasion he could talk of "substantial justice" and "fair play," and as a judge, when pressed too far, he could place a judicial restraint upon legislation that violated some irreducible minimum of individual right. The difference between the two attitudes appeared to depend mainly on whether he was theorizing about the law in general or whether he was adjudicating a case. In the former instance, his doctrine reflected the raw existentialism of his philosophy of life; in the latter, he reverted to traditional language of antecedent rightfulness and wrongfulness.

In legal theory, his utterances follow the familiar pattern. As shown, Holmes viewed life as a struggle between hostile forces. Since the *ultima ratio* was force, the right side was the side which prevailed in the struggle. The same realism applied to law. He defined law as the prediction of the circumstances in which force will be brought to bear upon men through the courts, "the prophecies of what the courts will do in fact, and nothing more pretentious." "So," he said, "when it comes to the develoument of a *corpus juris* the ultimate question is what do the dominant forces of the community want and do they want it hard enuogh to disregard whatever inhibitions may stand in the way."

In commenting upon this, Professor Harold Laski says that in his recognition of power in the community

Holmes was a Spinoza "proclaiming that might gives to right its letters of credit." Accordingly, Mr. Laski describes Holmes' doctrine by saying, "Rights are not the postulates of a pre-existing framework within which law must work. They are the product of law, maintained as the possession of citizens because that part of the community which has the power to maintain them is prepared to fight to that end. Law, therefore, becomes the expression of the will of the stronger part of society; and the state is the organization of the institutions which give form and coherence to the expression so maintained." In another place, Laski says that Holmes states law "in terms of an irresponsible and unlimited will such as Hobbes himself would have strongly approved." As a result of his philosophy, Holmes was much more concerned, said Laski, "with the ways of attaining ends than with the end themselves."

HOLMES DENIED EXISTENCE OF NATURAL LAW

To Holmes, natural law was a fiction which arose from the fact that certain habits and institutions, such as marriage, property, respect for contractural obligations and some protection of the person, seemed to be necessary elements in any society which from one's point of view would appear to be civilized. But these were not the product of any ethical *Ought*. They were merely rules that prescribed how we must behave if we wished to live in society. "I see no *a priori* duty," he said, "to live with others and in that way, but simply a statement of what I must do if I wish to remain alive." Pollock disapproved of the attack on natural law because it left no ethical background for law.

The legal positivism of Holmes is further illustrated in his doctrine of external standards. In that doctrine he complained of the confusion which resulted from inclusion of the moral element in law. His point was that positive law is not coextensive with morals; that law deals with external pacts rather than with motives; that it means the same thing to the bad man as to the good one; and that it is an actual expression of what the community wants, not a logical deduction from ideal premises. Therefore, said Holmes, "I often doubt whether it would not be a gain if every word of moral significance could be banished from the law altogether, and other words adopted which should convey legal ideas uncolored by anything outside the law. We should lose the fossil records of a good deal of history and the majesty got from ethical associations, but by ridding ourselves of an unnecessary confusion we should gain very much in the clearness of our thought."

Holmes' attempt at clarification is itself tinged with confusion. In the light of his philosophy, his reference to "morals" itself is of questionable meaning. In his philosophy, morals can mean nothing more than what at a given time and place the people think is right (although that, of course, might be the Nazi regime). True, Holmes used the *language* of morals. For example, on the issue of external standards, he defended himself against the imputation of cynicism, saying, "The law is the witness and external deposit of our moral life." But in a universe which is without meaning or *Ought,* in which the ultimate reality is force, and which is populated by beings essentially indistinguishable from baboons or grains of sand, there can be no morals in the real sense of the term. Another point of confusion lies in Holmes' misunderstanding of the relation between morals and law. Over and again he complains of the error of "deducing" laws from moral principles. The life of the law is not logic, he says, it is experience. One may not *deduce* a whole set of positive rules from some ideal absolutes. The answer is, of course not. But the answer is also that it was only the grossest caricature of the natural law which gave rise to such a claim and that a real acquaintance with the doctrine would have demonstrated that a positive law is the *determination* of a particular application of a natural moral principle, not a *deduction* from such a principle. A positive law is a realization of a principle of justice achieved by relating it to the facts and circumstances of a given environment, and it therefore possesses the relativity and changeability that are characteristic of the environment. Pollock attempted to correct Holmes on this issue, but Holmes stood his ground. In view of his gross misconception of the moral order, perhaps it was too much to hope that his concept of the relationship between law and morals could be any better.

On the whole, therefore, Holmes' legal theorizing, while containing some language indicative of an ultra-positive norm, remains essentially "realistic" in the modern connotation that law is fact explainable in terms of popular will.

A DIFFICULT PROBLEM OF INTERPRETATION

If we turn from his lectures, speeches and articles to his judicial statements and judgments, we are confronted with another difficult problem of interpretation. There were two aspects of his judicial thought. According to one aspect, his doctrine was a natural reflection of his amoral legalism and of his romantic concept of life as struggle, even meaningless struggle. It was a judicial *laissez faire*. The propriety of legislation was for the legislature, not for the courts. This was true even though the legislation was "shocking" or "noxious" to him. This of course was consistent with his doctrine of law as will, what the crowd wants. It is also consistent with the Spartan quality in Holmes' disposition. The latter was well described by the late Professor Morris R. Cohen, who described himself as "a grateful and admiring friend" of the Justice. Professor Cohen said that Holmes' liberalism was compromised by his economic backwardness which he got from the classical economists and also by the influence upon him of Malthus and Darwin, and he added, "Indeed, for a thoroughly civilized man, which Holmes was in the best sense of the word, he shows a remarkable absence of sympathy or compassion for the sufferings and frailties of mankind. His morality is thoroughly pagan or Stoic in that respect. His emphasis is on the pagan virtues of courage, temperance and justice, without any reference to the Hebrew-Christian view of God the Father, who is compassionate in His love for all men and sends down the beneficent rain on the just and the unjust alike. He is thus too ready to invoke the penalty of death in his theory of justice, and can think of no better remedy for the abuse of ownership than that the crowd will kill the man guilty of abusing the goods which the multitude needs." In another place, Professor Cohen said that Holmes' *laissez faire* was the product of his "militaristic philosophy" and of his belief "that the important thing is to build a strong race." At all events, Holmes thought little good could be accomplished by tinkering at social reform, especially by law.

ANOTHER ASPECT OF HIS JUDICIAL THINKING

But there was another aspect of his judicial thinking, in accordance with which he tested statutes by their reasonableness and justice, and although he usually upheld them he was not averse to striking them down, as in the case of a statute regulating coal companies (*Pennsylvania Coal Company* v. *Mahon,* 260 U.S. 393). Indeed, he once complained "that the judges themselves have failed adequately to recognize their duty of weighing consideration of social advantage." More than that, he said, "The result of the often proclaimed judicial aversion to deal with such considerations [of social policy] is simply to leave the very ground and foundation of judgments inarticulate, and often unconscious. . . ." The question at once arises, how can this be reconciled with the judicial *laissez faire* so often asserted by him? If law was what the majority wanted, even though shocking or obnoxious, if social policy was for the legislature and not for the courts, what justification was there for a court passing upon social policy or the validity of a statute?

HIS WORK AS JUDGE REPUDIATED SOME OF HIS THEORY

Max Lerner struggles with this question, but without any solution that I can discern. I think the reason is that there was a real inconsistency in Holmes' thought on this subject, and that in his work as a judge he actually repudiated some of the nihilism of his legal theory. His theorizing has been depicted above. Let us now look at his judicial work. The typical situation which he faced was a legislative exercise of police power, sometimes by Congress, usually by a state. His doctrine was that the legislature could do anything which was not expressly prohibited by the Constitution. The usual question was whether the statute under consideration violated the Due Process Clause of the Fifth or the Fourteenth Amendments. It may have been an act regulating wages or hours of labor, or the use of trucks on highways, or the right of parents to choose a school for their children, or some other aspect of our daily life. The question presented to the Court was whether the regulation was a valid exercise of police power or whether it deprived a person of "life, liberty, or property, without due process of law." And this "due process" included substantive as well as procedural rights. As stated by the Supreme Court, it included those "immutable principles of justice which inhere in the very idea of free government" (*Holden* v. *Hardy*, 169 U.S. 366, 389), those "fundamental principles of liberty and justice which lie at the base of all our civil and political institutions" (*Hebert* v. *Louisiana*, 272 U.S. 312, 316), and those immunities "implicit in the concept of ordered liberty" (*Palko* v. *Connecticut*, 302 U.S. 319, 325). In other words, it included the whole gamut of natural justice. It was a far cry from the jungle-toothed realism of "what the crowd wants." It was that very natural law that was rejected by Holmes' philosophy. It was the doctrine that was refused a place in the law as an implied limitation on legislative power, but that reëntered the law in the express garb of due process.

And Holmes accepted it as such. For example, in one of his greatest dissents, he said, "I think that the word liberty in the Fourteenth Amendment is perverted when it is held to prevent the natural outcome of a dominant opinion, *unless it can be said that a rational and fair man necessarily would admit that the statute proposed would infringe fundamental principles as they have been understood by the traditions of our people and our law.*" (*Lochner* v. *New York*, 198 U.S. 45, 76. Italics supplied.) And in another case, as indicated above, he based his decision on "fair play" and "substantial justice." (*McDonald* v. *Mabee*, 243 U.S. 90, 91, 92.) Moreover, he distinguished between claims which deserve protection under these fundamental principles and those which do not. He held that due process was not infringed by a law that forbade the use of any language in the schools but English (*Meyer* v. *Nebraska*, 262 U.S. 390), but he joined without dissent in a decision nullifying a statute that would have required all children to attend the public schools and that would therefore have outlawed parochial schools. (*Pierce* v. *Society of Sisters*, 268 U.S. 510).

NATURAL LAW DOCTRINE PROJECTED IN HIS WORK

The only solution I can make of the difficulty is that in spite of the rejection of the natural law by Holmes in his philosophy, the doctrine projected itself through his work as a judge. And it did that because it is inherent in human reason. Men may *talk* the language of the jungle, but they *act* like human beman beings. Holmes' action was a judicial *can't-help.* He was bound by his judgments as a reasonable man. Thus in a Massachusetts Supreme Court decision he said, "If I assume that . . . speaking as a political economist, I should agree in condemning the law, still I should not be willing or think myself authorized to overturn legislation on that ground, *unless I thought that an honest difference of opinion was impossible, or pretty nearly so.*" (*Commonwealth* v. *Perry,* 155 Mass. 117, 28 N.E. 1126, 1127.) This does not relieve Holmes of inconsistency. Even his ardent apologists do not attempt to relieve him of that. Thus Mr. Lerner says that it would take a bold man to say that the strains of legal realism in Holmes "are not balanced by strains of traditionalism rather than change, of belief rather than skepticism." And Mr. Biddle: "Contradictory? Certainly,]Holmes[would have answered, but so too is life full of contradictions." So, on the issue of a moral basis of law, Holmes was more "practical" than his philosophy, and he had some judicial *can't-helps.* On the bench he applied the *can't-helps* instead of the philosophy, and American law enjoyed an escape from disaster.

WHAT IS THE SECRET OF HOLMES' POPULARITY?

I return to the secret. What is the basis for the lavish popularity of Mr. Justice Holmes?

Perhaps it would be fitting to mention first some personal characteristics. He was a child of fortune: born of a distinguished family; tall, handsome, romantic; and a hero of the Civil War. "His conversation and bearing," says Cohen, "were like rare music that lingers in one's memory." Added to these qualities were his extraordinary health and vigor, which enabled him to remain active on the Court until his ninetieth year and to live until his ninety-fourth.

He was a talented writer. His opinions have a sharp thrust, a sure touch, a mastery, brevity, simplicity, pithiness and axiomaitc phrasing, an avoidance of verbiage and irrelevance, an originality and freshness that are the despair of his imitators, of whom there have been several. The result is that he continues to live in his phrases, which are standard quotations in legal literature: "clear and present danger"; "The common law is not a brooding omnipresence in the sky"; "The life of the law has not been logic; it has been experience."

His extrajudicial writings, too, have survived, at least until now. In general they reflect the underlying nihilism of his thinking upon fundamental subjects and his leaning toward a Darwinian evolutionism in place of a personal destiny. Some of them cloak an essential tawdriness of content with a lyric style. One of these may bear quoting. It is the conclusion of an address to the Harvard Law School Association of New York in 1913. He says,

"If I am right it will be a slow business for our people to reach rational views, assuming that we are allowed to work peaceably to that end. But as I grow older I grow calm. If I feel what are perhaps an old man's apprehensions, that competition from new races will cut depeer than working men's disputes and will test whether we can hang together and can fight; if I fear that we are running through the world's resources at a pace that we cannot keep; I do not lose my hopes. I do not pin my dreams for the future to my country or even to my race. I think it probable that civilization somehow will last as long as I care to look ahead—perhaps with smaller numbers, but perhaps also bred to greatness and splendor by science. I think it not improbable that man, like the grub that prepares a chamber for the winged thing that it never has seen but is to be—that man may have cosmic destinies that he does not understand. And so beyond the vision of battling races and an impoverished earth I catch a dreaming glimpse of peace.

"The other day my dream was pictured to my mind. It was evening. I was walking homeward on Pennsylvania Avenue near the Treasury, and as I looked beyond Sherman's statue to the west the sky was aflame with scarlet and crimson from the setting sun. But, like the note of downfall in Wagner's opera, below the sky line there came from little globes the pallid discord of the electric lights. And I thought to myself the Götterdämmerung will end, and from those globes clustered like evil eggs will come the new masters of the sky. It is like the time in which we live. But then I remembered the faith that I partly have expressed, faith in a universe not measured by our fears, a universe that has thought and more than thought inside of it, and as I gazed, after the sunset and above the electric lights there shone the stars."

In the realm of the common law, Holmes had immense learning. His lectures on that subject, which constitute his only book, are an evidence of his love, as well as of his mastery of it. The only blot on his record as a legal historian is his deprecation of the Roman law, for which Pollock chided him. In common law, however, few have equalled him.

HOLMES' DISSENTS VINDICATED BY TIME

As a Supreme Court judge, his fame rests upon that most popular of all foundations, vindication by time. During his tenure of office, the majority of the Court was engaging in what Roscoe Pound called a "carnival of unconsitutionality." Utilizing the newly discovered due process clause, it nullified statute after statute designed to curb the evils of economic *laissez faire*. Individual rights of property and of contract prevailed over social interests. Furthermore, due process was not limited to persons. It was held to protect corporations as well. The result was that the great majority of decisions involved the interests of corporations rather than of persons. The West was being built. Big investments were made by great corporations. The states began to regulate these companies in the interest of employees and consumers. Represented by the best legal talent, the companies rushed to the courts for protection against measures which threatened their objectives. The Supreme Court substituted its economic and political theories for those of the legislatures and destroyed the legislation. In protection of property, it nullified utility rates fixed by commissions. In protection of liberty of contract and of calling, it invalidated minimum wage laws and a statute which prohibited employment in a bakery more than ten hours a day or sixty hours a week and statutes prohibiting yellow-dog contracts by which a laborer became ineligible for employment by belonging to a union.

Against such decisions, Holmes wrote his famous dissents. As seen, his action was not due to any tenderness for the personal element, but to his doctrine that social policy was for the legislatures, not the courts. In an age that has gone to the other extreme, that has replaced frontier individualism with a cradling security, it is not surprising that Holmes is popular. Regardless of whether he would have liked the paternal legislation—he probably wouldn't—his dissents have triumphed as fixing the boundaries of judicial action, and therefore he is the logical hero of the day. The irony of it is that it was the reactionary spirit of those against whom he contended, rather than any ingrained liberalism of his own, which provided him with the triumph. But current history is a partial and a fickle judge. It acclaims those who provide the doctrine that facilitates its objectives. In that sense, Holmes above all others cleared the path in the federal courts.

HOLMES' PHILOSOPHY IS CONGENIAL TO OUR ERA

But what of his agnosticism and his philosophy of force and violence? What of his approval of law as will rather than reason? What of his dehumanizing man by his scorn of the essence which separates a person from brutes or clods of earth? What of the ignorance of purpose in life and the romantic, Hegelian exaltation of struggle and headship and command? Surely, such a philosophy would cut out from under us the very basis of the freedom and justice that we hold so dear. And surely lawmakers would seek in vain for any criterion of justice in a philosophy such as that. How, then, can a man be a national hero when his ultimate view of things strikes at the very principles on which our society was founded and rivals the thinking of those who would destroy us?

The answer lies in the simple fact that in the high realm of the intellect we have lost our principles. Holmes' agnosticism does not repel. On the contrary, Holmes is an agnostic prophet to an agnostic age. His bottomless relativism fails to create a reaction because in an age that denies the validity of any form of knowledge but the tentative findings of the positive sciences that relativism possesses the glamour of a war cry. This relation of Holmes to his age is well summarized by Max Lerner, who says, "The fact is that Holmes's 'bad man' standard, his rejection of natural law, and his definition of law as what the courts will in fact do, were all congenial to the mood and quality of a pragmatic American in whose practical business life the realm of fact had elbowed out the norms of morality."

The question naturally arises, which of the two will have the greater influence upon American life, Holmes the man and his decisions, or his philosophy? The answer is not difficult. In the long run, Holmes himself is not important. He is gone, and his personal influence, like that of every other man, will vanish. Even his decisions—whether this statute is valid, or that—will ultimately be buried in the stream of legal history. But a philosophy survives. In the final analysis, ideas command, for good or ill. As Holmes himself remarked, the abstractions of Descartes became a ruling force a century after they were made, and Kant rather than Bonaparte governs today.

Therefore the significant thing about Mr. Justice Holmes is not Holmes the genial, Holmes the charming, Holmes the romantic, or even Holmes the great and courageous judge. Those things are the stuff of biography and drama. The significant thing is that Holmes had a very bad philosophy, and moreover that that philosophy is congenial to our time. It is the latter fact—that Holmes' philosophy arouses few repercussions amongst us—that is the truly ominous thing and the end result of this study. For if we had not lost our principles, Holmes' voice would have been a negligible dissidence in our day. As it is, his philosophy is a symbol of our intellectual wretchedness, a conspicuous example of our abandonment of those spiritual, philosophical and moral truths that have been the life of the western tradition, the foundation of our law and the strength of our Republic. I mean the recognition that it *is* a father-controlled world in the sense that infinitely above the strivings of men is the Providence of God; that men are *not* means to society but spiritual beings whose right to happiness conditions the good of society; that the *ultima ratio* is not force but a truth and goodness that are founded in the Creator and are reflected in the nature of man and society; that law is not a product of irresponsible will but a branch of ethics because its whole purpose lies in being an instrument for the common good.

In harmony with the fashion of the day, Holmes said that traditional thought is childish in looking for superlatives. Actually, that was the fault of Holmes himself, who made such extravagant demands of proof that he was left with impoverished convictions. If he had only ceased asking for thunderclaps and been a little quieter and a little humbler he might have found that his famous *can't helps* were not merely the indefeasible offspring of his own mind but the cosmic first principles of human reason.

The crisis of Holmes is the crisis of modern society. If modern society does not solve it better than Holmes, then his dreadful philosophy may, as he himself said of all ideas, "one day mount a throne, and without armies, or even with them . . . shoot across the world the electric despotism of an unresisted power." If, on the other hand, we recapture without delay the perennial insight of the Judaeo-Christian tradition, then the electric despotism which is already a fact may yet be stemmed, and we may resume that march of mind and spirit which is the glory of human history. That, if we would only realize it, would be a happy solution of the secret of Mr. Justice Holmes.

THE DEMOCRACY OF JUSTICE OLIVER WENDELL HOLMES*

By Charles E. Wyzanski, Jr.†

Oliver Wendell Holmes is everywhere recognized as a great American. His life story has been depicted on the stage, fictionalized in a popular biography,[1] and majestically summarized in the *Dictionary of American Biography* by his successor and disciple.[2] Every undergraduate knows of Holmes' wounds in three Civil War battles, his seminal lectures on *The Common Law* delivered at the Lowell Institute, his pioneer decisions in labor cases in the Supreme Judicial Court of Massachusetts and his long and distinguished tenure as Associate Justice of the Supreme Court of the United States. But the recital of his public offices does not disclose Holmes' contribution to the fundamental need of our society. For he was not in title or in fact the commander-in-chief of his own generation. He sought the joy of the thinker "who knows that . . . men who never heard of him will be moving to the measure of his thought—the subtile rapture of a postponed power, which . . . is more real than that which commands an army."[3]

Instead of reviewing here the details of his biography or analyzing the precise contours of the cases he decided, I propose to concentrate on the democratic ideas which Mr. Justice Holmes embodies in three fields—the powers of popular government, the civil liberties of the citizen and the dignity of man. These will be admittedly mere strands plucked from a pattern. I should not want anyone to suppose that I am attempting an essay on the man as a whole. All I seek is to assay certain of his ideas which, though they will be, nay have been, to some extent superseded, seem to me to have eternal relevance to democracy and therefore to be of constant interest to every American.

I come first to Mr. Justice Holmes' views of the powers of popular government. Etymologically this clearly belongs at the forefront of any discussion of democracy. For from the Greek days when the word was coined, democracy has at the least embraced the idea of that form of state in which the people as a whole share public authority.

In the United States "democracy" has sometimes been defined with its original literal significance—the classic example being the triad in Lincoln's Gettysburg Address. Yet during the first century of the history of the United States—the period during which we were most often described as a "republic"—the actual role of the people diverged sharply from that in a Greek democracy.

Our orthodox eighteenth and nineteenth century view of popular government turned for philosophical justification not to Plate or Aristotle but to Locke and Montesquieu, and for practical techniques not to the colonies on the Eastern Aegean founded by Athens but to those on the Western Atlantic founded by England. The essence of the traditional American theory is that democratic government is limited in its methods and its objects, that the division of powers amongst the executive, legislative and judicial branches is the core of Anglo-American liberty, that the federal balance between the nation and the states is the secret of strength without tyranny and of self-government without provincialism, that the people express their wisdom not in determining policies but in choosing representatives and that the maximum goal of the state is to prevent force or fraud from interfering with the self-development of the individual man.

Whether this theory be labeled constitutionalism or the system of checks and balances or representative government or *laissez-faire,* it is the one set forth in most high school courses in civics. It is the picture of American government drawn by as serene and sophisticated observers as the omniscient historian Lord Acton and the knowledgeable ambassador Lord Bryce. More important, it was the view of popular government which nineteenth century Justices of the Supreme Court proclaimed not only from the bench but also from the platform, as the published lectures of Justices Miller, Brewer and Harlan reveal.

How far did Holmes subscribe to this theory?

Before I try to answer the main question I must not avoid a preliminary hurdle. Does a judge in his official capacity ever have a theory of government—or, to put it less in psychological terms and more in philosophical form—should a judge in his official capacity have a theory of government?

No informed observer supposes that a judge is a variety of impersonal calculating machine who merely applies the law. He does not automatically render an answer mechanically derived from learning first the facts from the litigants and second rules of law from books in a library. His judgments are not predictable by lawyers as eclipses are predictable by astronomers. He does not, Mr. Justice Roberts to the contrary notwithstanding,[4] decide a case by laying the text of a statute against the text of the Constitution to see whether it squares. Every constitutional judge to some degree, and self-conscious judges like Holmes to a large degree, applies in his judgments the policies which he believes represent the sober second-thought of the community and are suited to its inarticulate needs. Of course, I have not meant to indicate that a judge is always free to rule according to his discernment of the long-term public interest. The area of his freedom is limited—perhaps the boundaries have never been better described than by Judge Cardozo in *The Nature of the Judicial Process*—but nonetheless, as the multitude of dissents in the Supreme Court have incontrovertibly proved to our citizenry, there are some cases where there is an area of choice and, when he is within it, the judge consciously or unconsciously reveals his theory of government. Even an abstention from decision is a revelation of choice—a choice to entrust power to other hands more competent, more flexible or more responsive to popular will.

Before Holmes came to the Court and during most of his tenure the majority of the Justices were enforcing with full vigor and without abdicating much to the judgment of others what I have called the orthodox theory of American democracy. The majority held that the national government was severely circumscribed in its fields of interest. It had no right without an amendment to the Constitution to lay an income tax on individuals, or to prevent the shipment in interstate commerce of child-made goods, or to control monopolistic practices in manufacturing industries. The majority also held that both the national and the local governments must move warily where they trench on property rights. They could not in time of peace fix minimum wages or regulate maximum prices or preclude an employer from discriminating against union labor. And courts, if they were to be faithful to the Anglo-American tradition, must not allow the legislature to give administrative agencies a judicial power to find the ultimate facts in controversy and to enunciate and apply the governing rules of law.

The familiar decisions to which I have somewhat eliptically referred were, it is hardly necessary to say, superficially cast in terms of legal rather than political, economic or philosophical doctrines. The judges who wrote the majority opinions purported to find their reasons in the fundamental law of the land—in the scope of the taxing power conferred on Congress by Articles I, Section 8, Clause 1 of the Constitution or in the scope of the commerce power conferred on Congress by Article I, Section 8, Clause 3 of the Constitution or in the limits imposed by the "due process" clauses of the Fifth and Fourteenth Amendments to the Constitution or in the implications of Article III that judicial power can be reposed only in what are formally designated as courts of the United States. But there were no precise words in the test of the constitutional provisions which compelled this logic. And, as Holmes' opinions illustrated, a quite opposite course of reasoning was possible for one who started with a more enlarged view of constitutional democracy.

The starting point with Holmes was his awareness that "the provisions of the Constitution are not mathematical formulas having their essence in their form; they are organic living institutions transplanted from English soil. Their significance is vital not formal; it is to be gathered not simply by taking the words and a dictionary, but by considering their origin and the line of their growth."[5]

Our charter of government was intended to endure for ages and to be adaptable to a changing world and to the growth of men's experience and enlargement of their vision. It did not, as Holmes said, "enact Mr. Herbert Spencer's *Social Statics*"[6] or for that matter Locke's *Civil Government*. The provisions of the United States Constitution are not to be read as a pertification of past practice. They are set in a context calculated to remind us of the historical forces which originated, and of the contemporary allegiances which preserve, a balance between national and state governments. They are phrased in terms not of subject matters to be regulated by government but in terms of powers available to government. This is because just as individuals use their powers to create new forms of organization and to embark on new lines of activity to serve their own interests, so the people as a whole through their government are free to create new forms of regulation and to embark on new fields of welfare with the object of keeping all groups of private interests adjusted to each other. They are couched in language of utmost generality. For the Constitution excludes from the area of permissible regulation only a few topics, and those for the most part the so-called civil liberties. And even on the excluded topics the Constitution offers less an inflexible rule of limitation than a broad counsel of moderation—a constant appeal to the only half-articulated spiritual traditions that give substance to the promise of American life.

Applying these principles in litigation where the national government and the state governments conflicted, Holmes was one of the foremost in recognizing the overriding rights of the nation. Some may see in this the deeper impact upon his mind of his services as a soldier in the Union cause than of his services as a state judge. In any event he was alert to invalidate state tax or police action that revealed discrimination against, or even much theoretical interference with, the commerce among the several states. He said in an oft-quoted passage—

> "I do not think that the United States would come to an end if we lost our power to declare an Act of Congress void. I do think the Union would be imperilled if we could not make that declaration as to the laws of the several States." [7]

And as a corollary to that observation, he was more willing than most of his contemporaries to allow the national Congress to reach its regulatory arm into what were once thought to be local business concerns. His opinion in the first child labor case and his extension of the Sherman anti-trust statute to cover the packers' operations will serve as illustrations.

Of perhaps greater significance as an example of Holmes' democracy was the constancy with which as a judge he voted to allow governments both local and national to experiment with novel forms of regulation, of which as a voter or legislator he might have disapproved. The Supreme Court reports are replete with his explanations of these judicial votes, perhaps the most familiar being the statement in *Truax* v. *Corrigan*: [8]

> "There is nothing that I more deprecate than the use of the Fourteenth Amendment beyond the absolute compulsion of its words to prevent the making of social experiments that an important

> part of the community desires, in the insulated chambers afforded by the several States, even though the experiments may seem futile or even noxious to me and to those whose judgment I most respect."

The temper of that quotation explains how Holmes voted to sustain minimum wage and maximum hour legislation, state laws which imposed compulsory insurance for banking deposits, public regulations of employment contracts and many other measures which in his private correspondence the Justice would have characterized as socialistic humbug.

Holmes' willingness to tolerate change, variety and experimentation accounts for his attitude toward another facet of orthodox democratic theory. He was as familiar as any statesman with the oft-proclaimed virtues of the separation of powers, and he was aware how many interpreters of our Constitution have found these virtues enshrined not merely in certain constitutional clauses but in the very textual structure of the document—Article I dealing with the legislative power of Congress, Article II dealing with the executive power of the President, Article III dealing with the judicial power of the Courts. Yet Holmes was receptive to the needs of modern society to establish agencies of government which mingled these supposedly separate powers. He showed this in his votes in cases involving the Interstate Commerce Commission, the Federal Trade Commission and the government of the territories we acquired after the Spanish-American War. In many of these cases, however, he was less the pioneer than the second to Mr. Justice Brandeis, the chief judicial expositor of the most original affirmative powers of our twentieth century democracy—administrative agencies, governmental corporations and public authorities of mixed functions.

So far we have been considering Holmes' attitude toward the affirmative aspects of popular government—the powers which may be exercised by nation and state. But in a democracy limitations upon governmental power are equally significant. "The wise restraints that make men free" are restraints upon public authority as well as restraints upon private persons. And it is, therefore, appropriate to consider now Mr. Justice Holmes' attitude toward civil liberties.

Even before we adopted our Constitution we announced in the Declaration of Independence our belief in the inalienable rights of man—a doctrine whose genesis has been so admirably studied in Professor Carl Becker's famous historical monographs.[9] And this stress upon individual rights and civil liberties was carried further in the habaes corpus provisions in the Constitution of 1789 and the first ten amendments of 1791. The safeguards of these amendments, as Ambassador Thomas Jefferson's letter of March 1, 1789, to Congressman James Madison reminds us, were inserted because of "the legal check which it puts into the hands of the judiciary." Thus in the Jeffersonian and Madisonian no less than in the Hamiltonian and Marshall view the judges of our courts were specifically authorized to invalidate such public action as was repugnant to those particular civil liberties which are guaranteed by the Constitution.

But when Holmes ascended the bench in Washington in 1902 this authority had been sparingly exercised in the fields which most concerned Jefferson and Madison. A 1902 catalog of cases in which civil liberties had been successfully invoked would be surprisingly short. Property rights, to be sure, had been protected in the nineteenth century by invoking first the "obligations of contract" clause of Article I, Section 10, and later the "due process" clauses of the Fifth and Fourteenth Amendments. But what we ordinarily embrace within the concept of civil liberties or human rights had hardly been appreciated as constitutional rights subject to vindication by the Courts, as is convincingly shown in Professor Commager's slender though exhaustive volume on *Majority Rule and Minority Rights*. Indeed, Holmes himself applying constitutional principles as a Massachusetts state judge, had not been disturbed at a New Bedford police rule which denied a policeman the right to discuss political issues, or at the Boston ordinance which denied citizens the right to make a speech on the Boston Common without a permit from the Mayor.

The twentieth century, however, brought great changes in Holmes' viewpoint and later in that of the majority of the Court.

To my mind the most important change was not in the field of free speech as is sometimes asserted. It was the recognition that fair procedure in criminal trials conducted in state as well as federal courts is a civil liberty so fundamental to our democracy that it is covered by the constitutional assurance of "due process." When this point was first pressed it was denied by the Supreme Court of the United States. Indeed, as recently as 1915, in *Frank* v. *Mangum*,[10] where the defendant had been convicted by a Georgia state jury which was terrorized by a mob surrounding the courtroom, only Justices Holmes and Hughes thought that the Federal Supreme Court was warranted in invoking the due process clause or any other constitutional provision to set aside the sentence. The majority view was that so long as the state authorities outwardly followed the established form of trial the defendant could not successfully assert that his constitutional rights had been impaired by what was in substance lynch law. Today the dissent of Holmes is regarded as almost self-evident. And from Holmes' doctrine have stemmed the myriad of cases which lay down as fundamentals of our democratic system protected by the Supreme Court the right of a defendant in any criminal court in the land to a trial which is open to the public and free of outside pressure, which admits no evidence secured by torture or by third degree methods or by perjury known to the prosecution and which assures a defendant the right to the assistance of counsel in meeting a charge of undeniable gravity. Indeed, Holmes' dissents go further than the law has yet done in precluding the conviction of defendants upon the basis of evidence which had been procured by wire-tapping or other methods which he described as "dirty business." [11]

A second and much more widely known phase of Holmes' work in the field of civil liberties concerned freedom of speech. Here his influence not only on the law but on political theory and philosophy has perhaps been unmatched by any single American, although as I shall say in a minute it is not clear that this country now accepts his doctrines without qualification as adequate to meet the changed circumstances of the contemporary world.

It was in the aftermath of World War I that Holmes first faced a large volume of cases in which the free speech issue was predominant. In one of these, the *Schenck* case, he stated in a sentence familiar to every newspaper reader that "The question in every case is whether the words used are used in such circumstances and are of such a nature as to create a clear and present danger that they will bring about the substantive evils that Congress has a right to prevent." [12]

This is not the occasion to trace the origin of that doctrine, to show how much it owed to Holmes' youthful studies of the common law of criminal attempts and how much it owed to his reading of Milton's *Areopagitica,* to his knowledge of the history of John Adams' administration and to his personal friendship with John Stuart Mill, Frederick W. Maitland, Sir Frederick Pollock and Leslie Stephen. Yet without drawing that genealogical tree, we must recognize that Holmes' doctrine of the limits of free speech is the final crystallization of Nineteenth Century Liberalism. The doctrine is an admirably consistent series of deductions from two initial premises—that man is a reasoning animal and that, given time and space, reason will dissipate not merely error but danger as well. These deductions have captured countless readers partly because of the undeniably superb logic with which they move from the assumed premises, but even more because of the haunting poetry in which Holmes enshrined them. Let us stand in the back of the courtroom and hear him read his immortal opinion in the *Abrams* case: [13]

". . . when men have realized that time has upset many fighting faiths, they may come to believe even more than they believe the very foundations of their own conduct that the ultimate good desired is better reached by free trade in ideas—that the best test of truth is the power of the thought to get itself accepted in the competition of the market, and that truth is the only ground upon which their wishes safely can be carried out. That at any rate is the theory of our Constitution. It is an experiment, as all life is an experiment. Every year if not every day we have to wager our salvation upon some prophecy based upon the imperfect knowledge. While that experiment is part of our system I think that we should be eternally vigilant against attempts to check the expression of opinions that we loathe and believe to be fraught with death, unless they so imminently threaten immediate interference with the lawful and pressing purposes of the law that an immediate check is required to save the country."

Who can doubt the practical wisdom, the noble philosophy and the enduring strength of that passage—the most eloquent in all our court reports? Does it not belong with the two great memorial speeches of the democratic tradition—the one of 431 B. C. and the other of 1863 A.D.?

I am not prepared to deny the implication of these questions. Yet I want to invite you before applauding to consider carefully whether you agree not with Holmes' deductions but with his premises? Is man a reasoning animal and, given time and space, will reason dissipate not merely error but danger as well?

Holmes wrote before the world had fully appreciated the wickedness of which civilized man is capable. He knew not the Nazi concentration camps, nor the Goebbels propaganda for circulating the big lie, nor the Communist disciplined subordination of man's interest in truth to man's interest in material progress, nor the use of domestc dissidents as auxiliaries of a foreign state, nor the speed with which in our modern technological society forces of evil purpose may overwhelm the majority of peaceful men. Holmes wrote without reading Kierkegaard and Niebuhr and without hearing of Fuchs and Eisler.

If Holmes knew what we know would he ask the right to reconsider his premises and would he invoke as an avenue of retreat his most famous epigram, "the life of the law has not been logic; it has been experience"?

It is plain that some who have oft repeated their allegiance to Holmes' creed would do so. Consider the impressive opinion of Judge Learned Hand given in affirming the conviction of the eleven Communist leaders [14] and the action of the Supreme Court in affirming that decision [15] or the decision of the Supreme Court upholding that provision of the Taft-Hartley Act which denies the privileges of the National Labor Relations Act to unions which have Communist leaders; [16] or the action of the Congress in enacting the Internal Security Act of 1950 [17] over a presidential veto.

For one who has my other duties it would be inappropriate to make a personal comment upon those recent manifestations of our democracy. But I may without impropriety observe that it is only by rewriting Holmes' premises, recasting his critera of judgment and adding uncanonical qualifications to his formulas that judges and legislators of contemporary times have reached the results which the overwhelming majority of our contemporaries seem, at least in the pressure of the moment, to endorse.

We do not live in an era which looks with placid self-assurance upon nonconformity. We have not the civil courage, the confidence in other men's capacities, the consciousness of ultimate victory to admit as full partners in our society those who will not take without reservation the oaths we set before them. This is not the place to say whether we shall be justified before the bar of history. But those who subscribe to the dissents of Holmes in the *Schwimmer*[18] and *Maccintoch*[19] cases must recognize that in the circumstances of his day he was prepared to allow a broader liberty to dissenters, malcontents and radicals than are our statesmen in the circumstances of our day, a day in which this country has reached a new high in physical resources, in armament, in productive facilities, in employment and in liqiud capital, if not in spiritual leadership.

I turn now to the final point, Mr. Justice Holmes' attitude toward what some would regard as the central belief of the true democrat—the dignity of the individual man.

It is worth emphasizing at the outset what have been the sources of that belief—for, as we see, they include some currents in which Holmes was never caught up. One of the main sources has been natural law; another the Judaic-Christian religious tradition; and a third the classical influence of Greece and Rome on England and her offspring.

Holmes in letters, essays and legal opinions often attacked natural law concepts as a mere attempt to dress up as eternal verities our own limited experiences and hopes. He had no use for absolutes, legal or philosophic. Man did well to form generalizations of what was good and true and beautiful but the generalizations had no claim to be ultimate standards or to be final criteria of judgment. "The best that has been thought and said in the world" was of profound interest, but it was no copy of a Platonic set of universal ideas good *semper ubique,* marketable as coinage of the heavenly realm. Man could never find a pure gold fit for a universal standard. For him it was enough to learn how to mine, to refine, to use the alloyed metals of this earth. These mundane minerals were to be tested pragmatically. They were to be fitted into some workable and passable currency for our daily needs—on the understanding, of course, that the system of values was purely artificial, devised for convenience and subject to devaluation or revaluation whenever experience dictated.

To the Christian or any other formal religious discipline the mature Holmes never professed to be an adherent. He would not have denied that there was a power bigger than himself—he wrote that he knew he was in the belly of the cosmos and not the cosmos in him. But he irreverently referred to the deity as the Great Panjandrum who had not disclosed the plan of campaign, if indeed there is one. While he admired his father's friend, Ralph Waldo Emerson, and imbibed from him and older New England divines a sense of obligation and of Puritanical duty, he did not share their faith in God which gave New England its distinctive Transcendentalism.

Intellectually he was a skeptic. His ideas were not far different from those of the early Santayana—the author of *The Life of Reason.* And at times, as on his ninetieth birthday, Holmes could summarize in severely physical terms the insignificance of man's existence; "To live is to function. That is all there is in living." [20] But this rigorous separation of what he knew from what he did not know was never uttered in arrogance or pride. Indeed he disdained the impetuous defiance of our modern Prometheus, Bertrand Russell, who as Pollock said thought himself "a valiant fellow for throwing stones at God Almighty's windows." [21]

Yet this intellectual skepticism was to some extent balanced by a desire to plunge himself into the full tide of emotional forces in a way that would have astonished a complete Pyrrhonist like Montaigne. There was something far deeper than an imperturbable materialism in the judge who told a Harvard graduating class that a soldier's faith was "true and adorable" even "in a cause which he little understands," [22] in the Civil War veteran who told his former comrades in arms that "it is required of a man that he should share the passion and the action of his time at peril of being judged not to have lived," [23] and in the American citizen who saw mere belittling innuendo in Charles Beard's portrait of the framers of the American Constitution as businessmen motivated by concern for their own investments.[24] Holmes fully acknowledged the power of things of the spirit. He could never have enthroned as an ultimate trinity Freud, Marx and Darwin and said that the combination of their psychological, economic and biological theories explained the totality of life. For Holmes' rejection of the theological system was a rejection of all systems on the ground that life was too big, too multifarious, nay too mysterious to be comprehended. He rejected the parson for his certitude and his narrowness—but he did not delude himself with any lesser substitute of cocksureness.

Was then Holmes' attitude toward man classical in its origin? Some have persuasively argued that Holmes was an incurable romantic leading the younger generations to a wasteland where agnosticism, violence and force hold sway. But Holmes had none of the optimistic exurberance, love of the wildness of nature or the admiration for the varieties of eccentrictly which characterized his two great contemporaries in literature and philosophy, Walt Whitman and William James. The latter he regarded as a sentimental Irishman; the former's poetry is never quoted and never pulls at his vitals like Sophocles' *Philoctetes* or Dante's *Divine Comedy.*

If by the classical tradition in the Anglo-American world we mean the emphasis on the rounded man who conscious of the ideal of excellence disciplines himself to perform competently and unobtrusively and without being diverted whatever task falls to his hand, confident that every detail has significance and that every task greatly done makes the world more meaningful to the doer, then Holmes was a classicist. For Holmes, though he did not proclaim that human goals were eternal goals, never doubted that man could rise above the particulars of a sordid existence. If he could not discover God's purposes, he could nonetheless live a purposeful life of his own designing.

For himself, Holmes, at least after his Civil War years, chose as his design what may seem an austerely solitary life—first that of a scholar and then of an appellate judge. He never participated in the struggles of the market place nor of the political hustings nor even, to any substantial extent, of the trial court. He did not follow with reasonable closeness the diurnal conflict of other men's existences—going so far as often to avoid reading the daily newspaper. He never sought the spotlight of public attention and contemned those who advertised their own distinction. Cloistered in the library of his home he read voluminously mostly philosophical, historical, classical and juristic literature, interspersed with occasional French novels and current humorous books. He talked to and corresponded exclusively with the intellectual elite. His public appearances were virtually confined to four or five hundred hours a year on the bench in the former Senate Chamber in the Capitol. There he seldom spoke, but when he put one of his rare questions, it cut like a stingray to the heart of the case he was hearing. And then he went home to Eye Street to stand erect behind a tall bookkeeper's desk to write with a deft and sparkling pen opinions that "with a singing variety" epigramatically crystallized his profound insights.

In reading this description of Holmes you may have asked yourself whether I have shown the democracy of Holmes or his aristocracy. Quite plainly if democracy is the apotheosis of the lowest common denominator and if, to use Holmes' phraseology, every "great swell" is by definition an aristocrat, then the Holmes view of man was not democratic. But does democracy imply that the ideal man is the average man? Historically surely it does not, as Pericles would be the first and Franklin Roosevelt the latest to teach us. Democracy no less than aristocracy has always stressed the dignity or, if you please, the nobility of man. The difference between the aristocrat and the democratic philosophies is that in an aristocracy the terms dignity and nobility connote titles founded on the accident of birth or principles of invidious selection from an artificially restricted field.

In a democratic society the same terms are reserved for those who have so disciplined themselves that their countenances, their conduct, their code command respect. And it is in this sense that Holmes is a supreme instance of one democratic ideal of the dignity of man.

He has not, no man born in 1841 could have, given the answers suitable to our modern technological economy, to our new world order, to the rising tide of collectivism and, above all, to our crisis of faith. But like the Winged Victory of Samothrace he is the summit of hundreds of years of civilization, the inspiration of ages yet to come without being the foundation stone of any new school. He is the final authentic representative of the period of English democracy in America—the period that spans from 1607 to World War II.

But some of you may not be quite content to give Holmes that role unless I meet head-on a point now often pressed by detractors of the Justice. Despite the grandeur of the man and the style with which he carried off his life, was Holmes a believer in any durable values, democratic or otherwise? In his refusal of allegiance to any church, in his pervasive intellectual skepticism, in his praise of the soldier's faith apart from the soldier's cause, in his emphasis on adventure and on power, would he not have been as much at home in the world of Hobbes or of Hitler as of Jefferson or of Lincoln? Was he only a glorious specimen of Nietzsche's life force, a superman who but for the accident of birth into a Brahmin Beacon Hill family might have turned his theories and his talents to support an evil, destructive power?

One can make a superficial collation of Holmes' epigrams to fortify this sort of critical question. And there are some writers who have recently done so in theological pamphlets and bar journals. Holmes is himself not without blame for this criticism because he delighted to arouse his audience and stamp their memories with a witty or poetic phrase. He never spoke with cautious pedantic exactitude, qualifying every "bully generalization" with the express proviso that it was a mere apercu, understandable only as one of a series of partial visions. He invited the reader to cull his brocades out of context.

Yet we shall make a fundamental mistake if we assume that because Holmes was so happy a phrase-maker, because he was so disdainful of all absolutes and because he refused to accept or announce a systematic approach to the universe, his philosophy can be reduced to the two principles that "whatsoever thy hand findeth to do, do it with thy might"[25] and let thy neighbor go in peace.

Rigorous standards for himself and tolerance of his neighbor were, to be sure, two important articles of his creed. Yet each of these derived from this more basic postulate: although absolute truth, undiminished beauty, unalloyed good are not to be found by man, the never-ending quest for the true, the good and the beautiful is the activity most satisfying to man. Even if the quest serves no cosmic end, even if when the earth has made its last revolution round the sun not a trace of man's long journey will be left in any heaven or hell, nonetheless the search for truth and beauty and goodness seemed as desirable to Holmes as it was inevitable for him. And the final glory of the democratic life, as Holmes exemplified it and extended it, is that democracy keeps every door open to searchers for ultimate values and demolishes every irrelevant barrier standing athwart the oncoming adventures in ideas.

NOTES

THE DEMOCRACY OF JUSTICE OLIVER WENDELL HOLMES

By Charles E. Wyzanski, Jr.

* This essay is based on a lecture given by the author at Brown University in the fall of 1950. It was one of the Marshall Woods lectures delivered by various speakers depicting five outstanding exponents of American democracy and analyzing their contributions. The subjects included four presidents — Thomas Jefferson, Abraham Lincoln, Woodrow Wilson and Franklin D. Roosevelt — and one judge — Oliver Wendell Holmes.

† United States District Judge, District of Massachusetts.

1 BOWEN, YANKEE FROM OLYMPUS (1944).

2 *Frankfurter, Oliver Wendell Holmes,* 21 DICT. AM. BIOG. 417 (1944).

3 Lecture delivered to undergraduates of Harvard University, Feb. 17, 1886, reprinted in THE MIND AND FAITH OF JUSTICE HOLMES 31, 33 (Lerner ed. 1943).

4 United States v. Butler, 297 U. S. 1, 62, 56 Sup. Ct. 312, 80 L. Ed. 477 (1936).

5 Gompers v. United States, 233 U. S. 604, 610, 34 Sup. Ct. 693, 58 L. Ed. 1115 (1914).

6 Lockner v. New York, 198 U. S. 45, 75, 25 Sup. Ct. 539, 49 L. Ed. 937 (1904).

7 *Law and the Court* (1913), in COLLECTED LEGAL PAPERS 295-96 (1921).

8 257 U. S. 312, 344, 42 Sup. Ct. 124, 66 L. Ed. 254 (1921).

9 BECKER, THE DECLARATION OF INDEPENCENCES A STUDY IN THE HISTORY OF POLITICAL IDEAS (2d ed. 1942).

10 237 U. S. 309, 35 Sup. Ct. 582, 59 L. Ed. 969 (1914).

11 Olmstead v. United States, 277 U. S. 438, 470, 48 Sup. Ct. 564, 72 L. Ed. 944 (1928).

12 Schenck v. United States, 249 U. S. 47, 52, 39 Sup. Ct. 247, 63 L. Ed. 470 (1919).

13 Abrams v. United States, 250 U. S. 616, 40 Sup. Ct. 17, 63 L. Ed. 1173 (1919).

14 United States v. Dennis, 183 F. 2d 201 (2d Cir. 1950).

15 Dennis v. United States, 341 U. S. 494, 71 Sup. Ct. 157, 95 L. Ed. 1137 (1951).

16 American Communications Ass'n v. Douds, 339 U. S. 382, 70 Sup. Ct. 674, 94 L. Ed. 925 (1950).

17 64 STAT. 987 (1950).

18 United States v. Schwimmer, 279 U. S. 644, 49 Sup. Ct. 448, 73 L. Ed. 889 (1927).

19 United States v. Macintosh, 283 U. S. 605, 51 Sup. Ct. 570, 75 L. Ed. 1302 (1931).

20 Radio address on occasion of his ninetieth birthday, reprinted in UNCOLLECTED PAPERS 142 (Shriver ed. 1936), also in THE MIND AND FAITH OF JUSTICE HOLMES 451 (Lerner ed. 1943).

21 2 HOLMES-POLLOCK LETTERS 159 (Howe ed. 1944).

22 *Memorial Day Address,* 1895, reprinted in THE MIND AND FAITH OF JUSTICE HOLMES 18, 20 (Lerner ed. 1943).

23 *Memorial Day Address,* 1884, reprinted in THE MIND AND FAITH OF JUSTICE HOLMES 9, 10 (Lerner ed. 1943).

24 1 HOLMES-POLLOCK LETTERS 237 (Howe ed. 1944).

25 *Life as Joy, Duty, End,* reprinted in THE MIND AND FAITH OF JUSTICE HOLMES 42 (Lerner ed. 1943).

APPENDIX

NOTED EPIGRAMS, SAYINGS, THOUGHTS, ETC.,
Selected from the Writings of Mr. Justice Holmes.

ART

"The justification of art is not that it offers prizes to those who succeed in the economic struggle, to those who in an economic sense have produced the most, and that thus by indirection it increases the supply of wine and oil. The justification is in art itself whatever its economic effect. It gratifies an appetite which in some noble spirits is stronger than the appetite for food."—**Address at Northwest University. Collected Legal Papers (1920): 272-273.**

". . . the world needs the flower more than the flower needs life." —"Use of Law School." **Speeches (1913): 39.**

CASES, GREAT AND WEAK

"Great cases like hard cases make bad law. For great cases are called great not by reason of their real importance in shaping the law of the future but because of some accident of immediate overwhelming interest which appeals to the feelings and distorts the judgment. These immediate interests exercise a kind of hydraulic pressure which makes what previously was clear seem doubtful, and before which even well-settled principles of law will bend."—**Northern Securities Co. v. U .S., 193 U. S. 197, 400 (1904).**

"Some rather weak cases must fall within any law which is couched in general words."—**The Mangrove Prize Money, 188 U. S. 720, 725 (1902).**

COMPETITION

"Free competition is worth more to society than it costs." **Vegelahn v. Guntner, 167 Mass. 92, 44 N. E. 1077 (1896).**

CONDUCT

"If a man intentionally adopts certain conduct in certain circumstances known to him, and that conduct is forbidden by the law under those circumstances, he intentionally breaks the law in the only sense in which the law ever considers intent." **Ellis v. U. S., 206 U. S. 246, 257 (1906).**

"A man may have as bad a heart as he chooses, if his conduct is within the rules." **The Common Law (1881): 110.**

CONSTITUTION

"But the provisions of the Constitution are not mathematical formulas having their essence in their form; they are organic living institutions transplanted from English soil. Their significance is vital not formal; it is to be gathered not simply by taking the words and a dictionary, but by considering their origin and the line of their growth." **Gompers v. U. S., 233 U. S. 604, 610 (1913).**

"Constitutions are intended to preserve practical and substantial rights, not to maintain theories." **Davis v. Mills, 194 U. S. 451, 457 (1903).**

DIFFERENCES

"Most differences are merely differences of degree, when nicely analyzed." **Rideout v. Knov, 148 Mass. 368, 19 N. E. 390 (1889).**

DURATION OF THOUGHTS

"One of my favorite paradoxes is that everything is dead in twenty-five (or fifty) years. The author no longer says to you what he meant to say. If he is original, his new truths have been developed and become familiar in improved form—his errors exploded. If he is not a philosopher but an artist, the emotional emphasis has been changed." **Quoted by B. N. Cardozo in Mr. Justice Holmes, 44 Harv. L. Rev. 682 (1931); ante: 48.**

DUE PROCESS

Whatever disagreement there may be as to the scope of the phrase 'due process of law' there can be no doubt that it embraces the fundamental conception of a fair trial, with opportunity to be heard. Mob law does not become due process of law by securing the assent of a terrorized jury." **Frank v. Mangum, 237 U. S. 309, 347 (1914).**

". . . what is due process of law depends on circumstances. It varies with the subject-matter and the necessities of the situation." **Moyer v. Peabody, 212 U. S. 78. 84 (1908).**

EDUCATION see also TEACHER OF LAW

"No result is easy which is worth having. Your education begins when what is called your education is over,—when you no longer are stringing together the pregnant thoughts, the 'jewels five words long,' which great men have given their lives to cut from the raw material, but have begun yourselves to work upon the raw material for results which you do not see, cannot predict, and which may be long in coming,—when you take the fact which life offers you for your appointed task." **Profession of the Law. Speeches (1913): 24.**

"Learning, my learned brethren, is a very good thing. I should be the last to undervalue it, having done my share of quotation from the Year Books." **Learning and Science. Speeches (1913): 67; ante: 106.**

". . . if education could make men realize that you can not produce something out of nothing and made them promptly detect the pretense of doing so . . . I should think it had more than paid for itself." **Address at Northwestern University. Collected Legal Papers (1920): 274.**

"Mr. Ruskin's first rule for learning to draw . . . was, be born a genius. It is the first rule for everything else. If a man is adequate in native force, he probably will be happy in the deepest sense, whatever his fate. But we must not undervalue effort, even if it is the lesser half." **Address at Northwestern University. Collected Legal Papers (1920): 275.**

EIGHTEENTH AMENDMENT

"I cannot for a moment believe that apart from the Eighteenth Amendment special constitutional principles exist against strong drink. The fathers of the Constitution, so far as I know, approved it." **Knickerbocker Ice Co. v. Stewart, 253 U. S. 149, 166, 169 (1919).**

FICTION

". . . fiction always is a poor ground for changing substantial rights." **Haddock v. Haddock, 201 U. S. 562, 630 (1905).**

FOURTEENTH AMENDMENT

"If the Fourteenth Amendment were now before us for the first time I should think it ought to be construed more narrowly than it has been construed in the past. . . ." **Schlesinger v. Wisconsin, 270 U. S. 239, 241 (1925).**

"There is nothing that I more deprecate than the use of the Fourteenth Amendment beyond the absolute compulsion of its words to prevent the making of social experiments that an important part of the community desires. . . ." **Truax v. Corrigan, 257 U. S. 312, 344 (1921).**

"The fourteenth Amendment does not enact Mr. Herbert Spencer's Social Statics." **Lochner v. N. Y., 198 U. S. 45, 75 (1904).**

"The fourteenth amendment is not a pedagogical requirement of the impracticable." **Dominion Hotel v. Arizona, 249 U. S. 265, 268 (1919).**

FRAUD

"It is a question of how strong an infusion of fraud is necessary to turn a flavor into a poison." **Int'l News Service v. A. P., 248 U. S. 215, 247 (1918).**

FREE SPEECH

"But the character of every act depends upon the circumstances in which it is done. . . . The most stringent protection of free speech would not protect a man in falsely shouting fire in a theater and causing a panic." **Schenck v. United States, 249 U. S. 47, 52 (1919).**

"I do not doubt for a moment that by the same reasoning that would justify punishing persuasion to murder, the United States constitutionally may punish speech that produces or is intended to produce a clear and imminent danger that it will bring about forthwith certain substantive evils that the United States constitutionally may seek to prevent." **Abrams v. U. S., 250 U. S. 616, 627 (1919).**

". . . If there is any principle of the [U. S.] Constitution that more imperatively calls for attachment than any other it is the principle of free thought—not free thought for those who agree with us but freedom for the thought we hate." **U. S. v. Schwimmer ,279 U. S. 644, 654, 655 (1929).**

GAIETY

"Possibly gaiety is the miasmic mist of misery." **Letter to Pollock, Dec. 29, 1915. Ante: 163.**

GOSSIP AND PHILOSOPHY

"The difference between gossip and philosophy lies only in one's way of taking a fact." **The Bar as a Profession, Collected Legal Papers (1920): 159.**

HERE AND NOW

"Questions of here and now occupy nine hundred and ninety-nine

thousandths of the ability of the world." **Eulogy on Shattuck, 1897. Speeches (1913): 73.**

HISTORIC CONTINUITY

"I say that all society is founded on the death of men. Certainly the romance of the past is." **Letters to Dr. Wu. Sept. 6, 1925.**

"There is, . . . a peculiar logical pleasure in making manifest the continuity between what we are doing and what has been done. But the present has a right to govern itself so far as it can; and it ought always to be remembered that historic continuity with the past is not a duty, it is only a necessity." **Learning and Science. Collected Legal Papers (1920): 139; Ante: 106.**

IDEALS AND DOUBTS

"Man is born a predestined idealist, for he is born to act. To act is to affirm the worth of an end, and to persist in affirming the worth of an end is to make an ideal. The stern experience of our youth helped to accomplish the destiny of fate. It left us feeling through life that pleasures do not make happiness and that the root of joy as of duty is to put out all one's powers towards some great end." **The Class of '61. Speeches (1913): 96-97.**

"A man is bound to be parochial in his practice—to give his life, and if necessary his death, for the place he has his roots. But his thinking should be cosmopolitan and detached. He should be able to criticise what he reveres and loves." **John Marshall. Speeches (1913): 89.**

"We accept our destiny to work, to fight, to die for ideal aims. At the grave of a hero who has done these things we end not with sorrow at the inevitable loss, but with the contagion of his courage, and with a kind of desperate joy we go back to the fight." **Eulogy on W. A. Field. Speeches (1913): 81.**

"There is in all men a demand for the superlative, so much so that the poor devil who has no other way of reaching it attains it by getting drunk." **Natural Law. Collected Legal Paper s(1920): 310.**

". . . we all, whether we know it or not, are fighting to make the kind of a world that we should like . . . others will fight and die to make a different world, with equal sincerity or belief." **Natural Law, Collected Legal Papers (1920): 311-312.**

"To have doubted one's own first principles is the mark of a civilized man." **Ideals and Doubts. Collected Legal Papers (1920): 307.**

"If a man has the soul of Sancho Panza, the world to him will be Sancho Panza's world; but if he has the soul of an idealist, he will make—I do not say find—his world ideal." **Profession of the Law. Speeches (1913): 22.**

"When the ignorant are taught to doubt they do not know what they safely may believe." **Law and the Court. Speeches (1913): 99.**

"I do not pin my dreams for the future to my country or even to my race. I think it probable that civilization somehow will last as long as I care to look ahead—perhaps with smaller numbers, but perhaps also bred to greatness and splendor by science. I think it not improbable that man, like the grub that prepares a chamber for the winged thing it never has seen but is to be—that man may have cosmic destinies that he does not understand." **Law and the Court. Speeches (1913): 103.**

JUDGES

"I recognize without hesitation that judges do and must legislate, but they can do so only interstitially; they are confined from molar to molecular motions." **Southern Pacific Co. v. Jensen, 244 U. S. 205, 221 (1917).**

"It is not the will of the sovereign that makes lawyers' law, even when that is its source, but what . . . the judges, by whom it is enforced, say is his will. The judges have other motives for decision, outside their own arbitrary will, besides the commands of their sovereign. And whether those other motives are, or are not, equally compulsory, it is immaterial, if they are sufficiently likely to prevail to afford a ground for predicition. The only question for the lawyer is, how will the judges act?" **The Common Law (1881): 317.**

JUDGMENT OF DEATH

"Nature has but one judgment on wrong conduct—if you can call that a judgment which seemingly has no reference to conduct as such—the judgment of death. That is the judgment or the consequence which follows uneconomical expenditure if carried far enough. If you waste too much food you starve; too much fuel, you freeze; too much nerve tissue, you collapse." **Address at Northwestern University. Collected Legal Papers (1920): 272.**

JUDGMENT

"General propositions do not decide concrete cases. The decision will depend on a judgment or intuition more subtle than any articulate major premise." **Lochner v. N. Y., 198 U. S. 45, 76 (1905).**

"People often speak of correcting the judgment of the time by that of posterity. I think it is quite as true to say that we must correct the judgment of posterity by that of the time." **Eulogy on G. O. Shatuck. Speeches (1913): 73.**

JURISDICTION

"The foundation of jurisdiction is physical power." **Ex Parte Indiana Transportation, 244 U. S. 456, 457 (1917).**

JUSTIFICATION OF SCIENCE AND PHILOSOPHY

"I do not believe that the justification of science and philosophy is to be found in improved machinery and good conduct. Science and philosophy are themselves necessaries of life. By producing them, civilization sufficiently accounts for itself. **Speech at the Yale University Alumni Dinner. Speeches (1913): 50.**

LAW

". . . the law is not the place for the artist or the poet. The law is the calling of thinkers." **Profession of the Law. Speeches (1913): 22.**

"The law constantly is tending towards consistency of theory." **Hanson v. Globe Newspaper Co., 159 Mass. 293, 34 N. E. 462 (1893).**

"The life of the law has not been logic, it has been experience. The felt necessities of the time, the prevalent moral and political theories; intentions of public policy avowed or unconscious, even the prejudices which judges share with their fellowmen, have had a good deal more to do than the syllogism in determining the rules by which men should be governed." **The Common Law (1881): 1.**

"It is revolting to have no better reason for a rule of law than that so it was laid down in the time of Henry IV. It is still more revolting if the grounds upon which it was laid down have vanished long since, and the rule simply persists from blind imitation of the past." **The Path of the Law. Collected Legal Papers: 187; ante: 74.**

"It is perfectly proper to regard and study the law simply as a great anthropological document." **Law in Science and Science in Law. Collected Legal Papers (1920): 210, 212.**

"For the rational study of the law the black letter man may be the man of the present, but the man of the future is the man of statistics and the master of economics." **The Path of the Law. Collected Legal Papers (1920): 187; ante: 74.**

"The common law is not a brooding omnipresence in the sky but the articulate voice of some sovereign or quasi-sovereign that can be identified." **Southern Pacific Co. v. Jensen, 244 U. S. 205, 222 (1917).**

"It was affirmed, I believe, by a man not without deserved honor in his generation—the late Chief Justice Cooley—that the law was and ought to be commonplace. No doubt the remark has its truth. It is better that the law should be commonplace than that it should be eccentric." **Address at Northwestern University. Collected Legal Papers (1920): 276.**

"The law has got to be stated over again; and I venture to say that in fifty years we shall have it in a form of which no man could have dreamed fifty years ago." **Use of Law School. Speeches (1913): 34.**

"If we are to speak of the law as our mistress, we who are here know that she is a mistress only to be wooed with sustained and lonely passion—only to be won by straining all the faculties by which man is likest to a god. Those who, having begun the pursuit, turn away uncharmed, do so either because they have not been vouchsafed the sight of her divine figure, or because they have not the heart for so great a struggle." **The Law. Speeches (1913): 17; ante: 92.**

"If your subject is law, the roads are plain to anthropology, the science of man, to political economy, the theory of legislation, ethics, and thus by several paths to your final view of life. It would be equally true of any subject. The only difference is in the ease of seeing the way. To be master of any branch of knowledge, you must master those which lie next to it; and thus to know anything you must know all." **Profession of the Law. Speeches (1913): 23; Collected Legal Papers (1920): 29-30.**

"The law, so far as it depends on learning, is indeed, as it has been called, the government of the living by the dead." **Learning and Science. Speeches (1913): 67.**

LAW SCHOOLS

"I say the business of a law school is not sufficiently described when you merely say that it is to teach law, or to make lawyers. It is to teach law in the grand manner, and to make great lawyers." **Use of Law Schools. Speeches (1913): 30.**

LAWYERS

"The world has its fling at lawyers sometimes, but its very denial is an admission. It feels, what I believe to be the truth, that of all secular professions this has the highest standards." **The Law. Speeches (1913): 16; ante: 91.**

"The external and immediate result of an advocate's work is but to win or lose a case. But remotely what the lawyer does is to establish, develop, or illuminate rules which are to govern the conduct of men for centuries; to set in motion principles and influences which shape the thought and action of generations which know not by whose command they move." **Eulogy on S. Bartlett. Speeches (1913): 43.**

"The glory of lawyers, like that of men of science, is more corporate than individual. Our labor is an endless organic process. The organism whose being is recorded and protected by the law is the undying body of society." **Eulogy on D. S. Richardson. Speeches (1913): 47.**

LEADERSHIP see also HEROISM

"When a great tree falls, we are surprised to see how meagre the landscape seems without it. So when a great man dies." **Eulogy on S. Bartlett. Speeches (1913): 44.**

LIBEL

"A man cannot justify a libel by proving that he had contracted to libel." **Weston v. Barnicoat, 175 Mass. 454, 56 N. E. 619 (1900).**

LIFE

"Life is an end in itself, and the only question as to whether it is worth living is whether you have enough of it." **Speech to Bar Assoc. of Boston. Speeches (1913): 86.**

"One of the eternal conflicts out of which life is made up is that between the effort of every man to get the most he can for his services, and that of society disguised under the name of capital to get his services for the least possible return." **Vegelahn v. Guntner, 167 Mass. 92, 44 N. E. 1077 (1896).**

"I think that, as life is action and passion, it is required of a man that he should share the passion and action of his time at peril of being judged not to have lived." **Memorial Day. Speeches (1913): 3.**

"It was of this that Malebranch was thinking when he said that, if God held in one hand truth, and in the other the pursuit of truth, he would say: 'Lord, the truth is for thee alone; give me the pursuit.' The joy of life is to put out one's power in some natural and useful or harmless way. There is no other. And the real misery is not to do this." **Speech to Bar Assoc. of Boston. Speeches (1913): 84.**

"Life is a roar of bargain and battle, but in the very heart of it there rises a mystic spiritual tone that gives meaning to the whole. It transmuses the dull detail into romance. It reminds us that our only but wholly adequate significance is as parts of the unimaginable whole. It suggests that even while we think that we are egotists we are living to ends outside ourselves." **Class of '61. Speeches (1913): 97.**

"Life is action, the use of one's powers. As to use them to their height is our joy and duty, so it is the one end that justifie sitself." **Speech to Bar Assoc. of Boston. Speeches (1913): 85.**

"Life is painting a picture, not doing a sum." **Class of '61. Speeches (1913): 96.**

MEMORIAL DAY

"So to the indifferent inquirers who ask why Memorial Day is still kept up we may answer, It celebrates and solemnly reaffirms from year to year a national act of enthusiasm and faith. It embodies in the most impressive form our belief that to act with enthusiasm and faith is the condition of acting greatly. To fight out a war, you must believe something and want something with all your might. So must you do to carry anything else to an end worth reaching." **Memorial Day. Speeches (1913): 3.**

MISFORTUNE

"A man cannot shift his misfortunes to his neighbor's shoulders." **Spade v. Lynn & Boston R. Co., 172 Mass. 488, 52 N. E. 747 (1899).**

MORALITY

"We have to choose, and for my part I think it a less evil that some criminals should escape than that the Government should play an ignoble part." **Olmstead v. U. S., 277 U. S. 438, 470 (1918).**

"It is desirable that criminals should be detected, and to that end that all available evidence should be used. It also is desirable that the Government should not itself foster and pay for other crimes, when they are the means by which the evidence is to be obtained." **Olmstead v. U. S., 277 U. S. 438, 470 (1927).**

"Our system of morality is a body of imperfect social generalizations expressed in terms of emotion." **Ideals and Doubts. Collected Legal Papers (1920): 306.**

NATURAL LAW

"The jurists who believe in natural law seem to me to be in that naive state of mind that accepts what has been familiar and accepted by them and their neighbors as something that must be accepted by all men everywhere." **Natural Law. Collected Legal Papers (1920): 312.**

PHILOSOPHY see also GOSSIP AND PHILOSOPHY

"Philosophy does not furnish motives, but it shows men that they are not fools for doing what they already want to do." **Natural Law. Collected Legal Papers (1920): 316.**

"Men to a great extent believe what they want to—although I see in that no basis for a philosophy that tells us what we should want to want." **Natural Law. Collected Legal Papers (1920): 314.**

"The a priori men generally call the dissentients superfiicial." **Natural Law. Collected Legal Papers (1920): 314.**

POWER

"We fear to grant power and are unwilling to recognize it when it exists." **Tyson, etc. v. Banton, 273 U. S. 418, 445 (1927).**

PROHIBITION

"The notion that prohibition is any less prohibition when applied to things now thought evil I do not understand." **Hammer v. Dagenhart, 247 U. S. 251, 280 (1918).**

PURITANS

". . . The Puritans planted the democratic spirit in the heart of man. It is to them we owe the deepest cause we have to love our country—that instinct, that spark that makes the American unable to meet his fellow man otherwise than simply as a man, eye to eye, hand to hand, and foot to foot, wrestling naked on the sand." **The Puritan. Speeches: 19, 20.**

". . . the cold passion of the Puritan." **The Puritan. Speeches: 19, 20.**

PUBLIC OPINION

"The taste of any public is not to be treated with contempt." **Bleistein v. Donaldson Lity. Co., 188 U. S. 239, 252 (1903).**

"No falsehood is thought about or even known by all the world; no conduct is hated by all." **Peck v. Tribune Co., 214 U. S. 185 (1909).**

RIGHTS

[A feeble minded woman, whose mother and child were feeble minded, and an inmate of a Virginia State Mental institution, opposed sterilization under a statute.]

"It is better for all the world if, instead of waiting to execute degenerate offspring for crime or to let them starve for their imbecility, society can prevent those who are manifestly unfit from continuing their kind. The principle that sustains compulsory vaccination is broad enough to cover cutting the Fallopian tubes. Three generations of imbeciles are enough." **Buck v. Bell, 274 U. S. 200, 207 (1927).**

"In order to enter into most of the relations of life people have to give up some of their constitutional rights. If a man makes a contract he gives up the constitutional right that previously he had to be free from the hamper that he puts upon himself." **Powers v. Saunders, 274 U. S. 490, 497 (1927).**

"But the word 'right' is one of the most deceptive of pitfalls; it is so easy to slip from a qualified meaning in the premise to an unqualified one in the conclusion. Most rights are qualified." **Am. Bank & Trust Co. v. Federal Bank, 256 U. S. 350, 358 (1921).**

RUIN OF A STATE

"I have no belief in panaceas and almost none in sudden ruin. I believe with Montesquieu that if the chance of a battle—I may add, the passage of a law—has ruined a state, there was a general cause at work that made the state ready to perish by a single battle or law." **Law and the Court. Speeches (1913): 102.**

RULE OF JOY

"**The rule of joy and the law of duty seem to me all one. I confess that altruistic and cynical selfish talk seem to me about equally** unreal. With all humility, I think "Whatsoever thy hand findeth to do, do it with thy might,' infinitely more important than the vain attempt to love one's neighbor as one's self. If you want to hit a bird on the wing, you must have all your will in a focus, you must not be thinking about your neighbor; you must be living in your eye on that bird. Every achievement is a bird on the wing." **Speech to Bar Assoc. of Boston. Speeches (1913): 85.**

SOCIALISM

"When twenty years ago a vague terror went over the earth and the word socialism began to be heard, I thought and still think that fear was translated in todoctrines that had no proper place in the Constitution or the common law." **Law and the Court. Speeches (1913): 101-102.**

"The notion that with socialized property we should have women free and a piano for everybody seems to me an empty hum-bug." **Ideals and Doubts. Collected Legal Papers (1920): 306.**

SUCCESS

"I once heard a man say, 'Where Vanderbilt sits, there is the head of the table. I teach my sons to be rich.' He said what many think." **The Soldier's Faith. Speeches (1913): 56.**

". . . whether a man accepts from Fortune her spade, and will look downward and dig, or from Aspiration her axe and cord, and will scale the ice, the one and only success which it is his to command is to bring to his work a mighty heart." **Memorial Day. Speeches (1913): 11.**

"I have always thought that not place or power or popularity makes the success that one desires, but the trembling hope that one has come near to an ideal. The only ground that warrants a man for thinking that he is not living the fool's paradise if he ventures such a hope is the voice of a few masters. . . ." **Letter to B. N. Cardozo; ante: 49-50.**

"With regard to the chances of success, I remember that the late Lord Justice Bowen once told me, when he was at the bar and already successful, that he thought that beside patience and talent a man must have luck. But, so far as I have noticed, luck generally comes to patience and talent, if coupled with love of the thing, as the Lord Chief Justice so truly adds." **The Bar as a Profession. Collected Legal Papers (1920): 157-158.**

"One may fall,—at the beginning of the charge or at the top of the earthworks; but in no other way can he reach the rewards of victory." **Memorial Day. Speeches (1913): 3.**

"Only when you have worked alone,—when you have felt around you a black gulf of solitude more isolating than that which surrounds the dying man, and in hope and in despair have trusted to your own unshaken will,—then only will you have achieved." **Profession of the Law. Speeches (1913): 24.**

"No man has earned the right to intellectual ambition until he has learned to lay his course by a star which he has never seen,—to dig by the diving rod for springs which he may never reach." **Profession of the Law. Speeches (1913): 24.**

"We cannot live our dreams. We are lucky enough if we can give a sample of our best, and if in our hearts we can feel that it has been nobly done." **Speech to Bar Assoc. of Boston. Speeches (1913): 83.**

"Every calling is great when greatly pursued." **The Law. Speeches**

(1913): 17; ante: 91.

"No man can go far who never sets down his foot until he knows that the sidewalk is under it." **Report of speech in Boston Advertiser of Dec. 4, 1902.**

TAXES

"Taxes are what we pay for civilized society, including the chance to insure." **Compania General de Tabacos de Filipinas v. Collector of Internal Revenue, 275 U. S. 87, 100 (1927).**

TEACHER OF LAW see also EDUCATION

"[A teacher of law should send men] forth with a pennon as well as with a sword, to keep before their eyes in the long battle the little flutter that means ideals, honor, yes, even romance, in all the dull details." **Speech at Northwestern University. Collceted Legal Papers (1920): 278.**

THINKING

"The man of action has the present, but the thinker controls the future." **Eulogy on S. Bartlett. Speeches (1913): 43.**

"Many men, especially as they grow older, resent attempts to push analysis beyond consecrated phrases, or to formulate anew. Such attempts disturb the intellectual rest for which we long. Our ideal is repose, perhaps our destiny is effort, just as the eye sees green after gazing at the sun." **Eulogy on W. Allen. Speeches (1913): 53.**

"Most men think dramatically, not quantitatively, a fact that the rich would be wise to remember more than they do. We are apt to contrast the palace with the hovel, the dinner at Sherry's with the working man's pail, and never ask how much or realize how little is withdrawn to make the prizes of success (subordinate prizes—since the only prize much cared for by the powerful is power. The prize of the general is not a bigger tent, but command.)" **Law and the Court. Speeches (1913): 99-100.**

"It is one thing to utter a happy phrase from a protected cloister; another to think under fire—to think for action upon which great interests depend. The most powerful men are apt to go into the melee and fall or come out generals." **Eulogy on G. O. Shattuck. Speeches (1913): 73.**

"To rest upon a formula is a slumber that, prolonged, means death." **Ideals and Doubts. Collected Legal Paper s(1920): 306.**

"A new and valid idea is worth more than a regiment and fewer men can furnish the former than command the latter." **Letters to Dr. Wu, July 21, 1925.**

TRUTH

"I used to say, when I was young, that truth was the majority vote of that nation that could lick all others." **Natural Law. Collected Iegal Papers (1920): 310.**

". . . When men have realized that time has upset many fighting faiths, they may come to believe even more than they believe the very foundations of their own conduct that the ultimate good desired is better reached by free trade in ideas—That the best test of truth is the power of the thought to get itself accepted in the competition of the market, and that truth is the only ground upon which their wishes safely can be carried out." **Abrams v. U. S., 250 U. S. 616, 630 (1919).**

WAR

"War, when you are at it, is horrible and dull." **The Soldier's Faith. Speeches: 56, 62.**

WORDS

"But whatever the consequences we must accept the plain meaning of plain words." **U. S. v. Brown, 206 U. S. 240, 244 (1907).**

"Words express whatever meaning convention has attached to them." **Trimble v. Seattle, 231 U. S. 683, 688 (1914).**

"A word is not a crystal, transparent and unchanged, it is the skin of a living thought and may vary greatly in color and content according to the circumstances and the time in which it is used." **Towne v. Eisner, 245 U. S. 418, 425 (1918).**

MISCELLANEOUS

"A horsecar cannot be handled like a rapier." **Hamilton v. West End St. R. Co., 163 Mass. 199, 39 N. E. 1010 (1895).**

"Personally I like to know what the bill is going to be before I order a luxury." **Ideals and Doubts. Collected Legal Papers (1920): 307.**

"A dog will fight for his bone." **Natural Law. Collected Legal Papers (1920): 314.**